ANGER, GRATITUDE, AND THE ENLIGHTENMENT WRITER

Anger, Gratitude, and the Enlightenment Writer

PATRICK COLEMAN

OXFORD
UNIVERSITY PRESS

OXFORD
UNIVERSITY PRESS

Great Clarendon Street, Oxford OX2 6DP

Oxford University Press is a department of the University of Oxford.
It furthers the University's objective of excellence in research, scholarship,
and education by publishing worldwide in

Oxford New York

Auckland Cape Town Dar es Salaam Hong Kong Karachi
Kuala Lumpur Madrid Melbourne Mexico City Nairobi
New Delhi Shanghai Taipei Toronto

With offices in

Argentina Austria Brazil Chile Czech Republic France Greece
Guatemala Hungary Italy Japan Poland Portugal Singapore
South Korea Switzerland Thailand Turkey Ukraine Vietnam

Published in the United States
by Oxford University Press Inc., New York

First published 2011

British Library Cataloguing in Publication Data
Data available

Library of Congress Cataloging in Publication Data
Library of Congress Control Number: 2010936877

Typeset by SPI Publisher Services, Pondicherry, India
Printed in Great Britain
on acid-free paper by
MPG Books Group, Bodmin and King's Lynn

ISBN 978–0–19–958934–0

1 3 5 7 9 10 8 6 4 2

Preface

This book offers a new perspective on Enlightenment conceptions of sociability by exploring the ways eighteenth-century French writers define, express, and critique the two emotions of anger and gratitude. When is anger condemned as a failure of self-control, and when is it praised as a vindication of human dignity? Who is entitled to get angry, and at whom? Who is expected to be grateful, and is it always right to think of gratitude as a kind of obligation? Answers to such questions tell us much about how feelings are socialized and how social expectations shape emotional dispositions. They also provide a path to understanding a fundamental tension in modern culture: how the aspiration to personal independence may be reconciled—or not—with the recognition that the benevolence or hostility of other people, indeed, of the world itself, plays an essential role in the constitution of the self.

Conflicting judgments about the appropriateness of anger and gratitude also reveal a fundamental ambivalence in Enlightenment thinking about the kind of norms that should regulate human interaction. Should social life be based solely on legal rights and duties, applicable impersonally to all? Or should it be shaped by informal and more flexible rules of personal acknowledgment, backed by the pressure of opinion rather than the power of law? By eliminating occasions for personal slight or favor, the first of these schemes would provide welcome relief from the burdens of anger and gratitude. According to the second view, some readiness to give and take offense, and to grant and return a favor, is assumed to be a crucial dimension of human dignity, of what one owes to oneself or to others, and should be cultivated rather than curtailed. This dilemma is no less acute in contemporary thinking about managing human interactions in a globalized culture than it was to writers of the French Enlightenment.

Providing a comprehensive treatment of these topics would require marshaling a range of documentary and material evidence much wider than I can handle here. This book focuses more particularly on emotional transactions involving anger and gratitude—and the possibility or desirability of transcending such emotions—as they are dramatized in the work of four great eighteenth-century French writers, and especially of the one in whose person all these transactions find a symbolic focus,

Jean-Jacques Rousseau. Like Rousseau, Challe, Marivaux, and Diderot deploy the rhetoric of emotion to praise or to criticize, to urge their readers to protest against what they judge to be wrong or to foster appreciation for what they think is right. These writers enjoyed no official status as ministers of church or state, and so they navigated a perilous course between the prickliness of political authorities and the fickle expectations of their readers. As they did so, they also found in the language of and about anger and gratitude a resource for affirming in plausible ways the dignity of their vocation and the value of their work. The interplay between these two layers of their discourse gives their use of 'emotion' language a special richness and heuristic value for approaching the role of that language in the period as a whole.

Earlier versions of Chapters 3 and 5 were published as 'The Intelligence of Mind and Heart: *Reconnaissance* in *La Vie de Marianne*', in *Eighteenth-Century Fiction* 18.1 (2005–6), and 'Rousseau's Quarrel with Gratitude', in Victoria Kahn, Neil Saccamano, and Daniela Coli, eds, *Politics and the Passions, 1500–1850* (Princeton: Princeton University Press, 2006). I wish to thank the editors for their hospitality and the publishers for their permission to reprint. An early version of Chapter 2 was presented in 2005 at a conference sponsored by the Centre d'Étude de la Langue et de la Littérature Françaises des XVIIe et XVIIIe siècles at the Université de Paris-Sorbonne Paris IV; I am grateful to its director at the time, Sylvain Menant, as well as to Geneviève Artigas-Menant, an authority on Robert Challe, for their welcome and useful suggestions. I wish also to thank the Huntington Library, and its curator of rare books, Stephen Tabor, for the jacket illustration. It is the third of the set of engravings supervised by Rousseau for *Julie, ou la nouvelle Héloïse*, and it seemed to me to be particularly apt, since the scene to which it refers (Part II, letter 10) is one which moves from anger to gratitude. Thanks also to Bruce Whiteman of the William Andrews Clark Memorial Library for his advice, and to Michelle Lee for her work in compiling the bibliography.

This book would not have been completed without the help of many people. In my own academic field, Felicity Baker, Michel Delon, Bernadette Fort, Victoria Kahn, Judith A. Miller, Philip Stewart, and especially Benoît Melançon and Stephen Werner have provided me with encouragement and insightful comments; Peter Reill, as Director of the UCLA Center for 17th and 18th Century Studies, has been a constant source of support; and Julie Hayes has been a particularly attentive reader over many years. I am thankful to other friends, including Linda Leith, Gabriel Moyal, and Nancey Murphy, for expanding my literary, philosophical, and theological horizons. It has been a pleasure to work with the staff at Oxford University Press, and I especially appreciate the support I have received from my editor, Jacqueline Baker, as well as from Judith Luna at World's Classics. Above all, I am grateful more than I can say to my wife Susan and my daughter Judy, as well as to my brother John, my sister Veronica, and their families, for all their love.

P.C.

Contents

Abbreviations

C	Jean-Jacques Rousseau, *Confessions*, tr. Angela Scholar and ed. Patrick Coleman (Oxford: Oxford University Press, 2000)
CW	*The Collected Writings of Rousseau*, ed. Roger D. Masters and Christopher Kelly, 12 vols to date (Hanover, NH: University Press of New England, 1990–)
D	Robert Challe, *Difficultés sur la religion proposées au père Malebranche*, ed. Frédéric Deloffre and François Moureau (Geneva: Droz, 2000)
E	Jean-Jacques Rousseau, *Émile*, tr. Allan Bloom (New York: Basic Books, 1979)
G 1	*The Discourses and Other Early Political Writings*, ed. and tr. Victor Gourevitch (Cambridge: Cambridge University Press, 1997)
G 2	*The Social Contract and Other Later Political Writings*, ed. and tr. Victor Gourevitch (Cambridge: Cambridge University Press, 1997)
IF	Robert Challe, *Les Illustres Françaises*, ed. Jacques Cormier and Frédéric Deloffre (Paris: Livre de poche, 1996)
LLL	A. W. Preston, *Life, Love, and Laughter in the Reign of Louis XIV: A New Translation of Robert Challe's Novel 'Les Illustres Françaises'* (Brighton: Book Guild, 2008)
OC	Jean-Jacques Rousseau, *Œuvres complètes* (Paris: Gallimard, 1969–95)
RHLF	Revue d'histoire littéraire de la France
SVEC	Studies on Voltaire and the Eighteenth Century
V	Denis Diderot, *Œuvres*, ed. Laurent Versini, 5 vols (Paris: Laffont, 1994–7)

Note: In selecting translations of Rousseau for use in this book, I have considered both quality and wide accessibility. With the exception of *Émile*, all the works cited here are available in the *Collected Writings*, and since this translation is keyed to the pages of the French 'Pléiade' edition, readers using it should have no trouble locating particular passages. Translations of other authors that are not specifically credited are my own.

1

Anger, Gratitude, and Enlightenment Sociability

This book started with some questions about Rousseau. Did he think anger was ever an appropriate emotion, one it was good to feel and right to express? His writings present two diametrically opposed positions on the subject. The educational treatise *Émile* cites with approval Seneca's definition of anger as a disease of the soul and the enemy of reason.[1] By detaching himself from external goods and cultivating self-sufficiency, the Stoic sage limits his vulnerability to frustration and insult. Impervious to offense, he will not succumb to anger but rather maintain the equanimity of a rational being. Yet, Rousseau adopted as his motto a line from one of Juvenal's angriest satires.[2] Appealing in the *Lettre à d'Alembert* to the authority of the Roman satirist, he declared that in a corrupt society only righteous indignation proves the writer's personal commitment to truth and justice. To call for philosophical calm was to excuse complacency. As I explored the contexts in which these declarations are made and the intellectual traditions on which they draw I was intrigued by the ways in which the tension between them illuminates other aspects of Rousseau's thought. Indeed, looking at the ways anger is

[1] See the title page of *Émile*, in Jean-Jacques Rousseau, *Œuvres complètes* (Paris: Gallimard, 1969–95), iv. 239. See also *Emile, or On Education*, tr. Allan Bloom (New York: Basic Books, 1979), 31. References to these editions will henceforth be abbreviated as *OC* and *E*. The reference is to Seneca, *De ira*, II.13, which declares that anger is a curable illness. See Seneca, *Moral and Political Essays*, ed. John M. Cooper and J. F. Procopé (Cambridge: Cambridge University Press, 1995), 53.

[2] 'Vitam impendere vero' (to risk one's life on the truth), Juvenal, *Satires* IV.91. The poet is attacking the courtier Crispus, 'who never swam against the flood; he was not the kind of patriot who could speak his mind freely and risk his life for the truth'. *Juvenal and Persius*, ed. and tr. Susanna Morton Braund (Cambridge, Mass.: Harvard University Press, 2004), 205. Rousseau first publicly identified this phrase as his motto in his *Lettre à d'Alembert*, *OC* v. 120 n. He also placed it on the title page of his *Lettres écrites de la montagne* (1764), *OC* iii. 682.

discussed and dramatized by Rousseau and other writers of his day opened up fresh perspectives on conceptions of self and sociability in the broader French Enlightenment.

Important insights might be gained from a similar study of other passions or emotions, but in this study I have selected only one, the positive counterpart to anger that is gratitude. If, as de Jaucourt writes in the *Encyclopédie* article 'Passions', 'la haine que nous sentons envers ceux qui nous font du tort, c'est la colère' (the hatred we feel toward those who do us wrong, is anger), the opposite of anger is 'reconnaissance', or 'l'amour que nous avons pour quelqu'un, à cause du bien qu'il nous a fait, ou qu'il a l'intention de nous faire' (the love we have for someone because of the good he has done us or that he intends to do us).[3] As we shall see, Enlightenment writers take positions on gratitude that are as richly ambivalent as those they adopt on anger. Placing discussions of gratitude alongside those of anger gives us, I believe, a focused and economical way of framing what is new in Enlightenment debates about human interaction. Declarations of anger and gratitude often do more than illustrate a range of reactions to specific situations. They include judgments about whether the world as a whole favors or frustrates human happiness. In the face of evils offensive to reason, can the universe still be understood as the creation of a benevolent personal divinity to which we owe gratitude? Does it make sense, do we in fact owe it to our dignity as moral beings, to get angry with the world as it is? Or should we free ourselves from anger or gratitude altogether and dismiss such questions as reflecting a fundamental mistake about the nature and origin of the universe?

This debate has a long history, of course, as we can see from the Book of Job, and more generally from the tension between the wisdom and the prophetic books of the Hebrew Bible. Contrasting assessments of emotion and equanimity also feature prominently in classical antiquity. 'Anger' is the first word of the *Iliad*, and discussions of anger and

[3] Lists of contrary emotions have varied widely over the centuries, indeed what counts as an emotion or passion, of the body or of the soul, is a longstanding subject of dispute. For the discussion in early modern France, see Anthony Levi, *French Moralists: The Theory of the Passions 1585 to 1649* (Oxford: Clarendon Press, 1964). Most emotions are probably too multi-dimensional to have simple opposites. See Robert C. Solomon, *True to our Feelings: What our Emotions Are Really Telling Us* (New York: Oxford University Press, 2007), 176. Yet, anger and gratitude are often paired, beginning with Epicurus in his 'Letter to Herodotus'. See *Hellenistic Philosophy: Introductory Readings*, tr. Brad Inwood and L. P. Gerson (2nd edn, Indianapolis: Hackett, 1998), 13. In terms of our relationships with other people, at least, there is a good case for viewing anger and gratitude as opposites. Another pair of emotional dispositions that would be relevant for the kind of study I propose would be trust and suspicion.

gratitude are a recurring feature in Greek and Roman writers, of whom Lucretius is perhaps the most important for the French Enlightenment.[4] However, the philosophers of antiquity focused primarily on helping thoughtful individuals come to terms with their anxieties, not on changing the practices of society at large. Hellenistic thinking about emotions, for example, for all its conceptual boldness, never challenged the system of benefaction and gratitude pervasive in Mediterranean civilization, nor did it undermine the role of honor and status-consciousness in defining and defending social hierarchies. There were resources for such a challenge in Christian scripture and tradition,[5] but these were blunted by the church's political establishment, and counterbalanced by the otherworldly emphasis of its spirituality. In the cultural situation of Enlightenment Europe, however, insulating the inner lives of privileged souls from the general life of the world seemed a less appealing ideal, and one which in any case was proving difficult to sustain. The confessional wars that followed the Reformation had fostered widespread skepticism about religious certainties. Late seventeenth-century debates over theodicy, for example, engaged a broad section of the reading public. Scientific advances made large-scale transformations of the world conceivable, while the emergence of new conceptions of human association based on natural rights, consent, and contract invited—at least potentially—the involvement of all men in the legitimization and critique of political associations. Enlightenment analyses of emotions in individuals are thus often colored by questions about the religious or metaphysical underpinnings of human interaction, and concerns about the implications for social and political practices of unleashing or disciplining the emotions.

As a literary scholar, I am interested in the ways the resources of form, language, and genre of a text shape the articulation, illustration, and

[4] For Homer, see Leonard Charles Muellner, *The Anger of Achilles: Mēnis in Greek Epic* (Ithaca, NY: Cornell University Press, 1996). For an over view of Lucretius' influence on the *philosophes*, see Eric Baker, 'Lucretius in the European Enlightenment', in Stuart Gillespie and Philip Hardie, eds, *The Cambridge Companion to Lucretius* (Cambridge: Cambridge University Press, 2007), 274–88, and Silviane Albertan-Coppola, 'L'Anti-épicurianisme: l'épicurianisme des Lumières', *Dix-huitième siècle* 35 (2003), 309–18. In addition to the more general discussions of emotion in Greek and Roman antiquity cited below, see *Cicero on the Emotions: Tusculan Disputations 3 and 4*, translated and with commentary by Margaret Graver (Chicago: Chicago University Press, 2002) and Graver, *Stoicism and Emotion* (Chicago: Chicago University Press, 2007).

[5] For an overview, see David A. DeSilva, *Honor, Patronage, Kinship and Purity: Unlocking New Testament Culture* (Downers Grove, Ill.: Intervarsity Press, 2000).

imaginative testing of ideas in the text as what might be called a structure of feeling.[6] This book does not, therefore, seek to present a comprehensive account of Enlightenment philosophies of emotion.[7] Nor does it focus on the historical patterns of gift-giving or other forms of symbolic exchange that called for grateful or (in the case of failure or misfire) angry response. There is a burgeoning literature on these topics, and I can only refer the reader to some works I have found to be particularly relevant to this study.[8] Instead, I examine the ways in which the themes of anger and gratitude are presented in some key texts of the French eighteenth century. I also look at the role of these emotions in writers' reflections on the resources (literary, cultural, or social) available to them as authors, and on the public for which they write. I argue that because writers in eighteenth-century France were gaining new importance as public intellectuals and representative cultural figures, the exploration of anger and gratitude as themes in their works also reflects evolving attitudes toward the society that nurtures or frustrates their status claims. The way these emotions are appropriated, denounced, or transcended, I would argue, is more than a matter of individual psychology. It engages larger questions about the cultural life of their time. Sustained attention to key works of literature, broadly defined as including any work displaying a concern for shaping its material and the reader's response to it, can, I believe, offer a distinctive contribution to historical understanding.

[6] The term 'structures of feeling' comes from Raymond Williams, *Marxism and Literature* (Oxford: Oxford University Press, 1977), 128–35.

[7] Scholarship on this question has until recently focused mostly on the Enlightenment's 'rehabilitation' of the passions in general, in opposition to Augustinian critiques of the irrationality of emotion as a sign of humanity's fallen state. See Roger Mercier, *La Réhabilitation de la nature humaine 1700–1750* (Villemonble: La Balance, 1960). As mentioned below, we do not find French equivalents to Hume's or Smith's reflective analysis of particular passions as part of an overall moral philosophy.

[8] These include Natalie Zemon Davis, *The Gift in Sixteenth-Century France* (Madison: University of Wisconsin Press, 2000); Maurice Godelier, *L'Énigme du don* (Paris: Fayard, 1996), which reconsiders the legacy of Marcel Mauss's *Essai sur le don* (1924); Aafke E. Komter, *Social Solidarity and the Gift* (Cambridge: Cambridge University Press, 2005); Jacques Derrida, *Donner le temps* (Paris: Galilée, 1989) and *Donner la mort* (Paris: Galilée, 1999); Jean-Luc Marion, *Étant donné: essai d'une phénoménologie de la donation* (Paris: Presses universitaires de France, 1997); John Milbank, 'Can a Gift Be Given? Prolegomena to a Future Trinitarian Metaphysic', *Modern Theology* 11 (1995), 119–61. A good brief survey of this literature, secular as well as theological, may be found in Risto Saarinen, *God and the Gift: An Ecumenical Theology of Giving* (Collegeville, Minn.: Liturgical Press, 2005).

The chapters that follow look at writings in a variety of genres: narrative fiction, satirical dialogue, philosophical treatise, and polemical discourse. In each case, I have focused on the relationship between the discussion of anger or gratitude in the text, and the dramatization of these emotions in the rhetorical stance of the work as a whole. The emphasis throughout is on the singularity of each text, but my readings have naturally been prompted by a number of initial hypotheses about the contexts—historical and philosophical—within which the text might best be understood. The framing of these contexts has in turn been influenced by the work of reading, and so in what follows I sketch the approach to Enlightenment anger and gratitude that I have found fruitful in the work of interpretation. I hope it will show how attending to the discourse about emotions can be a valuable heuristic tool in studying aspects of eighteenth-century French culture which continue to shape the ways we understand our own.

ANGER AND CULTURAL STATUS

When is anger justified, and who may claim the right to be angry? Slights may be ignored or overlooked, wrongs may be redressed through negotiation, and either may be forgiven, but what makes them offensive in the first place, such that anger becomes an expected and appropriate emotional response? The answers to such questions as these tell us a lot about the ethos of a particular society. How the questions themselves are formulated, and whether the answers given are themselves matters of consensus or contest, can be important indicators of cultural self-understanding. The same is true for a related but different question: when and for whom is anger thought to be a good in itself and not merely a circumstantially justified emotion? The capacity to experience and express anger, on another's behalf, but also on one's own, might be a desirable feature of the kind of personality a society admires, at least in some of its members—a warrior nobility, for example—or, in an agonistic society like that of ancient Athens, in the citizen body as a whole.[9] On the other hand, and even in that same culture, the ability to resist or transcend anger may be made a marker of spiritual status; it may be viewed as a crucial qualification for a ruler, a judge—or a writer,

[9] See David Konstan, *The Emotions of the Ancient Greeks: Studies in Aristotle and Classical Literature* (Toronto: University of Toronto Press, 2006).

as illustrated by the famous *sine ira et studio* in Tacitus' preface to his *Histories.*[10]

In eighteenth-century France, the terms in which anger was discussed were inherited from a variety of sources. These included the poets and philosophers of classical antiquity, as well as the Bible and Christian tradition. The traditional vocabulary of the humors continued to play a role alongside the language of the new natural sciences, as we see in a work such as Descartes's *Passions de l'âme.*[11] However, 'enlightened' writing presents a number of distinctive features in its reflections on the relationship between emotion and sociability. The first is a growing tendency to give significant moral weight to the anger expressed by people of inferior status: to commoners, to women, even occasionally to children. This trend was by no means comprehensive. In literature, the anger of peasants, servants, and the like was still largely confined to comedy, since it was a traditional target for mockery. That such people might have the right to take offense, especially at the behavior of their betters, was still seen as absurd. For all their ironic questioning of social attitudes, Diderot's novel *Jacques le fataliste* and his satirical dialogue *Le Neveu de Rameau* continue to reflect this assumption in their depiction of the lower classes. Women's anger, too, was a longstanding object for derision, and it is still presented as such in the Mme Dutour episode of Marivaux's *La Vie de Marianne*, although here, as in other instances, it is the character's social status more than her gender that makes her anger comic. There was one important exception to the treatment of female anger: in noble heroines whose love was spurned anger took on tragic grandeur. Yet, if the heroine's anger led her to become implacable in revenge, pathos could easily shade into horror. Traditionally, the depiction of such horrors was mostly confined to theatrical tragedy, as in Corneille's *Médée*, where it is kept at a distance by strict conventions of speech and decorum. In the eighteenth century, however, it finds more contemporary and unfettered expression in novels such as Laclos's *Liaisons dangereuses* or Sade's *Juliette*, where the frustrations of women's

[10] Tacitus, *Histories* I.1, variously translated as 'without hatred or affection' or 'without either bitterness or partiality'. The Latin *ira* has of course a somewhat different range of meanings than does the modern *anger* or *colère*, and the same may be said for the Greek *thumos* or *orgē*, but these complexities of historical semantics (and the vexed question of how they were understood by French writers in our period) cannot be pursued here.

[11] Carole Talon-Hugon, *Les Passions rêvées par la raison: essai sur la théorie des passions de Descartes et de quelques-uns de ses contemporains* (Paris: Vrin, 2002).

lives were portrayed in more familiar domestic and social settings. In these works the woman's anger is directed not only at an unfaithful lover but at anyone who limits the scope of her action or the fulfillment of her desires, whatever form they take. Such novels represented a more direct challenge to readers' assumptions about gender roles than did tragedy or opera. Yet their subversive intentions only confirmed the longstanding view that female anger threatened the very fabric of society—a prospect that delighted Sade even as it made Laclos shudder. The exceptions to this paradigm are not always found where one would expect them. In his *Émile*, Rousseau, often decried as an anti-feminist, gave his ideal woman Sophie a legitimate claim to anger.[12]

The main novelty of the period, however, was to pay serious attention to the anger of men who believed their intelligence and sensibility entitled them to social recognition above and beyond what was warranted by their birth. Rousseau, again, is the outstanding case. His angry response to perceived slight, even on the part of those who offered to be his patrons and friends, and even more, his claim to determine for himself what *counted* as a slight, offended many people in return, but it also puzzled and intrigued them by the force of its conviction. Rousseau's protest at being wronged spoke to a slowly developing appreciation among traditional elites for the social, and not just the intellectual or artistic, dignity of talented commoners. Just as important was a corresponding shift in the attitude of the reading public. By virtue of their own felt capacity to respond with sensitivity and sympathy to the works of writers like Rousseau, ordinary readers saw themselves as sharing in the author's status—a claim manifested in their decision to take up the pen themselves and write to the author.[13] In their identification with the writer, they also appropriated for themselves his newfound entitlement to anger. In the generation of Robespierre which grew up reading Rousseau, this sense of justified indignation at the circumstances that blocked the careers of a growing class of educated but underemployed young men helped transform a revolt into a revolution. Anger at slights to the self and indignation at injustice done to the people as a whole were fused into one great emotion endowed with quasi-sacred significance. In the past, only a traditional authority figure

[12] Rousseau, *Émile*, in *OC* iv. 754.

[13] See Robert Darnton, *The Great Cat Massacre and Other Episodes in French Cultural History* (New York: Basic Books, 1984); Claude Labrosse, *Lire au XVIIIe siècle: 'La Nouvelle Héloïse' et ses lecteurs* (Lyon: Presses universitaires de Lyon, 1985).

such as the king bore general symbolic weight in his person; now intellectuals also viewed their lives as invested with a representative value they had a duty to honor.

An equally significant development can be observed in religion, where anger 'from below' also took on new significance. That human anger at God had a legitimate place in religious faith is explicitly recognized in the Bible.[14] Job's angry outbursts, however, like those of the Psalmist, were always set within an ongoing personal relationship with God, and indeed drew their legitimacy from God's own covenant promises. Getting angry at the way things were on earth made no sense outside that context of answerability. The anger of 'the nations', like their appeal to their arbitrary and ineffective gods, was only meaningless agitation.[15] This paradigm still held sway in eighteenth-century France, and nowhere more clearly than in that notoriously anti-Christian work, Sade's *Philosophie dans le boudoir* (1795). The hero of the dialogue, the atheist Dolmancé, is so angry at the God whose existence he denies that he wishes he could summon the divinity back into being 'pour que ma rage au moins portât sur quelque chose' (so that my rage might at least fall on something).[16] At the same time, many *philosophes* far less radical than Sade, and even some clerics, adopted a view of humanity's relationship to God that left no place for anger even within a religious worldview. Building on the views of the natural right lawyers of the seventeenth-century thinkers, they declared that the basis of moral law lay in the visible order of the universe rather than in God's personal will. This conviction arose in part as a reaction to the emphasis on the absoluteness of divine sovereignty in late medieval theology. In seeking to preserve the freedom of God's will from the constraints of human expectations or the claims of human merit, theologians of the late Middle Ages, followed after the Reformation by Calvinist and Jansenist writers, made it appear more arbitrary in its operation, less intimately attached to a stable earthly order.[17] For other thinkers dealing with the aftermath of the religious

[14] Lytta Basset counts the biblical occurrences of anger words in her *Sainte Colère: Jacob, Job, Jésus* (Paris: Bayard, 2004), 20; see also John Goldingay, 'Anger', in *New Interpreter's Dictionary of the Bible* (Nashville: Abingdon Press, 2006–9), i. 156–8; Matthew A. Elliott, *Faithful Feelings: Rethinking Emotion in the New Testament* (Grand Rapids, Mich.: Kregel, 2006).

[15] Acts 4: 25, adapting Ps. 2: 1.

[16] Sade, *Philosophie dans le boudoir*, in *Œuvres*, ed. Michel Delon, 3 vols (Paris: Gallimard, 1990–8), iii. 57.

[17] See Michael Gillespie, *Nihilism before Nietzsche* (Chicago: University of Chicago Press, 1995).

wars, eternal reason, manifested in the marvelously complex but regular laws of natural science, seemed to constitute a more dependable, and widely acceptable, reference point than a divine revelation mediated through texts based on special historical experiences. Various forms of a simple, 'natural' religion emerged as alternatives to a Christianity whose understanding of God was increasingly considered, not to transcend everyday reason, but to contradict it.

Ironically, however, the greater the trust invested in nature's ordered regularity, the more natural disasters, wars, and the perverse effects of good intentions became an affront to reason itself, an absurdity rather than a mystery. Since most enlightened thinkers still generally believed that the world was created by divine power, they continued to direct their frustration and anger at God, if only because there was no other obvious target. As Margaret Jacob puts it in a study of dissident writers of the early Enlightenment, 'to become a seeker given to heterodoxy required first a deeply personal anger'.[18] Yet, if moral dignity was no longer the free gift of a personal God but was grounded in humanity's own capacity to comprehend the natural order, then anger at disorder lost its relational dimension. Anger at the way of the world had nowhere to go, except to the bitter irony of Voltairean satire.

This was not a development entirely to be deplored. For the same logic that rendered anger pointless applied to the other side of the divine–human relationship. The prospect of divine wrath also lost much of its hold over the human imagination. Enlightenment writers were acutely conscious of the ways in which secular as well as ecclesiastical authorities could brandish the image of an angry God to instill fear and obedience in their subjects. 'Quel personnage fait-on jouer à Dieu?' (What character do we make God play?) exclaimed Du Marsais in his *Examen de la religion*, implicitly comparing the angry God to the undignified *barbon* of theatrical comedy.[19] Scientific investigation could also be inhibited by warnings that God would be offended if, repeating the sin of Adam and Eve, humanity overstepped the bounds supposedly set on human knowledge.

[18] Margaret C. Jacob, 'The Enlightenment Critique of Christianity', in *The Cambridge History of Christianity*, v. 7: *Enlightenment, Reawakening and Revolution 1660–1815* (Cambridge: Cambridge University Press, 2006), 270.

[19] César Chesneau Du Marsais, *Examen de la religion, ou doutes sur la religion dont on cherche l'éclaircissement de bonne foi*, ed. Gianluca Mori (Oxford: Voltaire Foundation, 1998), 170. In dismissing divine anger as a superstitious notion, Du Marsais and other *philosophes* could appeal not only to Lucretius but to the moderate and urbane Cicero as well. See *De officiis*, III.103–4.

Since in biblical tradition God's anger was prompted not only by human pretensions to divinity, but even more by the worship of other gods,[20] removing anger from the list of God's attributes also opened the way to greater tolerance of other religions. It made room for accommodating cultural practices (notably in the realm of sexuality) at odds with the beliefs of one tradition but considered natural in others. In all these cases, God is not necessarily banished from the scene; it is simply no longer plausible to think of him as taking offense at human waywardness, now largely redefined as cultural variety. Thus, while rational theodicy deprived human anger at God of much of its point, there was some compensation in that divine anger lost much of its sting.

On the level of human interaction, widening the right to take offense might ultimately serve the cause of equality, but restricting the range of acceptable justifications for anger had the more immediate benefit of reducing the level of social violence. Over the course of the seventeenth century, the advocates of *politesse*, haunted by the violence of France's civil wars, sought to limit the giving and taking of offense by those engaged in the worldly interactions of court and salon.[21] In some respects this effort paralleled the monarchy's efforts to limit the nobility's opportunities to defend its status outside the limits set by monarchical order. The outlawing of duels, an attempt not just to limit individual acts of revenge but to regulate the code of honor itself, is perhaps the best-known instance of this convergence of monarchical interest and civilizing concern. Yet, precisely because the ethic of politeness was formulated in universal terms, it challenged all forms of violent reaction to offense, even on the part of the sovereign. It did so by drawing on two widely influential currents of thought. The first of these is the neo-Stoic ideal of self-mastery, illustrated by Corneille's tragedy *Cinna* (1640). In this play, the Roman emperor Augustus meets the man who conspired against him with an offer of friendship instead of a threat of revenge. He declares that the mark of the truly noble person is his capacity to transcend his anger by an effort of will. Cinna is so impressed by this unexpected generosity that his rebellious anger

[20] Exod. 34: 6, 14.

[21] The classic work is Maurice Magendie, *La Politesse mondaine et les théories de l'honnêteté en France au XVIIe siècle, de 1600 à 1660* (Paris: Alcan, 1925). More recent works include Emmanuel Bury, *Littérature et politesse: l'invention de l'honnête homme (1580–1750)* (Paris: Presses universitaires de France, 1996); Marc Fumaroli, *La Diplomatie de l'esprit: de Montaigne à La Fontaine* (Paris: Hermann, 1994).

evaporates as he is moved to emulate his rival.[22] In a somewhat less sublime vein, Rousseau's *Lettre à d'Alembert* cites the story of Louis XIV throwing his cane out of the window to avoid striking one of his gentlemen (v. 66).

A more disenchanted form of thinking, often called Jansenist but more properly labeled Augustinian since it was not limited to one particular sect, maintained that the passions were essentially irrational impulses and so unamenable to the kind of education that would allow them to contribute to genuine well-being. We see this view reflected in the tragedies of Racine and novels such as Lafayette's *Princesse de Clèves.* As Pierre Nicole argued in one of his influential essays, even anger society considers to be appropriate, such as that of noble persons, is a form of sin.[23] Yet, as historians have shown, this Augustinian outlook could paradoxically encourage secular efforts to protect society against anarchy. Even if the sin itself could never be eradicated, earthly authorities should do what they could to limit anger's occasions and effects. While in other respects Augustinian pessimism stands in opposition to the more optimistic voluntarism of neo-Stoicism, here the two discourses converge in delegitimizing vehement emotion.

The discourse of civility lost some of its urgency as the threat of internal strife receded and as the pessimism of the seventeenth-century *moralistes* gave way to the more optimistic naturalism of the Enlightenment. References to anger, prominent in Montaigne and Charron, fade away in later theorists of *honnêteté* such as the Chevalier de Méré. They

[22] Corneille is drawing a contrast with the relationship between Brutus and Caesar. According to Seneca, 'it is commonly debated whether Marcus Brutus should have allowed our deified Julius to grant him his life, having decided to kill him'—which he later did anyway. Seneca, *De beneficiis*, III.2, *Moral and Political Essays*, 228.

[23] For Nicole, human beings are not 'aimables', and it is unjust to want to be loved and respected. 'La civilité nous gagne. L'incivilité nous choque. Mais l'une nous gagne, et l'autre nous choque, parce que nous sommes hommes, c'est-à-dire, tous vains et tous injustes' (Civility wins us over. Incivility offends us. But the one wins us over, and the other offends us, because we are men, that is to say, all of us vain and all of us unjust). Pierre Nicole, 'Des moyens de conserver la paix avec les hommes', in *Essais de morale* (1733–71; repr. Geneva: Slatkine, 1971), i. 293, 310. For the connections between Augustinianism and Epicureanism in seventeenth-century France, see Jean Lafond, *La Rochefoucauld: augustinisme et littérature* (Paris: Klincksieck, 1977), and Michael Moriarty, *Fallen Nature, Fallen Selves: Early Modern French Thought II* (Oxford: Oxford University Press, 2006).On the other hand, Nicole's position would seem to be incompatible with the Aristotelian tradition of ethics and its ideal of a proper mean between opposite dispositional extremes. In the works I will be discussing, references and even allusions to the language of the *Nicomachean Ethics* are notably absent, but accounting for this fact lies beyond the scope of this study.

are not to be found at all in paradigmatic discussions of sociability in the following century such as Charles Duclos's *Considérations sur les mœurs de ce siècle* (1750). It is as if violent reactions to slight were no longer viewed as an active possibility. No doubt Duclos assumed that the prospect of ostracism from polite company would deter any potential offender. It is significant, however, that, unlike Adam Smith in his almost contemporary *Theory of Moral Sentiments* (1758),[24] Duclos should not mention anger at all. Perhaps the threat of anger had not so much disappeared as gone underground.[25] The mid-eighteenth-century discourse of sociability preferred to celebrate the achievements of French civilization rather than draw attention to its fragility. The ideology of the salon, with its discourse of equality and friendship, could not, for example, openly admit any frank admission that the constraints of patronage might generate resentment on the part of its beneficiaries. Until late in the century, outsiders such as Rousseau who did take offense or who chafed at the obligations of gratitude were met with incomprehension and reproach.

If we turn from Duclos to the great eighteenth-century novelists, however, we find a tension between willed belief in the triumph of conflict-free sociability over hierarchy of status and a more skeptical view, which acknowledged an intractable conflict between the pressures of social opinion and the emotional autonomy of the self. As Jerrold Seigel has pointed out, Smith's notion of an 'impartial spectator' within the self, serving as a mediator between individual sensibility and the generality of social and moral norms, does not have a counterpart in French writers of the period. The latter tend to be more polarized in their conceptions of the self's interaction with society than their British counterparts. Shaped, perhaps, by the legacy of absolutism, or by the persistence, even into the Enlightenment, of Augustinian thought, they tend to view that interaction more in terms of domination and resistance to domination than as reciprocal enhancement. 'That selfhood was formed by social relations was evident, but some who observed it also felt that the reflective component of the self needed to be shielded from oppression and untrustworthy social powers, lest it become the

[24] Adam Smith, *The Theory of Moral Sentiments*, ed. D. D. Raphael and A. L. Macfie, in *The Glasgow Edition of the Works and Correspondence of Adam Smith* (Oxford: Clarendon, 1976–83), i. 11, 24, 36–7, 238, 240.

[25] The issue would re-emerge, of course, with the French Revolution. For a suggestive treatment of anger in this period, see Andrew Stauffer, *Anger, Revolution, and Romanticism* (Cambridge: Cambridge University Press, 2005).

entry-point thought which domination and corruption insinuated themselves into the interior of persons.'[26] For example, the Clarens community portrayed in Rousseau's *Julie, ou la nouvelle Héloïse* (1761) is presented as a model of mutual consideration, but the reader cannot forget the violent anger Julie's father displayed earlier in the book. When he discovered her affair with a commoner, he hit his daughter so hard she miscarried the baby she hoped would make her parents change their minds about forcing her to marry another man. In *La Vie de Marianne*, Marivaux also shows how in the absence of genuine bonds of affection the *égards* of polite sociability would never override hard-nosed assessments of social status. Once the smooth surface of politeness was cracked, the appeal to 'public opinion' lost some its power, since its authority was seen to rest, not on some universal consensus, but on the interests of a dominant elite.

The emancipatory potential of an ethic of polite sociability had no doubt been exaggerated to begin with, but disenchantment with it opened the door to an alternative but equally idealized conception of how offenses, and the anger they provoke, might be eliminated from social interaction. Instead of being disciplined by an ethic of propriety, mutual consideration, and self-control, the generation of unruly emotions could be checked at the source by creating a society governed by laws enforced equally on everyone in an entirely impersonal way. This is the solution Rousseau adopts in the first part of *Émile*. As a young child, the hero of the book will be free from anger because his environment is from the first so arranged by his tutor that the frustration and hurt he inevitably experiences never appears to him to be the result of another person's will, but only the effect of natural and necessary causes. When he is punished for misbehavior, Émile will feel no resentment because he can detect no hostile intention directed against him. Rousseau's vision of a world free from personal dependence, artificial and even oppressive as it may seem to us, had a powerful appeal for readers living in a society in which everyone was bound by ties of obligation to benefactors and clients of one kind or another and had to keep careful track of favors given and received. Even so, Rousseau will gradually abandon this approach to education as the boy grows up and enters society. The mature Émile must possess a capacity for anger if, as he should, he is to respond energetically to injustice in human interaction.

[26] Jerrold Seigel, *The Idea of the Self: Thought and Experience in Western Europe since the Seventeenth Century* (Cambridge: Cambridge University Press, 2005), 37.

On the level of the community as a whole, the institution of a rule of law powerful and pervasive enough to eliminate personal dependence and forestall the discomfort of its attending emotions could be imagined in at least two different ways. It might be focused, as in Rousseau's *Social Contract*, on a political compact in which obligation was founded on the general will of the citizens. The true general will is distinguished from the sum total of personal wills and intentions by its impersonal character. It is not simply what I (or we) want, but what 'one' wants when the passions are 'silenced'[27] and the self recognizes his deepest and truest interests. For Rousseau these interests will always be aligned with those of his fellow citizens, as long as the fundamental equality of citizens and the generality of law are respected.

Other Enlightenment writers, such as Morelly or d'Holbach, emphasized the ongoing regulation of behavior by philosophical rulers guided by their knowledge of natural laws. In a well-ordered society as these writers imagined it, there would be little occasion for anger in response to personal offense. Immediate physiological reactions to frustration could not of course be eliminated, but they would be correctible or at the very least containable, originating from the inevitable frictions of the social system rather than from expectations of personal consideration. That enlightened *dirigisme* of this kind would not provoke resentment in those whose behavior was being regulated is simply assumed. That the people might take offense at being disciplined, or that they might take exception to the regulators' claims to impartiality, is not a possibility these works imagine, let alone a right they are willing to grant, so intent are they on removing the burden of dependence on other people's will in the details of social organization, and so confident are they in the psychological relief that will result.[28]

It is easy to see today how such schemes suffer from simplistic notions about the malleability of human nature. After the Revolution, the

[27] See the first draft of the *Contrat social*, I.2 (*OC* i. 284).

[28] This is not true of Montesquieu, however, who occupies in this as in other respects a curious intermediate position. He is of course concerned to ensure that positive law is in harmony with the various kinds of natural and circumstantial laws that inform the spirit of a particular nation, but the latter may include patterns of angry or grateful behavior which are to be integrated into a complex whole rather than eliminated entirely. It would still be true, however, that offenses and obligations that deviated from those regulated patterns, and thus presumably more disruptive to selves otherwise culturally conditioned to expect them, would be eliminated. His view may be said to anticipate the nineteenth-century re-conceptualization of informal bonds in sociological rather than moral terms.

froissements they neglect to theorize will become an object of sustained attention by liberal constitutionalists such as Constant.[29] Materialist though he was, Diderot already had his doubts, expressed most memorably in his *Neveu de Rameau.* Yet, once again, we should not minimize how attractive these schemes might appear to eighteenth-century subjects of a regime still riddled by arbitrary authority. The books that proposed them appealed to the imagination and the affections as much as to the reason of contemporary readers. As in the case of natural religion, to see one's condition as the product of impersonal laws rather than of personal will could be experienced as emotionally liberating. We tend to think of deism as a halfway house between belief and unbelief, an intellectual attitude rather than a living faith, but it was for a time a worldview that fully engaged the sensibility of someone like Voltaire. Similarly, the prospect of a earthly life in which one owed obedience to impersonal laws, and not to persons, could be embraced as a relief from arbitrary rule and from invidious distinctions of status. We tend to forget how enthusiasm for the principle of obedience to laws, not men, was rooted in a crisis in the emotional regime of the period that gave that principle a particular affective coloration, and led some to overlook the oppressive potential even of the most rational system of laws.

We also tend to neglect another aspect of political thinking in the period. While the application of rational principles to social organization might be unproblematic once the opportunity to do so exists, those writers who considered the matter agreed that seizing that opportunity might require the decisive initiative of a founding genius or Legislator, as Rousseau called him. One consequence of this idea, acknowledged with varying degrees of explicitness, is to reintroduce emotion into political life. Anger might disappear, but the Legislator's founding act would place his fellow citizens in his debt and call for their gratitude. In the meantime, writers who showed potential legislators the way forward deserve the gratitude of their readers. Indeed, it might be argued that the historical originality of Enlightenment writers or intellectuals lies not only in articulating new entitlements to anger, but in staking new claims to public gratitude—even if, paradoxically, the burden of their proposals is to limit the salience of both these emotions in social and political life. Not for nothing could Paul Bénichou speak of a 'sacre de l'écrivain'

[29] See Patrick Coleman, 'Constant and the *Froissement* of Form', *Historical Reflections/Réflexions historiques* 28.3 (2002), 385–96.

in this period.[30] The writer's role in mediating social emotion can be seen as a secular version of the priest's mediation of social tensions through his access to a higher level of reality in which they can be reconciled or transcended. Yet, we should not too quickly accuse Enlightenment writers—even Rousseau—of narcissism or delusions of grandeur. In their writings, gratitude is no less problematic an emotion than anger, and the object of no less ambivalence.

GRATITUDE AS BURDEN AND GIFT

Like anger, gratitude can be seen as straddling the boundary between affective response and social interaction. In many traditional societies, such as those of the ancient Mediterranean, informal, personal favors were not clearly separated from the codified system of benefaction, material and symbolic, that cemented the relationships between patrons and clients.[31] As a consequence, classical writers such as Cicero and Seneca did not draw a sharp distinction between gratitude as a free response to a freely given favor, and gratitude as a formal obligation, the failure to fulfill which brings justified reprobation, and which may even provoke anger in the benefactor. In our post-Kantian world, moral and emotional obligations are two very different things, but this was not the case in pre-modern societies, which had other concerns.[32] For example, in antiquity, patrons bestowed favors to display their liberality to the public at large and so enhance their social prestige. Failure to

[30] Paul Bénichou, *Le Sacre de l'écrivain 1750–1830: sur l'avènement d'un pouvoir spirituel laïque en France* (Paris: Corti, 1973).

[31] Richard P. Saller, *Personal Patronage under the Early Empire* (Cambridge: Cambridge University Press, 1982); Andrew Wallace-Hadrill, ed., *Patronage in Ancient Society* (London: Routledge, 1989). It is more difficult for us to imagine anger as a systemic phenomenon, since such a system would seem to be incompatible with social cohesion, but our idealization of classical Greece and Rome may have led us to underestimate the pervasiveness of anger as an element of ordinary interaction in those societies. See William V. Harris, *Restraining Rage: The Ideology of Anger Control in Classical Antiquity* (Cambridge, Mass.: Harvard University Press, 2001) and Susanna Braund and Glenn W. Most, eds, *Ancient Anger: Perspectives from Aristotle to Galen* (Cambridge: Cambridge University Press, 2003).

[32] As for example, in Cicero's *De officiis*, the varying translation of whose title (as 'duties', 'obligations', or 'good offices') already indicates some of the difficulty. As P. G. Walsh suggests, Cicero is more interested in the contrast, at once aesthetic and moral, between the honorable and the dishonorable than in the difference between formal and informal obligation. Cicero, *On Obligations*, tr. P. G. Walsh (Oxford: Oxford University Press, 2000), liv.

acknowledge their benefaction constituted a serious slight to their honor.[33] A similar dynamic of benefaction and gratitude can be found in feudalism, but with the gradual emergence of centralized states, obligation came to be based on the impersonal bonds of political sovereignty or civil contract rather than on personal fealty. Patronage did not of course disappear. As Natalie Zemon Davis has reminded us, gift-giving and benefaction on a significant scale coexists with economic modes of exchange in any society, and thus one cannot identify any point in history at which the second can be said to replace the first.[34] Still, the assumption that the self's relationships with others should be understood in terms of a thick network of mutual consideration, of favors given and returned, began to be challenged by the idea that, at least in the public realm, these relationships should be subject only to general and impersonal laws. This would seem to leave little room for gratitude. Was this development a good or a bad thing? To eighteenth-century writers, the answer was not as obvious as some of the classical twentieth-century scholarship on the Enlightenment liked to believe.[35] Were Enlightenment writers, for example, obligated to society for the new prestige they were beginning to enjoy? Should they expect gratitude from their readers for their efforts to benefit the public? Or was the acknowledgment of merit a matter of impersonal reason only, and not of personal recognition?

Here again, Rousseau offers the paradigm case. Rousseau's friends and patrons often criticized his ingratitude. They were certainly justified in doing so, but Rousseau was also correct in thinking that such accusations missed a crucial point. His revolt against the burden of gratitude may have stemmed in part from a sense of his own entitlement, but it was also a principled protest against the whole system of benefaction that governed the life of anyone without enough status or income to give them a margin of independence. In an earlier era,

[33] Whether ingratitude constituted a slight, and the nature of the angry reaction to it, might depend in part on the status of the parties involved. The ingratitude of an equal, that is to say, of someone who should understand the subtleties of personal obligation, is not the same as that of a base person from whom one expects only material appreciation.

[34] 'The gift-exchange "system" and the commercial economic "system" . . . are two conceptions, or ideal types, of exchange behavior. They can function together, and economic activity of every sort is produced by their mix in greater, lesser, or equal degrees.' Barbara Rosenwein, *'To be the Neighbor of Saint Peter': The Social Meaning of Cluny's Property, 909–1049* (Ithaca, NY: Cornell University Press, 1989), cited (without a specific page reference) in Davis, *The Gift in Sixteenth-Century France*, 8.

[35] I think here of the works of Ernst Cassirer and Peter Gay.

Rousseau's protest would have been futile, even nonsensical, and his tortured responses to his friends' accusations show how difficult it was to separate the temperamental from the rational grounds for his discomfort. Still, in the context of the modern discourse of rights, and with the growing emphasis on intellectual achievement as a criterion for social advancement, it was possible for the 'republican' Rousseau to declare with some plausibility that rewards and recognition should be distributed on the basis of objective merit, rather than granted as favors. The rule of law and reason would lift the burden of personal dependence that made social inequality so hard to bear—and thereby, as in the ideal Geneva of Rousseau's *Lettre à d'Alembert* (1758), inspire in the citizens a free response of gratitude to their country for securing their freedom, and to each other for the unconstrained reciprocity in which that freedom finds its highest expression.

Rousseau's insistence on liberation from the obligation of personal gratitude may have irritated some of his friends, but his Enlightenment contemporaries shared a similar determination when it came to religion. Just as the *philosophes* had sought to banish the specter of divine wrath, they attacked the doctrine of personalized divine favor, especially as dramatized in the biblical account of a 'chosen' people. Such election was incompatible with the impartiality of divine justice. Likewise, the notion of particular Providence obscured the more truly divine institution of a natural order regulated by laws amenable to comprehension by human science.[36] It was of course still important to acknowledge the supremacy of God's will, but this was less a matter of personal obligation than of unconstrained appreciation for the sublime rationality of the cosmic order. The Vicaire savoyard of Rousseau's *Émile* may seem to be an exception to this general trend in that he experiences an impulse of gratitude for his philosophical insights, which he views, not just as the product of his reasoning, but as God's personal gift. As we shall see, however, the favor for which he gives thanks is the paradoxical one of liberation from any anxiety about what personal obligation God might expect from him in return. In this respect, his attitude almost certainly mirrors Rousseau's own.

The role played by the Vicaire's God may be likened to the one adopted, more or less explicitly, by the writer himself in relation to his public of grateful readers. Rousseau did his readers a favor by opening

[36] The most sustained effort to reconcile the two ideas is Malebranche's *Traité de la nature et de la grâce* (1680).

their eyes to social realities hitherto obscured from their view, and by giving expression to their own repressed or inchoate feelings. Instead of imposing a burdensome obligation on the recipient, this favor stimulated a free response from those who felt their reading experience had enhanced their capacity to think and feel for themselves. Rousseau owed his popularity among ordinary people to his independent spirit, to his refusal to acknowledge the humiliation of obligation. Yet, especially after the publication of his novel *Julie*, that acclaim was not based solely on esteem for his person or his philosophy. In unprecedented numbers, readers wrote to the author to express their gratitude for the way he helped them appreciate their own agency as feeling selves. This agency found confirmation of its vitality in the eager pleasure with which Rousseau's readers took up their pen and sent a letter to someone they did not personally know, but who seemed to offer a welcoming space for, indeed invite, their personal response.

This feature of Rousseau's relationship with his readers reminds us that gratitude is not always, or not only, a burden. Acknowledging one's obligations provides opportunities for displaying one's moral awareness, or at least one's good breeding. To express gratitude appropriately in many social situations, one must discern and conform to unwritten and often subtle rules. This cannot be done without some refinement of sensitivity and judgment. The classical theorists of gratitude always insisted on distinguishing the giving and returning of favors from the simple calculations of economic exchange, the world of civility from that of mere need. The kind of gratitude they single out for special praise is that which involves an activity of the mind and sensibility above and beyond the mechanical. Recipients may legitimately consider the quality of the gesture and the character of the giver in calibrating their response. The benefactor who acts only out of duty certainly imposes an obligation, yet he deserves no special credit, and one's gratitude may be measured accordingly. Favors done to humiliate the recipient are not really favors at all. Returning a favor too quickly, as La Rochefoucauld points out, is also a form of insult, since it indicates the recipient's unwillingness to live with his obligation any longer than absolutely necessary.[37]

[37] 'Le trop grand empressement qu'on a de s'acquitter d'une obligation est une espèce d'ingratitude' (Too much eagerness to discharge an obligation is a form of ingratitude). La Rochefoucauld, *Maximes* no. 226, in *Moralistes du XVIIe siècle: de Pibrac à Dufresny*, ed. Jean Lafond (Paris: Robert Laffont, 1992), 154. The English translation is from La Rochefoucauld, *Collected Maxims and Other Reflections*, tr. and ed. E. H. and A. M. Blackmore and Francine Giguère (Oxford: Oxford University Press, 2007), 65. This edition also contains the French text. The numbering used in both these works is that of the fifth edition of the *Maximes* (1678).

The capacity to return a favor with properly calibrated expressions of gratitude was not something every man or woman could be assumed to possess. Like delicacy in benefaction, it depended on gentle birth, education, good fortune, an exceptional temperament, or some combination of these.[38] Indeed, the ability to feel and express gratitude appropriately was an important factor in the establishment or reinforcement of cultural hierarchies. For the classical moralists, demonstrating the right kind and degree of gratitude evidenced a noble character, in which the advantages of birth had been refined by philosophical education. For theologians, of course, the capacity for gratitude was itself a gift, a sign of a prior divine favor that alone enabled a fallen human being to receive the particular grace now being bestowed. In short, to acknowledge obligation was, paradoxically, not only to display one's agency, but also to illustrate one's status.

In eighteenth-century French novels from *Manon Lescaut* (1731) to *Les Liaisons dangereuses* (1782), the capacity to appreciate favors and to return them with finesse are marks of high sensibility, sure signs of a character's distinction. In these stories, however, the relation of that distinction to other indicators of social worth has become problematic. The chevalier Des Grieux possesses an exquisite sensibility that prompts him to effusions of gratitude for M. de T . . . 's help in securing Manon's release from jail, and yet his cheating at cards, not to mention outright thefts, indeed the very fact of his relationship with a woman of Manon's class, violate the code of honor and propriety that should govern his conduct. Which form of moral refinement is to be given greater weight? *Les Liaisons dangereuses* is even more subversive of conventional morality. After Valmont seduces the young Cécile, he speaks of her with contempt, but not for giving in to his advances. Rather, by failing to learn from her experience how to play the libertine game to her own advantage, she shows a disappointing inability to appreciate the favor he has done her except at the level of physical pleasure. Whatever gratitude she might feel toward Valmont is thus of no value to him.[39] She

[38] 'Tous ceux qui s'acquittent des devoirs de la reconnaissance ne peuvent pas pour cela se flatter d'être reconnaissants' (Not everyone who discharges the duties of gratitude can flatter himself that he is really being grateful by doing so). La Rochefoucauld, *Maximes*, no. 224, in *Moralistes*, 154; *Collected Maxims*, 63.

[39] Compare Sade's Juliette, who scorns the idea of charity, since its only return is the 'cold gratitude' of the person who is helped. While that person may express genuine feeling, the gratitude means nothing to someone who enjoys self-sufficient power. See Sade, *Œuvres*, iii. 305.

therefore deserves to be scorned. The notion that Cécile's failure to become a self-conscious libertine might be a sign of her fundamental innocence is dismissed out of hand, and not only by the book's immoral characters. In both books, the exchange of personal favors is at odds with the larger system of moral and social interaction. They no longer rest on a common and coherent set of underlying values.

While Prévost and Laclos show how high-born figures distort and debase the merit of acknowledging a favor, other novels of the period focus on the unexpectedly refined forms of gratitude displayed by characters of humbler origin. The heroines of Challe's *Illustres Françaises* and Marivaux's *La Vie de Marianne* perform, and as narrators of their stories redefine, their expressions of gratitude in such a way as to secure recognition of their moral and social worth from the very people on whom they depend. In contrast with other characters in the same books, who acknowledge their debts in conventional and mechanical ways that confirm their low status, the heroines display in word and deed such a mastery of the subtleties of informal obligation as to expand their scope for autonomous action.[40] Marivaux's Marianne and Challe's Angélique convince their (male) benefactors that the free and gracious acknowledgment of their obligations is in itself the highest possible form of return for the favors done to them. To claim any more tangible, especially sexual, compensation would turn benefaction into a sordid and humiliating quid pro quo.

Not surprisingly, perhaps, arguments of this kind are most often employed by women characters, and appeals to female virtue as setting a limit to obligation had long been a familiar literary trope, although it could serve as a symbol for a wider protest against the oppressive side of gratitude. In the seventeenth century, writers such as Mlle de Scudéry insisted, for example, that a woman should not be expected to fall in love with her rescuer merely out of gratitude.[41] Passion could never be an obligation, and this theme was later echoed in a more pathetic mode by Prévost in his *Histoire d'une Grecque moderne* (1740). But in the eighteenth century, the claims of the weaker but virtuous character, male as well as female, began to include recognition of their social

[40] On the importance of the characters' reframing of their personal stories in their social advancement, see William Ray, *Story and History* (Cambridge, Mass.: Blackwell, 1990).

[41] Madeleine de Scudéry, *Clélie*, cited in Magendie, *La Politesse mondaine*, 663. On the other hand, the word 'ingrat' in the literature of the period is often used by women to condemn the man who has betrayed or ceased to love them.

dignity as well as of their moral integrity. This new emphasis can be seen in Rousseau's novel *Julie.*[42] Its principal male character, St Preux, exemplifies that class of educated but underemployed intellectuals we have mentioned earlier in relation to resentful anger. With certain significant exceptions, the virtuous St Preux is rarely angry. At the same time, he never retracts his bold claim to possess a sensibility as refined as that of any nobleman. Later, when he is adopted into the ideal community of Clarens, his gratitude to Wolmar is depicted not only as compatible with his moral independence; it is a mark that he truly belongs among the 'belles âmes'. In other works as well, Rousseau was by no means as categorical in his condemnation of gratitude as his prickliness would lead one to think. The last of his *Rêveries du promeneur solitaire,* which is also probably the last text he wrote, is a tribute of gratitude to Mme de Warens. He could never have become the writer he was had he not been empowered by the favors she had done him.

Like anger, therefore, gratitude could be a means of challenging as well as confirming status hierarchies. At the very least, the language of gratitude, encompassing as it did unforced reciprocity between intimates as well the obligations binding clients to patrons, was flexible enough to allow hierarchical relationships to be redefined in more egalitarian terms. Antoine Lilti has examined this phenomenon in his study of eighteenth-century salon life. In the relationships between writers and influential salon hosts, he writes, 'the key notion is that of protection'. Such protection differed from older forms of patronage: 'worldly protection draws its power and its utility for each of the participants from the fact that it borrows the language of friendship and sociability, of benefaction and gratitude' that characterizes relationships between moral equals. This allowed both hosts and writers to view themselves as disinterested parties rather than as seekers after glory.[43] Just as Enlightenment writers explored the emancipatory potential of a wider entitlement to anger while working to minimize the damaging effects of unbridled wrath, they also pondered the possibilities as well as

[42] For male characters, turning dependence to advantage is most often a strategy of the picaresque hero, whose gratitude generally operates on a more self-interested level. However, the Jacob of Marivaux's *Paysan parvenu,* while remaining within the comic mode and colloquial linguistic register, displays a gratitude of a more sensitive and refined kind.

[43] Antoine Lilti, *Le Monde des salons: sociabilité et mondanité à Paris au XVIIIe siècle* (Paris: Fayard, 2005), 182.

the limitations of adopting what the self-help books of today call 'an attitude of gratitude' as a means of enhancing individual agency.

EMOTIONS AS RELATIONS AND JUDGMENTS

The approach taken in this book to Enlightenment discourses on anger and gratitude builds on important recent philosophical and historical work on the role of the emotions in human life. For much of the nineteenth and twentieth centuries, emotion was primarily viewed in terms of individual psychology and biology. Indeed, as Thomas Dixon has shown in an illuminating recent book, the very use of the term 'emotion' in English as a category for what in earlier times was known variously as 'passions', 'affections', and even 'sentiments' dates to the early nineteenth century. This shift in vocabulary was part of a broader reconfiguration of knowledge in which psychology in the modern sense emerged as a discipline distinct from philosophical or theological approaches to human nature. As Dixon notes, the classification of feelings, dispositions, and drives has a very complex history, linked to shifts in the basic frameworks within which human nature is understood. 'The words "passions" and "affections" belonged to a network of words such as "soul", "conscience", "fall", "sin", "grace" ... "lower appetites", "self-love", and so on.' They were intimately linked to the discourses of Christianity and of the classical philosophers. This gave these terms a particular religious coloration, but at the same time they opened onto a comprehensive view of human action at its various levels: body, intellect, and will. 'The word "emotions" was, from the outset, part of a different network of terms such as "psychology", "laws", "observation" ... "behavior", and "viscera".'[44] As the study of human nature began to be modeled on the methods of modern science, emotions were conceptualized primarily in terms of physiological stimulus, response, and adaptation.[45]

There continued, of course, to be other, more philosophical approaches to human action. In France, Descartes had introduced the

[44] Thomas Dixon, *From Passions to Emotions: The Creation of a Secular Psychological Category* (Cambridge; Cambridge University Press, 2003), 5.

[45] One can also see in theology from the seventeenth century onwards a significant dissociation of affective emphases from rationalistic dogmatic systems, in ways at odds with both the mystical theology of earlier centuries and the patterns of biblical faith. See Mark A. McIntosh, *Mystical Theology: The Integrity of Spirituality and Theology* (Malden, Mass.: Blackwell, 1998).

term *émotion* to designate the passions, but his 'scientific' use of the term did not catch on at the time, or even later, with the development of modern psychology.[46] The historical semantics of emotion terms in France remain to be explored, but the influence of *ancien régime* usages seems to have been more lasting than in Britain. The *moralistes* and novelists of the later seventeenth century continued to speak of the 'passions', appealing in varying degrees to the moral judgment implicit in a word that in religious discourse was associated with humanity's fallen condition. 'Passions' are feelings to which human beings are subjected against their will; the central question is whether they can be mastered by the exercise of virtue. Eighteenth-century writers, on the other hand, employed the word 'sentiments' when they wanted to emphasize a closer relation between feeling and reasoned opinion, and between sensibility and enlightened sociability. The use of 'sentiment' in this broad sense by eighteenth-century British writers such as Adam Smith has become obsolete, but like the moralizing use of 'passion' it remains current in French. This difference of configuration may go some way toward explaining why the recent surge of philosophical interest in the emotions in the English-speaking world does not have an exact counterpart in francophone scholarship, despite a long-standing if heterogeneous tradition of writing on this topic from Staël's *De l'influence des passions* (1795) to Sartre's *Esquisse d'une théorie des émotions* (1939).[47]

The situation is very different today. While some scientists continue to view emotions primarily in terms of reactions to stimuli affecting the

[46] The word continues to be used to designate intense feeling in general, rather than a member of a class of feelings.

[47] The most comprehensive recent French-language work on the subject is Michel Meyer, *Le Philosophe et les passions: esquisse d'une histoire de la nature humaine* (Paris: Librairie générale française, 1991). For a discussion (which I cannot address here) see the review by Jack Abecassis in *MLN* 110 (1995), 918–42. Joan DeJean's *Ancients against Moderns: Culture Wars and the Making of a Fin de Siècle* (Chicago: University of Chicago Press, 1997), draws attention to the French rejection of Descartes's terminology and suggests that one of the reasons for it was the determination of writers such as Scudéry (in, for example, the 'Carte de Tendre' of *Clélie*) to keep the discussion of feeling within the framework of moral psychology, the better to highlight women's concerns about the gendered nature of personal and social relationships. As DeJean herself recognizes, however, the question is a complex one, involving theological as well as scientific and moral literature. DeJean herself does not engage the complex and politically fraught theological debates on the passions that (for example) so exercised Fénelon and his opponents. For an overview of some of the issues, see Susan James, 'The Passions and the Good Life', in Donald Rutherford, ed., *The Cambridge Companion to Early Modern Philosophy* (Cambridge: Cambridge University Press, 2006), 198–220.

balance of physical forces within the body, the 'object-relations' school of psychology has come to exercise important influence on the field. Without denying the reality of psycho-physiological processes, this approach considers the self's interactions with real or imaginary others to be more crucial for understanding human development than the more 'hydraulic' model of drives within the self. Psychoanalyst Melanie Klein's late work *Envy and Gratitude*, which describes the working of these emotions in the construction (and destruction) of psychic integrity, inspired my first explorations of emotion in eighteenth-century literature and is echoed in the title of this book.[48] More recent psychologists such as Carol Tavris have sought to combine an object-relations perspective with investigations into the broader social psychology of emotions such as anger. According to Tavris, anger is fruitfully understood as 'a process, a transaction, a way of communicating . . . Most angry episodes are social events. They assume meaning only in terms of the social contract between participants. The beliefs we have about anger, and the interpretations we give to the experience, are as important to its understanding as anything intrinsic to the emotion itself.'[49] Tavris's sensitivity to social contexts derives in part from her awareness of how earlier psychologists were influenced by stereotypes about the female mind, and she shows how manifestations of anger depend to a great extent on culturally conditioned ideas about gender roles. A similar approach is exemplified on a broader scale by the late Robert C. Solomon, whose work, based on a philosophically informed existentialist psychology, has some affinities with the object-relations school, and is also sensitive to the situational context of emotional transactions.[50]

Historians and anthropologists have also begun to look at the ways emotions have been defined, and their expressions evaluated, in the writings and other cultural productions of distant times and places.[51]

[48] Melanie Klein, *Envy and Gratitude* (1957); repr. in *Envy and Gratitude and Other Works 1946–1963* (*The Writings of Melanie Klein* III; London: Hogarth Press, 1975).

[49] Carol Tavris, *Anger: The Misunderstood Emotion* (rev. edn, New York: Simon and Schuster, 1989), 19.

[50] Solomon, *True to our Feelings*, and, among his other works, *The Passions* (Garden City, NY: Doubleday, 1976), and *Dark Feelings, Grim Thoughts: Experience and Reflection in Camus and Sartre* (New York: Oxford University Press, 2006).

[51] Recent collective works include Gail Kern Postan, Katherine Rowe, and Mary Floyd-Wilson, eds, *Reading the Early Modern Passions: Essays in the Cultural History of Emotion* (Philadelphia: University of Pennsylvania Press, 2004); and Victoria Kahn, Neil Saccamano, and Daniela Coli, eds, *Politics and the Passions 1500–1850* (Princeton: Princeton University Press, 2006). On anger see, for example, Barbara Rosenwein, ed.,

We have come to appreciate how remote from the categories of our own thinking are the ways in which certain emotions are named and acted out (or not) in different societies. Some scholars have even claimed that emotions are entirely constructed and regulated by norms arising from the cultures in which they are embedded, that there are no universals in human emotional life. In an important recent study, however, William Reddy argues that to say that emotional reactions are culturally constructed is to deny that they might serve instead to expose the stress-points and inadequacies of the cultural status quo, inspire reflective critique, and drive social change. Yet, this is in fact what happens. Emotions, Reddy writes, are 'badges of deeply-relevant goals', some of which are rooted in bodily needs while others are shaped by a complex of circumstances that vary even within a given culture.[52] The emotional suffering that results from conflict between individual and social goals may often be accepted and endured when it is given symbolic meaning and value, but it can also, in certain circumstances, lead people to demand a greater degree or different form of satisfaction from their marriage or career, to change the criteria for ascribing social honor and shame, or to modify other aspects of what Reddy calls the 'emotional regime' of the culture. Conversely, individuals are also sometimes led by emotional conflict to redefine their own high-level goals, 'converting' for example from one religion to another because they felt they 'had to' do so in order to preserve the unity or integrity of their self.

Such changes in overarching points of view indicate that cultural construction does not provide a sufficient explanation for the dynamic of emotions. Reddy insists, therefore, that without 'some conception of the universal features of emotional life' it is 'impossible to account for

Anger's Past: the Social Use of an Emotion in the Middle Ages (Ithaca, NY: Cornell University Press, 1998). While the notion of gratitude has been analyzed in recent works on gift-giving, it has received less sustained philosophical attention. One exception is Terrance C. McConnell, *Gratitude* (Philadelphia: Temple University Press, 1993). In theology, it occupies a more central role, as for example in B. A. Gerrish, *Grace and Gratitude: The Eucharistic Theology of John Calvin* (Minneapolis: Fortress, 1993). For a secular, or post-religious, commendation of general gratitude, see Ronald Aronson, *Living without God: New Directions for Atheists, Agnostics, Secularists, and the Undecided* (Berkeley: Counterpoint, 2008), 43–64.

[52] William Reddy, *The Navigation of Feeling: A Framework for the History of Emotions* (Cambridge: Cambridge University Press, 2001), 55. For the cultural constructionists, change would mostly be the product of outside forces such as colonialism and imperialism, or, as in Foucault, of paradigm shifts in an *episteme* largely inaccessible to reflection, since it provides the terms for reflection itself.

emotional change'.[53] Using the findings of cognitive science, Reddy suggests we look at emotions as a way of processing contradictions between learned habits or internalized norms and fundamental human impulses.[54] His concern is to defend the legitimacy of criticizing the emotional regime of a society other than one's own. While he is mindful of the dangers of judging other cultures by the standard of a single conception of human nature, itself culturally conditioned, Reddy insists on the legitimacy of judging the success or failure of these emotional regimes in minimizing emotional suffering. A key factor here is the degree to which individuals are allowed to adjust their higher-level goals, their definition and pursuit of overall values, in order to resolve contradictory thoughts and desires for themselves.[55] In this respect, Reddy's work stands in the best Enlightenment tradition. A closer look at that tradition may, in turn, help to refine Reddy's project.

Historically informed philosophers are also exploring the cognitive and relational dimensions of emotions.[56] Retrieving the somewhat neglected contributions of the Stoic and Epicurean thinkers of the Hellenistic age to this debate, writers such as Martha Nussbaum affirm that emotions are indeed evaluations. As Nussbaum puts it, emotions are 'intelligent responses to the perception of value'; they 'involve judgments about the salience for our well-being of uncontrolled external

[53] Ibid. 45.

[54] Reddy defines an emotion as 'a range of loosely connected thought material, formulated in varying codes, that has goal-relevance and intensity... that may constitute a "schema" (or a set of loosely connected schemas or fragments of schemas); this range of thoughts tends to be activated together (as in the examples... "angry at sister" or "in love") but, when activated, exceeds attention's capacity to translate it into action or into talk in a short time horizon. Its loose or variegated character is a reflection of the complexity of translation tasks (including the formulation and application of goals). Episodes of particular complexity give rise to the emotionally configured thought material in the first place; renewed episodes reactivate such configurations.' Ibid. 94. For a detailed account of mental processing that dovetails with Reddy's, but reacting to deterministic rather than to constructivist extremism, see Nancey Murphy and Warren S. Brown, *Did my Neurons Make Me Do it? Philosophical and Neurobiological Perspectives on Moral Responsibility and Free Will* (New York: Oxford University Press, 2007).

[55] There is an analogy here to what political theorists call the opportunity for 'exit' in social or political regimes. See Albert O. Hirschman, *Exit, Voice, and Loyalty: Responses to Decline in Firms, Organizations, and States* (Cambridge, Mass.: Harvard University Press, 1970).

[56] Martha Nussbaum, *The Therapy of Desire: Theory and Practice in Hellenistic Ethics* (Princeton: Princeton University Press, 1994), *Upheavals of Thought: The Intelligence of Emotions* (Cambridge: Cambridge University Press, 2001), among other works; Robert C. Solomon's *True to our Feelings* summarizes in a clear and helpful way both his earlier work and that of other emotion theorists.

objects'.[57] Nussbaum, whose work spans Greek and Roman antiquity as well as contemporary moral and legal philosophy, is well aware that cultural variables influence the ways particular emotions are defined and conceptualized. She therefore wants to analyze how human flourishing depends on certain kinds of emotional cognitions and judgments without committing herself to an overarching metaphysical conception of human nature. She contends it is possible to articulate normative conceptions about emotional regimes while still respecting the legitimacy of cultural variation. In this respect, Nussbaum's work departs from other contemporary appropriations of Hellenistic thought such as Michel Foucault's work on the 'care of the self' and Pierre Hadot's conception of philosophy as a way of life rather than a system of doctrine.[58] It shares with them an emphasis on the 'techniques' and 'therapies' that foster the kind of emotional equilibrium sought by selves who might have very different ultimate goals and values. But it acknowledges more frankly the challenges of reconciling an emancipatory appeal to normative liberal values with respect for cultural diversity. This dilemma also confronted the *philosophes* of the Enlightenment, although it was not always articulated so explicitly. Nussbaum's work can help us appreciate how writers in the period struggled with the implications of ascribing cognitive significance to feeling.

This approach to moral philosophy has some affinity with the 'virtue ethics' that has recently gained in popularity in comparison with Kantian and utilitarian theories. Virtue ethicists highlight the importance of tradition-formed practices in shaping moral norms and in giving moral vocabulary concreteness of meaning. In arguing for the importance of character-formation and the acquisition of practical wisdom, virtue ethicists such as Alisdair MacIntyre and Jean Porter also assign a key role to emotional dispositions in the discernment of appropriate action.[59] Thinkers in this tradition disagree, however, on whether a tradition-transcendent philosophical framework is required in order to

[57] Nussbaum, *Upheavals*, 1–2.

[58] Michel Foucault, *Histoire de la sexualité 3: le souci de soi* (Paris: Gallimard, 1984); Pierre Hadot, *Qu'est-ce que la philosophie antique?* (Paris: Gallimard, 1995), translated by Michael Chase as *What is Ancient Philosophy?* (Cambridge, Mass.: Harvard University Press, 2002); and *Philosophy as a Way of Life: Spiritual Exercises from Socrates to Foucault*, ed. Arnold I. Davidson, tr. Michael Chase (Oxford: Blackwell, 1995).

[59] Alisdair MacIntyre, *Dependent Rational Animals: Why Human Beings Need the Virtues* (Chicago: Open Court, 1999); Jean Porter, *Nature as Reason* (Grand Rapids, Mich.: Eerdmans, 2005).

meet the challenges of critique from within and without that tradition. Also in dispute is whether an overall religious or other meta-narrative is needed to reconcile the demands of the different virtues—including the emotions associated with them—and to sustain moral conviction and agency when they clash.[60] These debates give us a new perspective on tensions within Enlightenment writing, and in turn critics as well as defenders of what today is often dismissively called the 'Enlightenment project' may benefit from closer attention to the ways these tensions were acknowledged by writers of the period.[61]

Nor are these debates purely theoretical. They open onto practical issues about what constitutes the range of behaviors and conceptions of the good life that are compatible with a cohesive society, and about the legitimacy of regulating the 'emotional regime' of that society. As Robert Solomon puts it, defining and describing emotions is 'a political discussion. That is, it is part of a much larger discussion about how people relate and respond to each other, how they understand themselves, how they manipulate both themselves and others, in part by the very language they use in ascribing and describing the emotions.'[62] The eighteenth-century writers who are the subject of the following chapters are keenly aware of this broader context. The relation between theory and practice is illuminated by the interplay between analytical and dramatic examinations of anger and gratitude in their works. It is also a central issue in the writers' struggle to gain social recognition for themselves as authors as well as literary appreciation for their works.

My study opens with Robert Challe. His *Difficultés sur la religion proposées au Père Malebranche* (*c.*1710), while unpublished, circulated widely in different versions throughout the century, and has long been judged to be one of the most important critiques of Christianity in the

[60] This is true even within the Thomist tradition, with Porter taking rather a different approach to the relation of virtue to law than other prominent writers such as John Finnis. For the general issue of how public debate in such matters should be conducted, see Jeffrey Stout, *Democracy and Tradition* (Princeton: Princeton University Press, 2004).

[61] A question related to virtue ethics is the extent to which one can ever acquire genuine virtues through the imitation of them. On the history of this debate, including an incisive discussion of ethical thinking in early modern France that is relevant to the issues I raise in this study, see Jennifer A. Herdt, *Putting on Virtue: The Legacy of the Splendid Vices* (Chicago: Chicago University Press, 2008). This book appeared too late for me to do more than refer to it here.

[62] Solomon, *True to our Feelings*, 7.

French Enlightenment. The recent discovery of the original and complete text, however, shows that this is no ordinary deist tract but a remarkably self-involving attempt to define the grounds, limits, and affective tenor of religious belief, the most searching work of its kind in the period after Bayle. Challe's novel *Les Illustres Françaises* (1713) was one of the most popular fictions of the first half of the eighteenth century, and is now acknowledged to be the most formally inventive and thematically wide-ranging novel of its age. Not only does it weave seven separate stories into an intricate pattern of contradictory and convergent voices, it addresses social and religious questions in more realistic and emotionally varied detail than any other French novel of the period. By analyzing the rhetoric of anger, and the less salient, but no less significant articulations of gratitude in each work, I argue that the novel and the tract are complementary explorations of the relationship between the writing self and the various dimensions of his world, a relationship at once unmistakably individual and broadly resonant with changes in the culture at large.

I then turn to Marivaux, a less mercurial writer than Challe but an even keener observer of the complex interplay between emotional states and the negotiation of social convention. In his novel *La Vie de Marianne* (1731–42), the eponymous narrator tells the story of her rise from her beginnings as an orphan of uncertain parentage to the status of a well-married noblewoman. In her reflections on what she owes to those who helped her along the way, not just materially but by agreeing to see her as she wished to be seen, the emotional connotations of *reconnaissance* in the sense of gratitude are inseparable from the word's dramatic and epistemological uses to designate the 'recognition' or 'acknowledgment' of a person or a situation in Marianne's story. By also reflecting on the term's semantic complexity in the narrative commentary on that story, Marivaux's novel proves to be just as wide-ranging in its diagnosis of the philosophical and cultural complexities of gratitude as Challe's works are of anger.

The following two chapters are devoted to Rousseau, whose works and public personality are obviously central to any exploration of emotion in the Enlightenment. No eighteenth-century writer rivals Rousseau as a bellwether for the changes in sensibility occurring during this period, or as a catalyst for their mediation to a wide French, indeed European, readership. The extraordinary range of Rousseau's writing allows us to see how attitudes about anger and gratitude inform his conceptions of political no less than of personal life. Rousseau's self-consciousness about the precariousness of his position as a writer in France, about his duties as a citizen of Geneva, about the potential of his interventions to provoke outrage as well as appreciation in his public, to undermine as well as shore up the foundations of social peace in any country in which he is read, drives him to incorporate into his works an acute awareness—sometimes coolly strategic, sometimes anxiously defensive—of the emotional dimension in the relationship between author and reader. Instead of focusing in detail on one or two works, these chapters offer a more synthetic view of the role of the two emotions across the span of Rousseau's career. They examine the thematic role of anger and gratitude in his writings while at the same time attending to the ways the emotions appear in the author's articulation of his claims to cultural authority.

I conclude with Diderot, whose satirical dialogue *Le Neveu de Rameau* offers the fiercest exploration of sociability and emotional temperament in the late Enlightenment. The modulation of indignant anger into resentment, already present in Rousseau, constitutes a major development in the history of the relation between emotion and social status, one which will echo throughout the following century, from Tocqueville to Baudelaire and of course to Nietzsche. It is likely that Diderot had Rousseau in mind when he wrote or revised the book in the 1770s, and so *Le Neveu de Rameau* can be read in part as a commentary on the provocative role of anger in shaping Rousseau's career, as well as a reflection on Diderot's own contrasting position as what his friends called *le philosophe*. We see clearly how 'Lui's' envy and amoral conduct provoke anger in 'Moi'. As many critics have pointed out, the latter's claims to virtuous self-sufficiency are undermined by Lui's success in exposing the compromises Moi has had to make over the years, and they are even more severely challenged by the seductiveness of Lui's pantomimes of vice and corruption. We can see how Moi is tempted to counter Lui's resentments with a resentment of his own, and how Diderot's character seeks to shake off that emotion. But the dialogue is equally significant for the way it modifies the problematic of gratitude. More disturbing even than Lui's insidious resentment is the suggestion, implicit in the framing of the dialogue, that Moi should be grateful for the material Lui provides him, for without it he would fail to experience the full reality of the world around him. The idea of being obliged to someone like Lui is a source of acute moral as well as epistemological discomfort. Diderot's dialogue suggests that these tensions between dependence and independence cannot be resolved. They may, however, be transcended by adopting an aesthetic, and ironic, point of view. In this respect, *Le Neveu de Rameau* marks the literary culmination of French Enlightenment reflection on the writer's role as a mediator of emotional recognition-claims to and for the culture at large.

2

Anger and Reconciliation in Robert Challe

The recently rediscovered writings of Robert Challe (1659–1721) reveal him to have been one of the most vigorous and multifaceted writers of the early Enlightenment. Travel journals, fiction, memoirs, and religious controversies—in all of these Challe's curiosity and intellectual energy led him to discuss a wide range of subjects in an equally wide range of rhetorical modes. One element common to all his writing, however, is a readiness to express, indeed to cultivate, feelings of anger. In the *Journal d'un voyage aux Indes orientales*, which records his experiences in 1690 and 1691 as part of an expedition to advance France's commercial interests in the Far East, Challe recounts how he sought revenge on any shipmate who dared to insult his dignity as *écrivain du roi*.[1] He does so with the same attention to detail with which he records his observations on natural history and on local cultures. Indeed, his anger does not seem to distract him from his scientific investigations; both emanate from the same passionate engagement with the world around him.

Twenty years later, near the end of his career, we see the same sensitivity to slight. In 1713 Challe began a correspondence with the editors of the Dutch *Journal littéraire*, which had published a favorable review of his novel *Les Illustres Françaises*. It didn't take long before Challe's gratitude gave way to a more negative sentiment. In one letter, the Protestant writers of the *Journal* jokingly insinuate that the author of a book full of disobliging remarks about France's Catholic clergy might not be taking his Lenten fast too seriously. Given the context, the

[1] Robert Challe, *Journal d'un voyage fait aux Indes orientales (du 16 février 1690 au 10 août 1691)*, ed. Frédéric Deloffre and Jacques Popin (augmented edn, Paris: Mercure de France, 2002), i. 279, 428–30.

remark seems harmless enough to us,[2] but Challe bristles at the mere thought that his personal piety is being questioned. 'Si je suivais la colère où je suis contre vous, Messieurs, je lâcherais la bride à mon ressentiment, pour attirer la vôtre.'[3] Given the sometimes irrational prickliness of many of his novel's male characters, Challe's reaction may not be entirely unexpected, but it is curious in that we now know Challe to be the author of a major anti-Christian treatise, the *Difficultés sur la religion proposées au Père Malebranche.* This work is animated by an inexhaustible indignation at the bad faith, credulity, and other human weaknesses that Challe believes distort the search for truth.

The prominence of anger in Challe's work may in part be explained in biographical terms. He was disadvantaged in early life by his father's early death and his mother's preference for his brother, and his attempts to make his fortune were repeatedly frustrated by unfortunate circumstances.[4] But while Challe's writing may be spurred by an angry disposition, what makes it of enduring interest is that the workings of anger themselves become the object of wide-ranging intellectual and imaginative consideration. This is especially evident in *Les Illustres Françaises.* The novel consists of seven first-person stories about young people chafing under the restrictions of their family or class status. Gathered together at the end of their adventures as a community of friends, the characters reflect on each other's experiences. The more fortunate ones do what they can to reintegrate the others into society. They help them overcome their resentments, not by denying their force, but by creating a space in which they can be outweighed by gratitude for new opportunities. Anger is not just displayed; it is dramatized as an issue to be resolved within the overall structure of the book.

A more intellectual version of the same dynamic may be seen in the *Difficultés.* Although it is not the thematic center of the argument, anger

[2] Even from the practical point of view: the novel was published anonymously, and since Challe concealed his identity even in the correspondence, he had little to fear even if his letter was intercepted by the French authorities.

[3] Robert Challe, letter to the *Journal littéraire,* 30 April 1714, in *Mémoires, Correspondance complète, Rapports sur l'Acadie et autres pièces,* ed. Frédéric Deloffre avec la collaboration de Jacques Popin (Geneva: Droz, 1996), 496.

[4] These include the looting by the British of the Acadian outpost where he had gone in the 1680s to invest in the fur trade, and the untimely death in 1690 of his patron Seignelay, Colbert's son, who had been his classmate and who as minister responsible for the navy had helped protect Challe from the consequences of his sometimes turbulent behavior.

is the rhetorical starting-point for the process that leads to what one critic has aptly called the 'constructive deism' Challe develops in the fourth part of the work, where we see the author's resentment give way to thanksgiving.[5] My argument will be that the discussions of anger in the two books are in fact complementary. Although it would be just as wrong to neglect the formal variety of Challe's writings in an effort to discern a single underlying philosophical purpose as it would be to reduce them to expressions of his psychological temperament, it is nonetheless true that for Challe, as for many writers of his age, religion and sociability are the object of similar kinds of investigation. In both domains, we find an effort, characteristic of the early Enlightenment, to reconcile two ideas: that human autonomy flourishes only in a society (indeed, a universe) governed by impersonal, rational law, free of arbitrary rules, and that individual subjectivity demands recognition within personalized systems of meaning. Focusing on the different ways anger is expressed and overcome will allow us to explore this fundamental tension while attending to important differences of genre and context.[6]

DIFFICULTÉS SUR LA RELIGION

Unlike other clandestine manuscripts such as the *Traité des trois imposteurs* or the *Examen de la religion* that circulated in the early eighteenth century, denouncing the 'absurdities' of biblical chronology or

5 The phrase is the title of chapter 3 of the first volume of Leslie Stephen's *History of English Thought in the Eighteenth Century* (London, 1876), and applied to a version of Challe's treatise (whose authorship had not yet been identified) by Ira O. Wade, *The Clandestine Organization and Diffusion of Philosophic Ideas in France from 1700 to 1750* (Princeton: Princeton University Press, 1938), 63.

6 Jean Goldzink has criticized those who have looked for connections between Challe's theological speculations and his fictional narrative, arguing that religious issues are not themselves in question in the novel. Yet, Challe's discursive persona, in its combination of truculence and anxiety, is so consistent across the different genres of his work that scholars such as Marie-Hélène Cotoni and Geneviève Artigas-Menant are surely right to maintain that the novel is grounded in the same existential and metaphysical concerns as the religious treatise. See Jean Goldzink, 'Des *Difficultés sur la religion* aux *Illustres Françaises*: écarts et interprétations', *RHLF* 101 (2001), 313–24, and the responses by Cotoni and Artigas-Menant, 324–6. In the *Journal*, anger is of a piece with Challe's passionate curiosity about the details of other peoples' behavior, and about the laws governing the operations of the physical world. This topic would require a separate study.

Christian metaphysics,[7] the *Difficultés sur la religion proposées au Père Malebranche* are shaped by the author's existential involvement in the controversy. True to his rationalist convictions, Challe sets out a series of what he considers to be his irrefutable syllogisms according to the models of Descartes's *Règles pour la direction de l'esprit* (*Rules for the Direction of our Native Intelligence*, 1628/9).[8] But the relish with which Challe savors the triumph of his logic sets him apart. So does the rhetorical framing of the work. Not only does he preface the work with a personal 'Lettre d'envoi', the treatise itself takes the form of a lengthy brief (it is too long to call it a letter), addressed to an imagined 'you'. This conversational approach, famously illustrated by Pascal's *Lettres provinciales*, allows Challe to adopt a variety of styles from the informally autobiographical to the most austerely intellectual. Unlike Pascal, however, or other controversialists who used this device, such as Fréret,[9] Challe does not write to a fictional character or to a real person distanced by death or disguise. The personal address is not merely a rhetorical strategy. Challe writes to Malebranche, the most famous philosopher of his day, and in a manner that suggests he would like a response, even if, practically speaking, he does not expect one.[10]

For Challe, Malebranche is no venal churchman, but a genuine philosopher for whom the 'search for truth' is not just the title of a book.[11] For that very reason, he cannot understand why Malebranche's

[7] See *Le 'Traité des trois imposteurs' et 'L'Esprit de Spinosa'*, ed. Françoise Charles-Daubert (Oxford: Voltaire Foundation, 1999); César Chesneau Du Marsais, *Examen de la religion, ou, doutes sur la religion dont on cherche l'éclaircissement de bonne foi*, ed. Gianluca Mori (Oxford: Voltaire Foundation, 1998).

[8] See Mladen Kozul, 'Péril extrême du discours d'autrui, ou le destinataire piégé: *Difficultés sur la religion* entre Descartes et Malebranche', in Jacques Cormier, Jan Herman, and Paul Pelckmans, eds, *Robert Challe: sources et héritages* (Louvain: Peeters, 2003), 263–78.

[9] See Fréret, *Lettre de Thrasybule à Leucippe*, in Gianluca Mori and Alain Mothu, eds, *Philosophes sans Dieu: textes athées clandestins du XVIIIe siècle* (Paris: Champion, 2005), 51–185.

[10] For a similar blend of personal engagement and philosophical argument, we need to wait for Rousseau's *Lettre à Christophe de Beaumont* (1763). However, it is very unlikely that Challe actually sent his book to Malebranche.

[11] Nicolas Malebranche, *De la recherche de la vérité* (1674–5). Challe was not wrong to distinguish Malebranche from other apologists of his day. A recent study of Malebranche's writing strategy underscores his respect for the reader's independence: while the author may develop convincing philosophical and theological arguments, he can only be the occasion for the reader's being illuminated by God. His seductive and ostensibly non-coercive stance irritated more intransigent writers such as Arnauld. See Véronique Wiel, *Écriture et philosophie chez Malebranche* (Paris: Champion, 2004). Later writers such as Voltaire wondered why Malebranche's rationalism didn't lead him to deism. For

philosophical integrity does not lead him to disavow the errors of Christian apologists. 'Je présume que vous vous trouverez assez engagé à une réponse lorsque vous ferez réflexion que je ne suis pas [le] seul que ces difficultés aient frappé et ébranlé' (I presume that you will find yourself sufficiently committed to reply when you consider that I am not the only one who has been struck and shaken by these difficulties).[12] The lengthy personal letter from which this quotation is taken makes it clear that Challe is looking for a personal response as much as for a philosophical reply. He wants Malebranche to admit that he shares Challe's doubts about the possibility of providing philosophical foundations for theological claims, and this mode of this sharing is depicted by Challe in strikingly intimate terms. When he writes, 'je me regarde, mon R.P., comme élevé avec vous dans un désert avec une mère muette, sans autre guide que de notre raison, et sans autre instruction que nos réflexions et méditations' (I think of myself, Reverend Father, as having been raised with you in a desert with a mother incapable of speech, without any other guide than our reason, and without any instruction other than our reflections and meditations) (*D* 71), Challe evokes a picture of family closeness in the very way he insists on the absence of emotional connection.[13] Indeed, it has been persuasively suggested that the vehemence of Challe's contradictory appeal to Malebranche—pleading for a reassurance he knows the other cannot give, and then blaming him for his failure—suggests that the figure of Malebranche is a double of Challe himself, onto whom the writer can project his own inner tensions.[14]

Challe writes as if he were estranged from Malebranche, even though the two men had never met. The anger expressed in the *Difficultés* stems not only from the slight Challe experiences as a thinking human being whose autonomy is precious to him, but from a frustrated desire for

the way Malebranche was read in the eighteenth century, see Stuart Brown, 'The Critical Reception of Malebranche, from his Own Time to the End of the Eighteenth Century', in Steven Nadler, ed., *The Cambridge Companion to Malebranche* (Cambridge: Cambridge University Press, 2000), 262–87.

[12] Robert Challe, *Difficultés sur la religion proposées au Père Malebranche*, ed. Fréréric Deloffre and François Moureau (Geneva: Droz, 2000), 67. This edition gives the text of the complete manuscript as it stands, and references to it, abbreviated *D*, will be included in the text. The translations are my own.

[13] The passage is all the more resonant because we know that Challe was jealous of his own brother, his mother's favorite. Here, the mother's mute silence makes it possible for the brothers to think alike.

[14] Kozul, 'Péril extrême', 271.

reconciliation. Seen in this light, the 'infinite gratitude' (*D* 72) that Challe offers in return for an answer is no mere formula of courtesy. This gratitude would be as much a personal response as the assertion of difference and distance in the anger out of which Challe writes.[15] It is also conditional on an exchange of views that would extend indefinitely into the future. Challe's gratitude would be infinite if Malebranche sent him a response as expansive as his own text. This is quite a requirement, since Challe's book is a very long one, but Challe adds that he would be happy to develop any point in as much detail as Malebranche would wish. Quantity would eventually turn into quality, exchange into relationship, in an ultimate meeting of the minds.

In the *Difficultés*, the complexity of the rhetorical stance, with its peculiar mixture of intellectual and emotional demands, is matched by that of the argument itself. It presents itself as objective and dispassionate. As Frédéric Deloffre has remarked, Challe's positive theology is not primarily concerned with issues of faith. Rather, it is at heart a theodicy; in other words, it is chiefly concerned with God as the guarantor of justice.[16] Challe is determined to find answers to the problems of revelation and predestination, which seem to give some men insights or privileges unfairly denied to others. Like other early modern thinkers,[17] Challe believes divine and human attributes to be univocal, not analogical, concepts. 'La force de Dieu et l'existence de Dieu, n'étant simplement que force et existence, sont de même genre et de la même espèce que la nôtre, et proportion gardée, on en peut parler en même terme, et avec la même idée' (God's power and God's existence, being just that, power and existence, are of the same kind and species as our own, and even though on another scale, we can speak of them in the same terms, and with the same idea in mind) (*D* 518).

The criteria for defining divine and human justice must therefore be the same, and they must hold for all people everywhere. There is no room for awe or mystery, for the cautious awareness of metaphorical approximation, or for any hesitation about applying the standards of ordinary human reason. All of this stems from Challe's insistence that a

[15] Like the *Difficultés* themselves, the 'Lettre d'envoi', as the editors call it, was never sent. Perhaps just for this reason, Challe could take liberties with its tone.

[16] Frédéric Deloffre, 'Challe et la justice', in Michèle Weil-Bergougnoux, ed., *Séminaire Robert Challe: 'Les Illustres Françaises'* (Montpellier: Université Paul-Valéry Montpellier III, 1995), 54.

[17] See William Placher, *The Domestication of Transcendence* (Louisville, Ky: Westminster John Knox Press, 1996).

true idea of God must respect human dignity. But this concern extends beyond the realm of intellectual and moral standards. Challe wonders how God's declared wish that all men be saved can be reconciled with the necessarily impersonal distribution of rewards and punishments that justice demands. This is the classic question of the relation between divine goodness and divine justice. As we shall see, Challe will deny there is any real problem as long as these notions are clearly defined. Yet, in responding to the question Challe also appeals to a vocabulary of anger and gratitude that by their subjective connotations do not work in the same way as terms such as 'force' and 'existence'. This vocabulary gives the text not just a personal reference, but an element of unquantifiable affective resonance at odds with its rationalist framework.

This shift appears in the fourth and final part of the work. There, Challe outlines an idiosyncratic deist theology in which anger, not science, is the rhetorical starting-point for thinking about the order of the universe and man's place in it. Unlike other writers of the period, Challe does not ground his conviction in a conception of nature's rational and esthetic order. This is striking, because even the self-preoccupied Rousseau has his Savoyard vicar start his 'Profession of Faith' in this manner. Instead, he begins with anger. This is not just the indignation of an independent thinker whose rationality is scandalized by religions claiming the authority of special revelation. It is the anger that arises from an interpersonal encounter between self and other. Indeed, anger is the primary evidence that there is such a self. Where does Challe find a stimulus for thought? Not in experience of the natural order; nor, like Descartes, in that he knows he thinks, but in that he is sensitive to insult thrown at him by another person.

Mon camarade me dit sérieusement que je suis un coquin, j'en ressens un chagrin violent qui me porte à risquer ma vie, à perdre ma fortune, à recevoir des blessures qui me feront longtemps souffir. Qu'y a-t-il dans ce mot qui ait pu blesser mon corps? Rien ... J'ai cependant reçu un coup, une atteinte, une blessure véritable, cruelle, c'est donc dans une partie de moi qui est un être réel et véritable sans être corporel, que je connais sans pouvoir l'exprimer, que je sens être le véritable moi, auquel la machine n'est point essentielle, mais un simple annexe. (*D* 581–2)

If my comrade tells me in all seriousness that I am a scoundrel, I react with a violent distress that leads me to risk my life, to lose my fortune, to receive wounds that will make me suffer a long time. What is there in this word that could have hurt my body? Nothing ... Nonetheless, I have received a blow, an assault, a real and cruel wound; thus it is in a part of myself that is a real and true if not corporeal being, of which I have knowledge without being able to express it, that I feel is the true me, to which the mechanical self is not essential but a mere adjunct.

Lest we think that his anger is an automatic response to the insulting word in itself, that is, to a material stimulus, Challe adds that if 'un fol, un enfant, une femme, quelque prêtreau me l'avait dit du même ton, je n'y aurais pas pris garde' (a madman, a child, a woman, some priestling had said it to me in the same tone, I would have taken no heed) (*D* 581). The power to determine what *counts* as an insult is further proof of the self's independence and freedom of response.

Anger also plays a key role in the self's discovery of the moral order of evaluative judgments in which, as the preceding quotation shows, the self is enmeshed from the start. Along with its opposite, gratitude, it mediates to our understanding the more abstract notions of good and evil.

Les sentiments d'indignation et de reconnaissance prouvent encore invinciblement l'idée du bien et du mal. Le premier étant l'effet du tort souffert, et l'autre celui du service reçu. Nous avons, indépendamment d'aucune réflexion ou instruction du penchant à témoigner de la gratitude, nous en avons de même à nous venger. Donc qu'il y a de la justice et de l'injustice, et que nous en avons une idée naturelle. (*D* 598)

The sentiments of indignation and gratitude also provide irresistible proof of the idea of good and evil. The first being the effect of wrong suffered, the other that of favor received. We have, independently of any reflection or instruction, an inclination to show gratitude just as we have one to take revenge. Thus that there is justice and injustice, and that we have a natural idea of them.

The implications of this statement extend beyond social relationships. They affect the way Challe defines humanity's relationship to God. Challe's use of the vocabulary of emotion is at odds with the appeal elsewhere in the *Difficultés* to more impersonal notions of divine and human justice. Thus, he denies that one can attribute 'goodness' or 'love' to God, since that would imply he could be swayed by an emotional connection to humanity. Divine justice must be immune to the kind of likes or dislikes that affect human judgments, or to that need to possess the object which is a crucial element in human love (*D* 640, 646). We would need another word to designate the true divine goodness, which is simply God's steady will to reward virtue (*D* 641–2).

Such statements echo those of other deists, who seek to purge divine justice of the 'irrationality' of its biblical representations. These include the ascribing to God of feelings of anger, an emotional attribute enlightened men should now understand as reflecting a primitively anthropomorphic idea of the divinity. Just as important, the Bible considers human anger at suffering and injustice, such as displayed by Job and in some of the Psalms, to be an appropriate and meaningful response in the anguish of the moment. If anger is not Job's final word, however, it is not as a result of any intellectual argument about divine justice. He is answered in a way that puts his anger in the context of a cosmic mystery, but more important than the content of the response is the very fact that God does answer him, and in so doing acknowledges Job as a person.[18] It is true that for Challe the dynamic of anger and gratitude remains grounded in the language of favors and slights developed by Cicero and Seneca and their heirs, the seventeenth-century theorists of sociability, more than in that of the Bible. Yet, the very fact that Challe invokes anger and gratitude shows that he, too, thinks of the divine–human relationship in terms of personal recognition. In this respect, his starting-point is very different from that of philosophical deism.[19]

A first explanation for Challe's concern with recognition may be found in other passages of the *Difficultés*. He tells us that before working through the ideas articulated in that book, the force of his education was such that despite the 'mille raisons et mille lumières' (thousand reasons and thousand insights) that would for a moment dissipate the darkness, 'je retombais toujours dans les transes que donnent les affreuses menaces dont on a été bercé' (I would always fall back into the convulsions caused by the horrible threats with which we've been kept in thrall) (*D* 721). As several critics have pointed out, Challe never quite overcame his fear of eternal punishment. Despite his claim to have arrived at a satisfactory intellectual resolution, this fear haunted him throughout his life.[20] Indeed, one might say that what angered Challe most about

[18] The idea may be found in many recent commentaries, but see also, from a psychological perspective, Lytta Basset, *Le Pardon originel: de l'abîme du mal au pouvoir de pardonner* (Geneva: Labor et Fides, 1994); and Carol A. Newsom, *The Book of Job: A Contest of Moral Imaginations* (New York: Oxford University Press, 2003), which draws on the work of Mikhail Bakhtin.

[19] It remains true that for Challe, God is impervious to personal offense. But in another passage of the *Difficultés*, Challe assumes that God's reactions to human displays of gratitude and liberality would be similar to his own: a desire to respond with a reward, with this difference, that 'ces sentiments sont en l'Etre parfait au plus haut degré et sans mélange de faiblesse' (*D* 613).

[20] On Challe's religious views, see the essays of Geneviève Artigas-Menant collected in *Du secret des clandestins à la propagande voltairienne* (Paris: Champion, 2001), 65–159; for religious anxieties in the period as a whole, see Jean Delumeau, *Le Péché et la peur: la culpabilisation en Occident, XIIIe–XVIIIe siècles* (Paris: Fayard, 1983).

the Christianity of his youth was precisely that he was made to feel so anxious about the future. Thus his investigation of divine justice is driven by a need, not just for a rational solution he can use to refute superstition, but for personal reassurance. In contrast to Job, however, Challe the enlightened thinker maintains that such reassurance can only come from intellectual satisfaction and the self-respect that follows from it.

Challe's first argument in answer to the problem of theodicy is thus based on a high view of human capacities. He declares that human beings have the power to do good. Since God's justice cannot demand the impossible, virtue lies within our grasp. Those who fail to meet a standard tailored to human possibility deserve their punishment. From this point of view, divine justice is in fact fairer than human justice. A man seized by the police may succeed in escaping, but no one escapes God; on the other hand, the criminal cannot look to the judge for forgiveness, while the sinner is 'le maître absolu' of securing pardon by his repentance. For Challe, the church is at fault for instilling in us an irrational fear (*crainte*) of God far greater than our natural and appropriate fear of human justice. The fear of divine punishment is not the same kind of feeling as the fear of human punishment; the one is as different from the other as *indignation* is from *colère* (*D* 642). It is a 'misuse' (*abus*) of language to identify them, for it is only 'la disette de mots' (the dearth of words) (*D* 642, 682)[21] that obliges us to use the same word for both.

Curiously, Challe does not explain what he means in saying the difference between the two kinds of fear is similar to that between indignation and anger. In light of his use of anger to explain the origin of our fundamental notion of justice the comparison is surely significant. According to most definitions, including those of Furetière's dictionary, indignation is a form of anger directed at an action that does not involve us personally. It is a response to injustice suffered by another, or to the general fact of injustice. The inference is that fear of God, properly understood, is similarly general in nature. It should not derive from a conviction that we ourselves are unworthy. The latter idea is the invention of priests who want to control us. In fact, Challe seems to be arguing that the fear of God is less opposed to one's sense of self-worth than is our fear of human justice, precisely because it is less personal. The conclusion seems paradoxical, but its paradoxical quality

[21] As Challe's editors point out (*D* 557 n.279), Challe's complaint is similar to that of Locke, *Essay Concerning Human Understanding*, III.19.

may be attenuated if we keep in mind that for an independent-minded writer in the twilight of Louis XIV's reign, personal justice is, all too often, arbitrary justice. Challe criticizes the church for the same tendency to manipulate the fear of God for its own ends. He rejects any analogy between different kinds of *crainte* not because he wants to impose a reductively literal and univocal view of language (and thus of humanity), but in order to open up a space in which the self's emotional and intellectual capacities find room to flourish.

To this end, Challe is willing to be creative as well as critical in his use of words. It is not enough to distinguish, and so moderate, the various meanings of fear by emphasizing the impartiality of God's justice. Challe is not satisfied with a God who acts only as the referee of a game whose rules are fair. 'Je ne puis résister à un torrent qui m'entraîne dans le sentiment que Dieu voudrait que tous les hommes se rendissent dignes de ses bienfaits, et qu'aucun ne méritât de sentir sa sévérité' (I cannot resist a torrent that carries me into the conviction that God would like all men to become worthy of his benefits, and that none should deserve to feel his harshness) (*D* 680–1). He wants God's will to be good as well as just. At the same time, God's will cannot be divided against itself. Here, the resources of the French language are of no help. There is no distinction comparable to that between indignation and anger that would allow him to distinguish between different kinds of willing. Thus, in what is one of the most original passages of his book, Challe feels compelled to invent a new word.

In the proper sense of *vouloir*, he says, God impartially wills justice. In another sense, to which Challe gives the name *olouvrir* (an anagram of *vouloir*), God wills every man's happiness.[22] The former is absolute, the latter conditional. By way of example, Challe imagines he is running a lottery, and that a friend of his has purchased a ticket. 'Je veux d'un vouloir simple tirer ma loterie sans partialité. Je veux conditionnellement que mon ami ait le prix, c'est supposé que je le puisse faire tomber sans fraude' (I want with a simple act of will to draw my lots without bias. I wish conditionally for my friend to win the prize, that is, on the assumption that I can have his number come out without fraud) (*D* 682). Similarly, God cannot will that all men be saved—that would not be just. But he can will that all men be worthy of salvation.

[22] This twofold approach to the question may be contrasted with the semantic distinctions drawn by Jansenist and Reformed theologians to harmonize the thesis that Christ died for all men with the idea of double predestination.

'C'en est assez pour contenter le sentiment de la préférence des biens aux maux, que nous ne saurions abandonner' (This is enough to satisfy the sense that goods should be preferred to evils, which we would not want to abandon) (*D* 684).

This conclusion does more than subordinate the idea of God to human reason; it offers the prospect of personal reconciliation with the divine. Thanksgivings (*D* 635) and prayers for forgiveness (*D* 701) now become meaningful once more, but (to restate the earlier paradox in another way) precisely because they have no effect on God's fundamental disposition. If Challe is able to worship God, it is because first he can respect him. Geneviève Artigas-Menant has explored the ambiguity of Challe's notion of prayer, which hovers uneasily between the address of a personal petition to God and an impersonal wish for justice in general.[23] One can add to her analysis the observation that whereas in the fear of God it was important to distinguish the personal and the impersonal on the analogy of indignation and anger, in expressions of gratitude such distinctions become less important. Once the articulation of God's *vouloir* and *olouvrir* is comprehended, one no longer need worry too much about the personal (or psychologically dependent) as opposed to the impersonal (or intellectually appreciative) dimensions of one's prayer.

One might wonder why not. Ever since the Desert Fathers, the Christian tradition has been preoccupied in one way or another with exposing the vanity or self-interest prayer may conceal. In Challe's time, the issue had become particularly salient in the debates around Fénelon's idea of *pur amour* and Jansenist suspicions of the ruses of *amour-propre*. But despite Challe's anxieties about the afterlife, he does not seem to be troubled by the problem of mixed motives within himself. One reason is that, as we see in his descriptions of anger and gratitude, Challe's focus is outward-directed. Whether and when it is right to feel anger at a slight is not an issue; his focus is on the response itself and the *riposte* that follows from it. The other is the importance for Challe of resolving any mystery or ambiguity in the actions of the other. Having resolved the puzzle of God's will to his satisfaction, it is as if he were relieved of the burden of self-examination. The success of his intellectual enterprise, it seems, not only restores the relationship to the other, it makes it subjectively unproblematic.

[23] Geneviève Artigas-Menant, 'La Prière dans les *Difficultés sur la religion*', in *Du secret des clandestins*, 65–75.

And this is where Challe stops. Challe's God manifests an intention that makes an emotional response to it meaningful, but this interaction does not lead to the further development or differentiation of the relationship. Indeed, it seems to render it unnecessary. The same is true of Challe's response to Malebranche. Having addressed the book to the great philosopher, and through imagined debate with him arrived at satisfactory answers to his difficulties, he need not seek any further contact. All this suggests that what matters most to Challe in both relationships is the validation of his own act of speaking. To achieve this, he presents his self-assertion, not as his own initiative, but as a response to provocation. The anger sparked by that provocation then makes manifest an order of justice in which both parties can be said to participate.

The fact that no answer comes, or is actually sought, from the opposing party does not finally matter. The very fact that (like Job, in a way) Challe is able to challenge the other directly, and experiences the freedom of being able develop his thought with the other in mind, is compensation enough. Address, one might say, is in itself a form of redress. In the language of the passage cited earlier, it is, implicitly, a favor received, for which thanksgiving is the natural, appropriate response. It is out of this matrix that Challe finds his voice as a writer.[24] One may usefully compare the rhetorical stance of the *Difficultés* with that of literary satire or invective, which also seeks to make the moral order manifest through the expression of anger. But the range of satire does not usually extend to expressions of gratitude, which belong more to the realm of encomium. One might say that Challe's *Difficultés* are a somewhat awkward attempt to combine the two stances in a work of intellectual prose. He does so more successfully in *Les Illustres Françaises*, the extraordinary novel which offers a tribute to women's gracious power, but does so through the voices of seven angry men.

LES ILLUSTRES FRANÇAISES

It is widely recognized that while *Les Illustres Françaises* consists of seven interlocking stories about love, justice is a central concern both of the

[24] If we accept that the adversarial 'Malebranche' is to some extent a projection of Challe's inner tensions, then what has been achieved is a greater degree of personal integration, achieved in and through the process of writing itself.

individual narratives and of the narrative framework that unites them.[25] Philosophical considerations of the rights and obligations of parents and children, or husbands and wives, are integral to the discussion of personal relationships. On the most basic level of the plot, Challe's self-respecting heroines will not risk their reputation and self-respect in a love affair without the guarantee of marriage and the legal protection it affords. In Challe's novel, marriage is not just a pledge of faithful love, but a realistically presented institution involving contracts, negotiations over money, and concerns about the civil or ecclesiastical validity of the ceremony. Attending to such matters as whether secret marriages will hold up in the face of parental opposition, or whether godparents are entitled to wed, does not imply a coarse preoccupation with material concerns at the expense of romance; on the contrary, it is part of what makes the characters worthy of our attention and respect. They are careful to preserve documents that might be needed as evidence, their speeches sometimes recall lawyers' briefs, and those who feel offended are ready to take their disputes to the courts. Finding one's soul mate is important, but defending one's dignity is the first priority.

Of course, legal institutions and procedures cannot resolve all questions involving personal relationships. The characters need to negotiate many issues beyond the purview of the law, and it not surprising that for Challe the most prominent of these is whether to forgive a partner who has given offense, or how to overcome one's resentment at the adverse circumstances of life. The law can protect the autonomy of the individual, but it provides no procedure for reconciling people with each other or with the world in general. For this, the characters must seek other forms of mediation. In Challe's novel, it is notable that this search does not involve exploring the inner resources of the self. The first-person narrators rarely pause to reflect on their inner life or to weigh their conflicting emotions. There is no inner deliberation such as we find in *La Vie de Marianne.* Nor do the narrators probe the inner lives of others. Instead, we have civil conversation among the various narrators and their friends. Indeed, almost all the characters are linked by interlocking relationships of kinship and acquaintance. Challe also devises a frame story, in which the main characters of each narrative assemble to discuss each other's experiences and help those whose search for love has ended badly find a second chance of happiness. The group of friends also acts

[25] In addition to the Deloffre article cited above, see Christian Biet, *Droit et littérature sous l'Ancien Régime: le jeu de la valeur et de la loi* (Paris: Champion, 2002), 198–224.

as an informal love tribunal, to whose judgment its participants agree to submit their problems. It thus exercises a judicial function, but one which is discreet rather than inquisitive in its approach, since one of its goals is precisely to overcome people's susceptibility to offense. Through the intervention of this tribunal (in which women and men play equally active roles) even the most recalcitrant heroes agree to marry and thereby become fully integrated members of society.

The image of a free and flexible community of *devisants* has led some critics to define the overarching spirit of the novel as one of gaiety. Françoise Gevrey, for example, notes that the expression *en riant* (the expression means 'laughing' or 'smiling', according to the context) occurs eighty-seven times in the book, adding that 'laughter and good form put into proper perspective the behavior described in the stories'.[26] Yet, at a number of places in the novel, the laughter takes on a resentful edge. Toward the middle of the book, for example, when the characters are enjoying dinner and taking a break from their storytelling, one of the young men, Condamine, turns a joking discussion among husbands into a critique of marriage that drives his wife to tears:

Comme ces pestes nous déchirent, dit la belle Mme de Jussy, en haussant les épaules et en riant . . . —Je ne me plains pas de ma femme, répondit Condamine; il y en a de bien moins raisonnables qu'elle, le nombre en est même très grand. Cependant quelque bien marié que soit un homme, il se rencontre très souvent des moments où il regrette sa liberté. Je ne parle pas, comme vous voyez, de ceux qui sont mal mariés, je parle des mariages les mieux unis tel que le mien . . . —Quoi, interrompit sa femme toute surprise, et presque les larmes aux yeux, ai-je eu le malheur de faire quelque chose qui vous ait déplu?—Tu es une sotte, dit-il en riant, ce que tu me demandes là, me déplaît, laisse-moi poursuivre. Je ne crois pas, ajouta-t-il, qu'il y ait au monde un mariage plus uni que le mien . . . cependant . . . c'est cette union-là qui me fatigue quelquefois.[27]

How these creatures malign us! said the beautiful Mme de Jussy with a shrug and a laugh . . . I do not complain about my wife, answered Condamine. There are some women, even a large number, who are far less reasonable than she is.

[26] Françoise Gevrey, *L'Illusion et ses procédés: de 'La Princesse de Clèves' aux 'Illustres Françaises'* (Paris: Corti, 1988), 283, 286. This would also seem to be the judgment of A. W. Preston, whose recent translation of the novel is published under the title *Life, Love, and Laughter in the Reign of Louis XIV: A New Translation of Robert Challe's Novel 'Les Illustres Françaises'* (Brighton: The Book Guild, 2008).

[27] Robert Challe, *Les Illustres Françaises*, ed. Jacques Cormier and Frédéric Deloffre (Paris: Livre de poche, 1996), 359. Subsequent references to this edition, abbreviated *IF*, will appear in the text. The translations are Preston's (identified as *LLL*), occasionally modified where it was important to bring the wording closer to that of the French text.

But however happy one's marriage, there are many moments when a man regrets the loss of his freedom. I am not talking, as you see, about those with unhappy marriages. I am talking even of people with the most loving of marriages, like myself.

What is this I hear! his wife interrupted in great surprise, with tears almost springing to her eyes. Have I done something to displease you? You silly thing, he said with a smile, what you are asking me now displeases me. Let me continue what I was saying. I do not think there is a closer marriage than mine anywhere in the world . . . nonetheless . . . I am sometimes tired of that very closeness. (*LLL* 294–5, tr. modified)

Condamine scolds his wife because she doesn't understand his point, which is that he feels tied down even though he has no complaint about the marriage itself. He is not merely expressing a rueful awareness of the imperfection of human relationships, which, like Mme de Jussy's exclamation about male prejudice, would be unproblematic. Rather, Condamine is insisting that allowance be made for his continuing ambivalence. His free speech must not be stifled for the sake of a superficial harmony.

We can understand Condamine's gesture as a way of compensating for a persistent weakness of character. He had been unable to stand up to his mother, who was reluctant at first to let him marry a woman who, though well born, was poor and had few social connections. Now he finds himself dependent on the equally strong-willed Angélique. But his edginess is also a sign that the unity of the little community is not to be taken for granted as something fully achieved. The very fact that the community initially comes into focus as a love tribunal points to the characters' difficulty in having their various goals—recognition of their dignity and autonomy as individuals, but also reconciliation into a world of mutuality and interdependence—adjudicated in a satisfactory manner.

A closer look at the text reveals that expressions of anger and resentment appear with remarkable frequency throughout Challe's novel. In addition to ambiguously comic moments such as the one just cited, explicit references to anger or indignation occur more than sixty times in Challe's text.[28] For purposes of comparison, we may take Sorel's novel *Les Aventures de Francion*, whose hero is no paragon of civility and is cited by one of Challe's characters as a model (*IF* 504). *Francion* is

[28] The count was done by hand, and includes both *colère* along with an occasional synonym such as *indignation*.

roughly the same length as *Les Illustres Françaises*, but in Sorel's novel the word *colère* appears a mere half-dozen times.[29] Certainly, for a novel ostensibly focused on courtship and marriage, the number of references to anger in *Les Illustres Françaises* is exceptionally large. Yet it does not strike the reader as totally incongruous. One reason is that Challe's characters are adults engaged in urban life and commerce, not idealistic adolescents like Prévost's Des Grieux, students like Francion, or bohemians like the comic players of Scarron's *Roman comique*. Nor do they belong to the world of romance, where the only slights that matter are the conventional ones of scorned love or challenge from a rival. Respect is what matters to Challe's characters, but they live in a world where that respect cannot be gained simply by revealing one's identity through some spectacular demonstration of passion or prowess.

But perhaps the most important reason is that Challe gives a new and disenchanted social concreteness to the conventions of the marriage plot by linking it to issues of practical justice. In its conventional form, the marriage plot dramatizes the process by which the unique merits and claims of an individual come to be recognized so that he or she can then be properly integrated into the social world, for which marriage serves as a symbol. In *Les Illustres Françaises*, however, this process is stripped of the elements that in other literary works disguise or mediate its functional or transactional character. There is little suggestion that love is the meeting-point of the real and the ideal, such as we find in the romance, including a satirical romance like *Francion*. Nor does Challe's novel adopt the naturalistic perspective of comedy, according to which marriage guarantees and celebrates the renewal of families, as children become adults and future parents in their turn.[30]

In the absence of generic conventions to support the process, it becomes difficult for the novel to persuade us that recognizing individ-

[29] Charles Sorel, *Histoire comique de Francion*, édition de 1633 présentée par Fausta Garavini, établie par Anne Schoysman et annotée par Anna Lia Franchetti (Paris: Gallimard 'Folio', 1996). Sorel's work is also more satirical in nature than *Les Illustres Françaises*, whose title, far from being ironic, reflects not only Challe's admiration for female heroism, but his belief that women of modest backgrounds (though of good family) may deserve to be called 'illustrious' just as much as those born into the highest nobility.

[30] On the peculiarities in the relationships between parents and children in the novel, see René Demoris, 'Parents et enfants: jeux de l'inconscient dans *Les Illustres Françaises*', in Geneviève Artigas-Menant and Jacques Popin, eds, *Leçons sur 'Les Illustres Françaises' de Robert Challe: actes de la table ronde de Créteil* (Université de Paris XII-Val de Marne: Champion-Slatkine, 1993), 151–65.

ual differences and reconciling distinct individuals into a larger whole can both be achieved without recourse to some arbitrary solution. There is, of course, always some tension between the two aims. Obstacles to resolution may include mistaken identities, the distorting effect of the passions, and the economic or status concerns of families. Yet, the marriage plot rests on the premise that whatever the difficulties, recognition and reconciliation are not in themselves contradictory goals. The suggestion of such a contradiction does emerge in what we have come to call the realist novel, and in this sense *Les Illustres Françaises* can legitimately be called realistic. And yet, its structure is still that of the earlier *nouvelle* or exemplary tale: the considerations of historical relativity and social change through which the realist novel of the nineteenth century mediates the contradiction between the two goals are not on Challe's horizon. As a result, his novel manifests a starkness of tension that is more characteristic of baroque or gothic fiction. On the surface, most of its stories end happily (there are two exceptions, which serve as instructive contrasts). But, as in Condamine's speech, the leitmotiv of anger sounded throughout the entire text shows that the cultural forms such as marriage which are supposed to mediate the recognition of the characters' dignity and autonomy, on the one hand, and their reconciliation to the pressure of social conformity on the other, fail to do so in a satisfactory way.

In this respect, Challe's novel may best be illuminated by comparing it, not with another novel, but with the author's own *Difficultés sur la religion*. The novel's questioning of marriage is similar to the treatise's questioning of divine justice. In structural terms, however, the novel's search for a way to mediate between recognition and reconciliation differs in one crucial respect from the approach taken in the treatise. In *Les Illustres Françaises*, the community of friends plays a key role, whereas Challe's theological quest is a purely individualistic one. The institutional church has been discredited, and in the absence of free public discussion of religion there can be no mediating community to help Challe resolve his anger or his anxiety. At most, as we have seen, there is the imagined fellowship with Malebranche. Challe does not consider that the code of natural morality to which he appeals in his discussion of justice might itself be socially conditioned. From his point of view, its premises are self-evident. We see something similar in the novel. Challe's characters never question the legitimacy of their society's legal institutions. They may get angry when their desires are frustrated by a particular law or custom, and the bolder ones exploit procedural complexities for their own ends, but they do not cast doubt on the overall rationality of the system as such. But when it comes to the unwritten and uncertain rules of personal relationships, Challe's characters cannot go it alone. They need the mediation of their friends. The role assigned to community opinion gives to the dramatization and resolution of anger in the novel an interpersonal dimension already hinted at in the treatise's address to Malebranche.

A hard-won harmony

The first story of *Les Illustres Françaises* offers a striking example of the way recognition and reconciliation may be at odds with each other. Old M. Dupuis knows Des Ronais loves his daughter Manon, but he withholds consent to their marriage. A widower himself, he likes having his daughter at home taking care of him. Yet, far from forbidding Des Ronais from courting Manon, he welcomes the young man into his home. He even allows the couple to spend time alone, knowing that Manon is too virtuous to let herself be seduced. Des Ronais is as well treated as a son-in-law could be, except that he has neither the status nor the privileges of a husband. He finds himself torn between anger at Dupuis's selfishness and appreciation for his trust and friendship. Des Ronais's ambivalence becomes even stronger when a servant girl he has seduced to relieve his sexual frustration announces she is pregnant and demands that he marry her. Old Dupuis sends the girl packing but says not one word of reproach to Des Ronais. Dupuis's lack of concern with propriety is, we learn, a fundamental trait of his character. He only married his own wife when he thought he was about to die from a battle wound and his confessor pressured him to do the right thing. Now, he and Des Ronais live in what we might call reconciliation before the fact. The struggle for recognition which should be a precondition for reconciliation is short-circuited rather than resolved. Des Ronais puzzles over his own ambivalent reaction to the situation. 'Je voyais tous les jours un homme, dont la vie me faisait mourir de chagrin, et que je ne pouvais haïr' (Every day, I saw a man whose very existence caused me the utmost despair, yet whom I could not dislike) (*IF* 117/*LLL* 51).

Des Ronais's frustrated anger finds expression only after Dupuis's death. Instead of marrying Manon right away, he puts off the wedding. The reasons he gives are unconvincing. Later, he finds a pretext for rejecting Manon altogether. He finds a letter which suggests Manon is involved with another man. He refuses to listen to her explanation or to the friends who try to settle their quarrel. Clearly Des Ronais *wants* to be angry. It is as if refusing to be reconciled now could offer compensation for the false harmony of his earlier life with Manon. Even if the circumstances don't really fit, he insists on being recognized as someone who has suffered offense. This is not merely a question of vanity. His inability to get angry earlier had a consequence he was reluctant to acknowledge: it blocked his desire for Manon. After admitting that he could not bring himself to hate Dupuis, he adds in reference to Manon that 'je ne ressentais aucun de ces mouvements impétueux, auxquels l'amour rend si sujets ceux qui sont remplis de passion' (I felt none of those wild impulses to which love subjects those who are filled with passion) (*IF* 117/*LLL* 51, tr. modified). It takes the intervention of his friend Des Frans to get Des Ronais to meet Manon and eventually to apologize for his obstinacy. The couple's happiness is quickly restored, but the choice of go-between is significant. Des Frans had been absent during the years of Des Ronais's courtship of Manon. It is his return to Paris from the provinces that opens the book and launches the telling of the stories. He is thus not just another friend, but a crucial mediator for the group as a whole. He is an insider who is also an outsider, and thus his presence opens up a space in which Des Ronais is freed to adopt a more flexible attitude toward Manon. Des Frans is an outsider, not just because he has been away from Paris, but, as we discover in the sixth story, he himself has been the most stubbornly angry of all the men in the novel, the one whose unhappy relationship with Silvie has alienated him the most from the idea of marriage. That the intransigent Des Frans should join those who want to reunite the couple gives Des Ronais the cover he needs to reconcile with Manon.

We have already mentioned Condamine, the hero of the second story, whose anger emerges only after his marriage. He, too, was unable to get angry at a parental figure who opposes his marriage, but in his case the cause lies in his own weakness of character. He cannot stand up to his own mother. It is Angélique who proves to be firm in seeking the respect of his family even at the risk of driving Condamine away by her concern for decorum. In the event, Condamine cannot get angry with Angélique either. He sets her up in her own apartment, but when Angélique insists instead on moving in with a respectable family in the same building, he expresses no resentment at losing the opportunity of seeing her alone. On the contrary, 'il n'en eut que plus d'estime pour elle' (he esteemed her the more for suggesting it) (*IF* 168/*LLL* 101). This is less because of any moral principle than because her precautions make Condamine feel for the first time that he is a man whose virility has to be reckoned with. 'Il le lui témoigna en riant, disant qu'il voyait bien qu'il n'était pas tout à fait si peu à craindre qu'il avait cru' ([he] told her so with a smile, saying he was pleased to see he was not quite as harmless as he had thought) (*IF* 168/*LLL* 101). Here is another instance in which Condamine's remark is more than a good-humored joke. It is a desperate and somewhat pathetic effort to affirm his masculine dignity in the midst of dependence.

Over the course of his story, Condamine's strategy for impressing Angélique relies, not on displays of aggressive energy, but on his financial generosity, which he hopes will earn her gratitude. At the beginning of the story, he helps Mlle de Vougy, Angélique's protector, resolve a legal dispute with his mother on very favorable terms. Angélique is indeed grateful (*IF* 146), and so Condamine continues by helping Angélique herself escape her somewhat humiliating position as Mlle de Vougy's companion and establish her own household. 'Je ne vous demande pour toute reconnaissance des présents que je vous ferai, que la seule satisfaction de vous les faire', he tells her (in return for the presents I give you, I ask only the pleasure of giving them) (*IF* 155/*LLL* 88). Of course, it is clear he has fallen in love, and Angélique gradually allows herself to imagine the possibility of marriage. Her reaction must be described in these neutral terms, since Challe leaves some doubt as to whether Angélique is really in love with Condamine. She may simply be taking advantage of an opportunity to better herself without ceasing to be virtuous in the eyes of society. In a moment of desperation triggered by the influential Mme de Cologny's remark that, based on the finery she wears, she must be a kept woman, Angélique does admit to Condamine that she feels for him 'un amour de reconnaissance et d'inclination' (my love stems from both gratitude and inclination) (*IF* 174/*LLL* 107). The word *inclination* does suggest spontaneous feeling, but in contrast with the hierarchy of Madeleine de Scudéry's 'Carte de Tendre', the less passionate *reconnaissance* is ranked first. The priority of gratitude is given an additional layer of meaning when she goes on to tell him 'vous n'êtes point plus cher que ma réputation' (you are not so dear to me as my reputation). The *reconnaissance* owed to the other gives way to the 'recognition' she owes to herself.

Angélique, it must be said, is merely turning Condamine's own strategy back on him. While the favors he did her during his courtship were expressions of love, they arose from fear that his lack of personal magnetism would prevent Angélique from responding to him with anything other than gratitude. Condamine's resentment at Angélique after their marriage suggests that, despite her protests, he might not have been entirely wrong. The married Angélique seems be more attached to Condamine's mother than to her husband. Not only have her merits now been recognized by that distinguished lady; to everyone's astonishment the two women are now practically inseparable. It is certainly true that Angélique has good reason to be grateful to Mme de Condamine. The social validation she receives is more valuable than anything she got from her son. The result is an almost excessive integration of Angélique into the family. That is to say, we have here another instance of a reconciliation that outweighs the recognition given the male hero. Condamine is all the more resentful in that, like Des Ronais in his relationship with Dupuis, he has no socially acceptable reason for complaint.

The third story, about Monsieur de Terny and Mademoiselle de Bernay, is very different from the first two. Terny shows more independence and strength of will than either Des Ronais or Condamine. His anger at learning that his beloved Clémence, the beautiful sister of his army friend de Bernay, is being pressured to become a nun so that the inheritance (and thus the marriage prospects) of her older siblings can be enhanced, is all the more fierce in that he is a Protestant. Not that he is especially attached to his faith. He looks forward to the social benefits of becoming a Catholic, and the only reason he has postponed his conversion is to avoid offending his staunchly Calvinist aunt, from whom he expects a substantial legacy. After her death, Terny is reconciled to the 'true religion', but this is a matter of expediency: the door is now open to a career in government service. Certainly he never changes his mind about the evils of monasticism. Secure in his sense of self, Terny is less concerned with belonging and gratitude than with negotiating his way through the social maze.

In the story of how Terny succeeds in winning Clémence, therefore, the resolution of anger is stymied by premature or ambiguous reconciliation. Terny's initial attempts to get Clémence's father to consent to their marriage are a failure: the parties are too angry with each other to arrive at a settlement (*IF* 206/*LLL* 140). Terny fights a duel with the family's chosen husband and flees to England. Forced to re-enter a convent, Clémence manages to send him a letter about her impending vows, and he manages to return to Paris just one day before the ceremony. Terny's account of his state of mind is characteristic. 'J'étais si las et si fatigué, que je ne pouvais me soutenir; mais la colère et la passion me donnaient des forces' (I was so weary and tired, I could scarcely sit upright, but love and anger gave me strength) (*IF* 238/*LLL* 173). Yet, instead of pushing ahead blindly, Terny uses his knowledge of the technicalities of secular and canon law to turn the ceremony of Clémence's profession into a wedding ceremony with himself as the groom.[31] He and Clémence exchange vows before the altar and in the presence of a crowd of witnesses, so that even though the priest refuses his blessing, a canonically valid marriage has taken place.

Secure in his triumph, Terny can now settle down to a quiet life. He fails to win over Clémence's parents, but the public's approval of his marriage guarantees his personal, as well as legal, integration into society. Terny can now act in turn as an agent of reconciliation for others. It is he who proves to Des Ronais that the letters apparently addressed to Manon Dupuis by the mysterious 'Gauthier' were in fact written by himself to Clémence. Manon was only their intermediary. Like Des Frans, Terny enables Des Ronais to abandon his attitude of distrust without losing face. Not only is Terny's testimony unimpeachable, the self-respect he displays qualifies him as a trustworthy mediator. He knows what justice owes him, and so he can adjudicate other people's obligations.

The reconciliation of Des Ronais and Manon concludes the first set of stories in *Les Illustres Françaises*, so it is worth pausing at this point to compare the dynamic of recognition and reconciliation in Challe as it appears thus far with the treatment of the same topic in other novelists of the early eighteenth century. In Prévost, and even more in Marivaux, the characters are able to explore and rectify their relationships with other people by retelling their personal stories in ways that allow them to be reframed in more constructive ways.[32] As we will see in the next chapter, Marivaux's Marianne, for example, responds to slight, not with an open display of anger—as an orphan of uncertain social status, and as a woman, she cannot do so and expect a positive response—but with an appeal to wounds suffered by the delicacy of her feelings that encourages others to see her in a new light. She benefits from the prevailing

[31] For the technical details, see Biet, *Droit et littérature.*

[32] See William Ray, *Story and History: Narrative Authority and Social Identity in the Eighteenth-Century English and French Novel* (Cambridge, Mass.: Blackwell, 1990).

ambiguity about what it means to possess a refined sensibility (is it a sign of high birth or a mark of individual distinction?), an ambiguity which allows her to negotiate her way to respect and social integration. Because the social world she inhabits makes some allowance for the metaphorical mobility of language, the nature of things can be revealed and redescribed at the same time without the sense that redescription and revelation are mutually exclusive.

As we have seen in the *Difficultés*, this flexibility is foreign to Challe, and the same intransigence is apparent in the novel. Unlike Marianne, Manon cannot overcome Des Ronais's anger by invoking shared ideas about the relationship between personal identity and patterns of conduct. He needs an explanation of the facts and the testimony of witnesses. His expectations are shaped by legal procedures rather than by the forms of civility. Yet, although his behavior is viewed by the others as foolish, it is not presented, nor should it be read, as a sign of coarseness or moral blindness. His friends make fun of him, but they do not scorn him as a boorish inferior. Part of the reason is that Challe's characters are in general less preoccupied with proving their refinement than those of Marivaux or Prévost. Another factor, and I believe a more crucial one, is Challe's fascination with truculent characters like old Dupuis, whose actions are all out in the open yet frustrate any attempt to make them culturally understandable.

The fact that Challe does not make Dupuis give a more intimate account of his feelings may result less from his alleged lack of curiosity about his characters' inner lives than from his conviction that there is no further explanation to be had. Or, since Challe does not announce his intentions, perhaps it is better to say that the novel dramatizes some puzzlement, not about the inner workings of the self, but about the reactions of other people. This formulation is more in line with Challe's 'reactive' perspective, typified by his focus on anger. The question would then be, should one look for a secret hidden behind a person's behavior, when one cannot understand that behavior, despite the fact that one has in hand all the evidence one can expect to obtain in the normal course of things? From the legalistic, externally focused perspective of Challe's male characters, the answer should be 'no', but the novel shows how inadequate this response proves to be in the negotiation of personal relationships.

In the case of Des Ronais and Manon, an explanation based on factual evidence and reliable third-person testimony does resolve the problem. The same is not true in Condamine's relationship with

Angélique. Everything she does is also open to scrutiny, yet Condamine does not really know what she thinks, and since she has no confidantes there is no third party who can help him either. It is this inability to uncover the secrets of characters who do not seem to be hiding anything that in Challe's work produces the deepest form of anger. It is the same kind of anger that emerges in Challe's attempt to understand the actions of God. It is important to note that, when it comes to religion also, Challe believes that all the evidence one needs is readily available. No appeal to special revelation is required. Yet, the need for explanation remains unsatisfied. Since for Challe this need, whether in religion or in love, is intimately connected with the investigator's demand for recognition, it cannot be met simply by adducing another fact. It requires a reconfiguration of the whole problem. In the treatise, this happened through the author's creative use of language to redefine the terms of the question and so dispel the mystery. In the world of the novel, such a reconfiguration involves concerted action on the part of the characters, and this is not always an easy thing.

Thus, it is interesting that Terny's story is followed by another one of those uneasy moments in which anger is said to be an occasion for laughter. Mme de Condamine (the former Angélique) pretends to be angry at Manon's cousin Dupuis (the nephew of 'old' Dupuis and referred to simply by that name), when he reveals that his mother and his fiancée have sent him away while they discuss his marriage plans. She complains that she and her friends are only a 'pis-aller' (second-best entertainment) for Dupuis (*IF* 245/*LLL* 180). He, in turn, 'affectant un air de colère' (putting on a pretense of anger), reproaches her for turning on him after she has mocked Des Ronais and Des Frans. He seems to be joking, but as in the other incident with Condamine, the laughter is tinged with frustration and resentment. In his reply, Dupuis says that to punish Mme de Condamine, he won't tell her details about the marriage and the money his mother is going to settle on him. She counters that she and her friends won't participate in the wedding until he stops being angry (*IF* 246/*LLL* 181), and meanwhile she wants to hear Des Frans tell the story of Jussy. This interlude of banter follows on the reconciliation of Des Ronais and Manon, but its undertones suggest the fragility of the harmony achieved, even in the midst of wedding preparations.

The moral relief of clear judgment

The fourth and fifth stories of *Les Illustres Françaises* pursue Challe's exploration of anger and its mediations by offering two sharply contrasting tales. The mood of puzzlement that makes the stories of Des Ronais and Condamine so intriguing is dispelled, since each story leads to a judgment of the characters' behavior—in the first case positive, in the second, negative—that leaves no room for ambivalence. In this respect, and despite the somber tone of the fifth story, these stories provide a kind of epistemological and moral relief in the middle of the book, while also tracing the upper and lower boundaries of the novel's problematic.

The story of Monsieur de Jussy and Mademoiselle de Fenouil is the most straightforward of the book. It arrives at its happy end with a minimum of drama because the anger it dramatizes is a tactical device rather than a genuine reaction to slight. From the perspective of social interaction, of course, anger is always to some degree an attempt to gain tactical advantage. If this is all it is, there is no cause for anxiety.

The story itself combines elements drawn from the earlier stories of Condamine and Terny. Like Condamine, Jussy is less than heroic in his approach to love, but his timidity has some justification. Angélique was poor, but Babet de Fenouil is much richer than Jussy. Babet is also a woman of initiative. She tells Jussy how to get out of the marriage his family has arranged with a Mademoiselle Grandet. He is to find a plausible pretext for quarreling with his fiancée and then walk out in anger. Like other meek people, however, Jussy doesn't know how to be angry properly. He decides to stage a scene of jealousy and accuse Mademoiselle Grandet of entertaining other suitors, but he goes too far, accusing her of immodesty and reducing her to tears (*IF* 257/*LLL* 193). Jussy's reputation for docility is such that Mademoiselle Grandet's own family turns against her. They do so with such vehemence that Babet reproaches her lover for exposing the innocent young woman to her relatives' wrath (*IF* 258/*LLL* 194).

Jussy himself regrets his action, and in the course of the story becomes a model of virtue and strength in adversity. His affair with Babet is discovered by her family, which has him banished from France for seven years. He fakes his own death in Spain in order to lull them into thinking he is no longer a threat, but he keeps Babet secretly informed of the truth. She, too, is faithful to him, while also caring secretly for the child they have had out of wedlock. When his ban is lifted, Jussy gets proper certification of his freedom and returns to Paris incognito, securing permission from the archdiocese to marry Babet and legitimize their son. He then invites his unsuspecting in-laws to the wedding reception, where they have to accept the facts. Like Terny, Jussy has mastered the rules of the legal system. In his case, however, the triumphant *coup d'éclat* does not need the support of anger, faked or real. It is enough that Jussy can display documents whose validity cannot be questioned.

All that remains is for Jussy to apologize to Mademoiselle Grandet. By this time, she has become the widowed Mme de Mongey and a member of the little community of friends. She has been listening as Jussy's story has been told by Des Frans. The latter is an old friend of Jussy's, and also (if his friends' efforts are successful) Mme de Mongey's next husband. Des Frans thus apologizes himself for not having defended his lady's honor when Jussy had attacked it. His excuse is that he had not yet made her acquaintance. Mme de Mongey responds reassuringly that she bears no 'ressentiment' toward Jussy or his wife. 'Je le sacrifie à ce que je viens d'entendre' she says, at the end of the story (I give it up on hearing what I've just heard) (*IF* 278/*LLL* 214–15, tr. modified). The fact that she is in love with Des Frans no doubt makes it easier to give up her anger. In any case, this is all ancient history; there is no real unfinished business. Challe thus need not bring Jussy into the frame story to apologize to Mme de Mongey in person. His forgiveness can be taken for granted.

Des Prez, the protagonist of the fifth narrative, also makes no appearance in the frame story, but for the opposite reason. His anger leaves no room for negotiation, and his conduct toward his lover Mademoiselle de l'Épine cannot be redeemed. The community of friends can do nothing with or for him.

The roots of Des Prez's anger lie deep in his family situation. His early life was dominated by fear of his angry father (*IF* 291, 294/*LLL* 229, 232). Instead of asserting himself directly, Des Prez decides to marry Marie-Madeleine de l'Épine in secret. She comes from a good but poor family, but unlike the canny Angélique, whose situation is somewhat similar to hers, Marie-Madeleine pays no attention to practical issues. The marriage's validity could be challenged because the young Des Prez does not have his father's permission, but this young woman's only concern is her moral conscience. As long as the marriage is properly blessed by a priest, she is reassured. She resembles Des Prez in being unable to assert herself openly. Her mother, Mme de l'Épine, depends on Des Prez's father for help in a lawsuit and is also, as the latter knows, 'fort intéressée' (a fortune-hunter) (*IF* 294/*LLL* 231). Money is more important to her than her daughter's happiness. When she discovers Marie-Madeleine is married and pregnant, she is so consumed by rage that even old Des Prez is moved to pity for his daughter-in-law (*IF* 347/*LLL* 283). But he does not accord the young woman any more respect, and it is obviously difficult for Marie-Madeleine to demand it. She cannot get angry.

Marie-Madeleine's social timidity seems also to reflect her lack of instinctual energy. As Des Prez tells Dupuis, who narrates his story, 'le plaisir des sens ne la dominait pas' (the pleasure of the senses was not a dominant part of her nature) (*IF* 285/*LLL* 222). This surprisingly frank remark says as much about Des Prez's character as it does about hers. His two displays of anger in the first part of the story are in fact related to sexual desire, the only domain in which he dares to assert himself, and in which his fundamental resentment emerges. On one of his visits to his wife in their secret apartment, he finds her sleeping and, thinking she might be ill, leaves without disturbing her. He later returns to find a note in which she teasingly accuses him of lack of ardor in not waking her up, 'surtout dans un lieu où il sait bien que l'envie de dormir ne l'amène pas' (particularly in a place where he is well aware it is not the need for rest which has brought her there) (*IF* 326/*LLL* 262–3). Des Prez is pleasantly surprised by this recognition of his sexuality, and decides to respond with an equally witty expression of irritation. Telling the landlady to report to his wife that the note made him angry, Des Prez writes his wife that she has so often received his advances with reluctance that he has decided not to return for three months, to give himself time for his ardor to return (*IF* 327/*LLL* 283). The effect recalls that of Condamine's jokes about marriage. Marie-Madeleine bursts into tears. Des Prez emerges from hiding to reassure her, but his triumph is a mean and hollow one. He can assert himself only against a weaker opponent.

The second episode makes the same point even more dramatically. Walking in the country with his wife soon after their marriage, Des Prez is overcome with sexual desire and drags her into a rye field, thinking they won't be seen making love among the stalks of grain. He is mistaken. A peasant, assuming they are tramps, attacks them. Des Prez responds with equal anger. The peasant apologizes for his mistake, but Des Prez accepts no excuses. He keeps the man at sword's point until his wife can get away and then has him beaten by his lackeys. Adding insult to injury, he also 'sacrifices' the reputation of an unknown woman passing by in the distance by pretending to the assembled villagers that she was his sexual partner (*IF* 328–9/*LLL* 285). His declared intention is to protect his wife's reputation, but the contrast with Mme de Mongey's 'sacrifice' in the preceding story is significant (the same verb is used in both episodes). Whereas Mongey let go her right to be offended so as to be reconciled with Jussy, Des Prez's anger leads him to compound his offense.

Des Prez behaves very differently when his father pressures him to marry someone else. Des Prez avoids a confrontation by saying he wants to become a monk. It is suggestive that the only response he can imagine on the spot involves renouncing his real desires. Des Prez never does get openly angry at his father, even when his marriage ends in tragedy. The pregnant Marie-Madeleine is so distraught by her mother and her father-in-law's accusations that she tricked Des Prez into marriage that she falls down a flight of stairs and dies in hospital. Furious, Des Prez resolves to avenge her by punishing his mother-in-law in whatever way he can. By contrast, his anger at his father takes a more passive-aggressive form: he vows never to get married again. The family name will die with him.

Dupuis tries to salvage Des Prez's reputation by saying that 's'il a témoigné, et s'il témoigne encore une colère et un ressentiment implacable contre ceux qui lui ont été contraires, il a aussi témoigné sa reconnaissance à tous ceux qui lui ont été favorables, et qui lui ont rendu service, ou bien à la défunte' (if he showed, and still shows, an anger and implacable animosity toward all those who thwarted or opposed him, he demonstrates equally his gratitude to those who helped him or to his late wife) (*IF* 352/*LLL* 288, tr. modified). It is true that Des Prez is devastated, and that he did really love his wife. Yet, his gratitude carries no weight in the resolution of his story; we never see any instances of his gratitude. Des Prez cannot be reconciled to society because he has never found an appropriate way to assert himself. Angélique condemns Des Prez for contracting a secret marriage he knew his father would contest. Even more damning is that even after Marie-Madeleine's death, he keeps his marriage to her a secret. Des Prez says it is to avoid revealing his wife's shameful death in the Hôtel-Dieu, but he is also sparing his father the shame of having his cruel behavior to her exposed (*IF* 351/*LLL* 287). In the context of a novel celebrating virtuous women, whatever their station in life, such concealment clearly warrants censure. Des Prez's unwillingness to let the truth be known and face the consequences makes him unworthy to enter the community of friends.

Anxiety about answers

Des Prez's exclusion from the group stands in sharp contrast to the reception given the heroes of the novel's last two episodes. Des Frans and young Dupuis (Manon's cousin) display a capacity for anger just as fierce as Des Prez's, their actions display an equal cruelty, and yet their friends treat them with sympathy and even indulgence. One reason, of course, is that they were already friends before the story starts, while Des Prez is an outsider. Moreover, they are each loved by a female member of the group, who gives the man a second chance to become reconciled with society through marriage. It is worth noting that these relationships are not entirely new. The couples were acquainted before the men's adventures. Now the men are available and ready to settle down, while the women are widowed and also free to start afresh. By contrast, Des Prez does not seem to have inspired love in, or be attracted by, any woman other than Mademoiselle de l'Épine. This lack of wider affective connections is just as damning as the neglect of social convention by the more libertine men.

Des Frans and Dupuis enjoy a privileged position on the narrative level as well. As narrators themselves, they are central to the storytelling process, while the information they provide helps answer other people's questions and calm their anxieties. Des Frans mediates the conflict between Des Ronais and Manon, while Dupuis plays a crucial role in bringing closure to Des Frans's unhappy experience with his wife Silvie. It would seem that their ability to mediate conflict through superior knowledge is what makes these men lovable despite the excesses of their behavior. Again, the contrast with Des Prez is instructive: the latter can use his superior knowledge only to punish, not to heal. But the most crucial difference is that whereas Des Prez's rage is only a reactive resentment toward his father, the anger of Des Frans and Dupuis includes a crucial cognitive dimension. They are frustrated because they cannot solve a mystery. Their stories are also the longest in the book. The plots are more complex because they dramatize, not the pursuit of a clearly perceived goal, as in the earlier stories, but the quest for an elusive truth. The group of friends would not be the community Challe imagines if it did not honor that quest.

That enigmatic situations may provoke anger was already a theme in one of the earlier stories. Des Ronais's refusal to accept Manon's explanation about the letters from 'Gauthier' was clearly a projection of his own inability to understand what was going on in his peculiar *ménage à trois* with Manon and her father. But father figures, fascinating as they may be, are not the objects of Challe's greatest curiosity in *Les Illustres Françaises.* Challe's heroes do not have a problem with their identity or genealogy. Their quickness to take offense shows they know who they are. What they seek is reassurance about their place in a universe whose order they can comprehend and in which they can feel comfortable. This is a theme that might well have been dramatized through the relationship of son to father, as in Fénelon's *Télémaque.* After all, the somewhat similar quest in the *Difficultés* involved figuring out the relationship between God's justice and his will that all men be saved. Yet, although finding a satisfactory answer to that question led Challe to accept (with qualifications) the goodness of a personal God, the relationship that resulted was limited in nature. It certainly did not include the subordination of the human to the divine, which for Challe can only provoke resentment. Instead, the two final stories of Challe's illustrate a move toward a more personal experience of justice through relationships with women that culminate in marriage. The women may be idealized as the mediators of integration into society and, more implicitly, of life itself, but the men retain the initiative. In the *Difficultés,* this initiative is represented by an epistemological drive whose goal is the satisfaction of both Challe's intellectual curiosity and his sense of self-worth. In the novel, that drive is one component of a more comprehensive erotic urgency in the two most forceful male characters.

For Des Frans, the mystery is that of his wife Silvie's infidelity. Before they were married, doubts had already been raised about her past. The people who could best vouch for her good birth and character had died, and so Silvie resorted to some complicated and somewhat dubious measures in order to show Des Frans she was a socially suitable bride. Des Frans himself is an orphan dependent on the patronage of relatives, but instead of making him be more flexible in judging the relationship between the appearance and the reality of merit, this background predisposes him to anger whenever he feels the least bit slighted. Still, the marriage was a happy one until Des Frans returned early from a trip to find Silvie asleep in bed with his best friend Gallouin. Enraged, Des Frans's first thought is to kill them both, but his sense of honor stops him from killing a sleeping man. Also, as he is ashamed to realize, he is still in love with Silvie. So he leaves without taking any action except to steal Silvie's necklace as proof that her infidelity has been discovered.

The next day, Des Frans provokes Gallouin to a duel, wounds him badly, and in his rage would have gone on to kill him had not other people intervened. Yet, having taken his revenge, Des Frans never questions Gallouin about his behavior. In a sense, there is no need to ask: Silvie is beautiful and Gallouin is a notorious libertine. Des Frans also has too much pride to stoop to Gallouin's level. Silvie's behavior, on the other hand, Des Frans cannot understand at all. He questions her with angry relentlessness, but to no avail, for Silvie herself does not know the truth, which is that Gallouin used a secret charm to overcome her resistance. Only later in the book will Dupuis reveal, in his own narrative, that Gallouin had borrowed Silvie's necklace on the pretext of having it repaired. He then contrived to prick her finger so as to draw a drop of her blood onto a handkerchief and mixed her blood with his on the necklace ribbon. In the course of his debaucheries, Gallouin had learned that the mixture of the two bloods would make Silvie powerless to resist him as long as the necklace touched her skin (*IF* 614/*LLL* 545).[33] Because Des Frans had taken the necklace during the night, the spell was gone when Silvie woke up, and she was even more shocked than her husband had been to find Gallouin in bed beside her.

Meanwhile, Des Frans's inability to discover the truth drives him mad. He is convinced Silvie was lying, but the spectacle of her grief is so authentic that he cannot stop loving her. His continuing attachment makes him torment her all the more: she *should* have the solution to the mystery, and the very fact that she can't supply it is all the more painful because he continues to idealize her. For Des Frans, no reconciliation is possible without an explanation. In this respect, he resembles the Challe of the *Difficultés*. Like the Challe of the treatise, too, Des Frans cannot appeal to any community through which understanding could be mediated. Third parties, he assumes, lack the knowledge he needs, and in any case, Des Frans wants to avoid the humiliation of consulting anyone. He takes Silvie to a remote location far from Paris, and forces

[33] As the editors point out, there is some ambiguity as to whether the charm is supposed to be a natural or supernatural one (*IF* 614n.). Gallouin claims that he was armed with 'les puissances de l'enfer et les secrets de la nature' (the powers of hell and the secrets of nature) (*IF* 612/*LLL* 544, tr. modified), but it seems that Challe believed the power of mixed blood to be a scientific fact. Since Gallouin abandons the occult only to become a devout Catholic monk, it seems likely that the belief in diabolical powers reflects the character's perspective rather than the author's.

her—and himself—to live in complete isolation. His anger turns into cruelty as the abject Silvie undergoes one punishment after another. Finally, at wit's end, Des Frans runs away. The misfortunes he experiences on his travels open the way to a change of heart, but neither affection nor remorse can outweigh his frustration at not knowing the truth. Before he can return to Silvie, she dies in the convent to which he had consigned her. Des Frans is left alone, his rage now turned to grief.

The tragedy might have been avoided had Des Frans—or Silvie, for that matter—spoken with Gallouin. In this respect, Des Frans resembles Des Ronais, who refused to see Manon and hear her explanation, except that whereas the friends had mocked Des Ronais for his obstinacy, they feel pity for Des Frans. Since Silvie has died, this is understandable, but why do they not criticize his rash behavior? Another remarkable difference is that Des Frans, unlike Des Ronais, is spared the humiliation of learning the truth in public. Before Dupuis reveals the mystery of the love charm to the group, he tells Des Frans in private (*IF* 501–2). These two features of the narrative suggest that for Challe the dubious morality of Des Frans's actions is less important than the fundamental legitimacy of his demand for an explanation. Des Ronais, as a courteous lover, should have taken Manon's declaration on faith, but Des Frans deserves to know the facts. A possible explanation for these differences of attitude is that the facts in question here, while not exactly supernatural in character, could not be explained by common-sense reasoning. Only someone familiar with the secrets of natural philosophy would have access to the answer, and even more important, would be able to trust one's lover in the absence of an explanation, given the shocking nature of the evidence. Des Frans deserves consideration because he stands for all those (not least the Challe of the *Difficultés*) who legitimately demand the solution to mystery. The ambiguity of the love potion, half scientific secret, half occult force, allows Challe to give the story a religious resonance without transgressing the boundaries of the realist novel.

In drawing this kind of parallel between Des Frans and the Challe of the *Difficultés*, I am taking issue with the claim that it is the explicitly religious anxieties felt by Gallouin after his duel with Des Frans which represent the most significant connection between the novel and the treatise.[34] When he woke up beside Silvie, Gallouin was mystified at the necklace's disappearance, and like his former friend he was distressed

[34] See Melâhat Menemencioglu, 'Gallouin-Don Juan, une clé pour Robert Challe', *RHLF* 79 (1979), 981–93.

not to find any answer. The outraged Silvie refused to speak to him, and the subsequent duel has wounded him so badly that it prevented him from pursuing the matter with Des Frans, who when he challenged Gallouin had not said he had taken it. From Dupuis's story we learn that Gallouin later repented of his crimes, which along with the seduction of Silvie included the death by overdose of Silvie's companion Mme Morin. Full of remorse, and frightened by the way events spun out of his control, Gallouin's interest in the occult turns to superstition. An astrologer once predicted he would die by hanging, even though as a nobleman he was entitled to be beheaded, a less humiliating form of execution. After he recovers from his wounds, he tells Dupuis that his crime against Silvie is so dishonorable that a judge might well find him unworthy of that privilege. Haunted by the astrologer's prediction, Gallouin decides to become a monk, 'tant pour faire pénitence de mes péchés et de mon crime, que pour en prévenir les suites' (both to do penance for my crime and my sins and to forestall their consequences) (*IF* 622/*LLL* 552). Ironically, however, during the course of a charitable mission, he is set upon by robbers as he crosses through a dark forest. They kill him and hang his body high in a tree whose thick foliage will delay its discovery. Thus Gallouin's conversion and subsequent saintly life do not prevent the astrologer's prediction from being fulfilled.

Gallouin's anxiety about his fate may well echo Challe's, but he cannot be considered a stand-in for the author. Unlike Des Frans, or Challe's other strong male characters, Gallouin is not really interested in the truth. Nor does he get angry at failing to get a rationally satisfactory answer. One might infer that, just as he believes he does not deserve an honorable death, he does not deserve a rational explanation, even for the apparently inexplicable. The result is paradoxical, but consistent with Challe's constant emphasis on the dignity of the individual who knows what is owed to him. Gallouin's remorse might be thought morally more admirable than Des Frans's grief, but it is Des Frans who is given social redemption. To be sure, the religious dimension of Gallouin's story (including the significant detail that he dies on Holy Saturday, that moment of divine 'absence' between Good Friday and Easter) is presented seriously and without irony. But the suggestiveness of Gallouin's pathetic end is diminished because it is more conventionally novelistic than Des Frans's surprising integration into the community of friends in spite of (indeed, with full recognition of) his intransigence. *Les Illustres Françaises* is just as original as the *Difficultés* in the way reconciliation is achieved through the recognition, not the repression, of anger.

Anger and integration

The final tale, the story of Dupuis and Mme de Londé, is comic rather than tragic in tone. No one dies, and the irrepressibly libertine Dupuis stands in sharp contrast to the somber Des Frans. And yet, Dupuis displays the same readiness to take offence and seek revenge. Readers may well feel uneasy about the way several incidents of his violent and mean-spirited behavior are dismissed as pranks. Nor are we told how exactly it happens that such a cynical man, who after many adventures seemed to have settled into a long-term affair with an equally freethinking widow, leaves her and begins a desperate pursuit of the widowed and respectable Mme de Londé, whom he had sought in vain to seduce while her husband was alive. Mme de Londé is the sister of Gallouin, Dupuis's intimate friend, a fact which does not prevent Dupuis from looking at her initially as a potential mistress to be taken by force. She forgives him, however, and Dupuis's decision to marry her and settle down concludes both his story and the book. All this suggests that Dupuis must have found an answer to some question that provoked him. We may assume that his success in finding resolution carries a broader meaning for the novel as a whole.

What this question might be is never formulated explicitly, but a closer look shows Dupuis to be obsessed by what to the male imagination is the most classic of mysteries, the nature of women. Challe's treatment of this issue is original, at least in novelistic terms, in that the mystery does not turn on anything as specific as what prompts a wife to be unfaithful. Dupuis's restlessness and seemingly inexplicable rage suggests that the real issue is a deeper one. And indeed, Dupuis's anger seems to originate in his childhood, in the fact that his mother loved his older brother more. There is no more of an explanation for this than for why Dupuis won't let go of his daughter. Dupuis begins his angry career by arranging for his mother to discover his brother entering a brothel. She in turn gets angry at the brother, but unfortunately this does Dupuis himself no good (*IF* 514/*LLL* 450). Dupuis's early experience of inferiority makes him particularly susceptible to slight as he grows older. In one remarkable episode, he is swimming in the Seine when a soldier shovels some excrement onto him from a bridge (*IF* 536/*LLL* 472). Dupuis flies into a rage, climbs onto the bridge without stopping to get dressed, and throws the soldier into the river. The people who had been watching the incident with great amusement stop laughing when the man almost drowns, but Dupuis's anger is not yet satisfied. After the soldier is rescued from the river, Dupuis lays into him again and breaks a walking stick over his back. The most disturbing aspect of the story is the sense that Dupuis could have gone on hitting the man indefinitely. As in the relationship between Dupuis and his mother there is no way, and no one, to reconcile the parties. The incident only comes to an end because, following the pattern of the picaresque tale, Dupuis moves on to a new adventure.

From a very early age, Dupuis is equally aggressive in chasing women. Yet, he seems to be motivated more by curiosity than by desire. This may be natural enough given his age, except that his curiosity has an angry edge. We see this first in his relationship with a young woman named Célénie. Tired of waiting for Dupuis to make good on his promise to marry her, Célénie marries another man. Dupuis's anger is immediately rekindled (*IF* 550/*LLL* 485) even though he doesn't want her for himself. As in the river incident, when he ran up the steps without pausing to get dressed, his revenge is marked by a deliberate flouting of decency. Wondering how Célénie will convince her new husband of her virginity, Dupuis has his servant hide in the room where the marriage is to be consummated. Against expectations, Célénie succeeds in her deception, and so Dupuis reveals to the husband that someone witnessed the fraud of his wedding night. Again, however, the result is unexpected. Dupuis tells us Célénie's loss of her husband's esteem satisfied his anger, yet he reports with equanimity that Célénie's husband must have forgiven her, since they live together quite contentedly (*IF* 558/*LLL* 493). Dupuis's reaction suggests that satisfying his curiosity was ultimately more important than destroying the marriage. Success in that enterprise allows Dupuis to be indulgent about the rest.

Curiosity is dramatized in a more disturbing way in Dupuis's next adventure. He discovers that his friend Grandpré's mistress, Mademoiselle Récard, had 'le secret de pourvoir à ses besoins, sans le secours de ses amants' (to satisfy her needs without the help of her lovers) (*IF* 559/*LLL* 494, tr. modified). Like Bunuel's 'Belle de jour', she uses a rooming house run by a libertine woman as a safe house where she can have anonymous sex with strangers. The discovery sparks Dupuis's own desire, which is, however, quickly dampened when Récard falls in love with him and suggests they get married. Then, because Récard goes back to Grandpré, Dupuis feels duty-bound to tell his friend the truth. In this case, however, the rival refuses to believe the story. Even the testimony of an eyewitness fails to sway him. In contrast with the easy victory over Célénie, Dupuis's evidence is trumped by a clever woman's ability to keep her secrets. The angry Dupuis then arranges for Grandpré to confront Récard in the bawdy house. Grandpré's eyes are finally opened. In a gesture of contempt he tells his erstwhile fiancée to lie down on the bed as if he were going to take advantage of her and then walks out. Dupuis takes the woman's humiliation a step further. 'Je fis dessein dans le moment d'épuiser toute la colère de Grandpré et de l'obliger à me demander pardon pour elle' (at that moment, I decided to take out all Grandpré's anger on her and to force him to ask me for forgiveness on her behalf) (*IF* 571/*LLL* 505, tr. modified). He makes her strip naked and examines her closely. 'Je lui visitai partout le corps', he tells us (I examined every part of her body). It is as if he hoped to learn who or what Récard really is by reading the truth on her skin. Like Grandpré, Dupuis shows his contempt by refusing to have sex with Récard, but the fact that he goes on humiliating her, to the point where even Grandpré comes back to stop him, shows that Dupuis's contempt is mixed with continuing anger at not finding the truth he hoped to discover.

Dupuis's quest might have gone on indefinitely had he not chanced one day to overhear a conversation in which a young widow consoles a female friend upset by her husband's infidelity (*IF* 573–80/*LLL* 507–12). Far from appealing to the rhetoric of sentiment, the widow discusses sex and marriage in a completely matter-of-fact way. 'Ce n'est pas l'innocence des plaisirs qui les rend plus chers' she says; 'la volupté ne dépend point d'un contrat, ni de la bénédiction d'un prêtre' (it is not legitimacy that makes pleasures more precious; rapture is not dependent on a contract or on the blessing of a priest) (*IF* 575–6/*LLL* 509, tr. modified). So calmly does this widow accept the naturalness of desire and the inconstancy of human nature, and so openly does she confess her thoughts, that Dupuis is instantly transformed. His anger is miraculously turned into feelings of gratitude toward this woman. He realizes the widow thought she was speaking in confidence to a woman who is probably her sister. 'Cependant je la remerciai dans mon âme, de s'être expliquée avec tant de franchise; et je la remerciai avec tant de reconnaissance que si elle m'eût parlé à moi-même' (Nevertheless, I thanked her in my heart for having spoken so honestly, and thanked her with a gratitude as sincere as if she had actually been speaking to me) (*IF* 581/*LLL* 513).[35]

[35] The word *reconnaissance* appears again soon afterwards in a speech Dupuis makes about the gratitude befitting a lover (*IF* 593/*LLL* 525).

Here, it seems, is the 'explanation' Dupuis was looking for. Not that he learns anything new: what the widow says, in fact, mostly confirms what Dupuis himself believed all along. What matters is that the widow 'explained herself', that is to say, freely revealed her inner being. Because the explanation comes to Dupuis without any effort on his part, he can receive it as a gift. We are never told the widow's name: her identity is all in what she says. Dupuis is so gratified that not only does he enter into a relationship with her that lasts longer than any of his other affairs; he even suggests they get married. The widow refuses because she cannot stand any kind of constraint. Their relationship is based on complete openness and acceptance of each other's desires, and she has no wish to return to the servitude of marriage. After five years of happiness, however, Dupuis decides to separate from the widow. He gives no reason, but it seems clear that his transformation has reached another stage. He now wants to get married, that is, to be fully reconciled to the society he had scorned up to now.

What accounts for Dupuis's change of heart? Challe does not say so explicitly, but a comparison with Des Frans points to the answer. The mystery at the center of Silvie's story involved occult knowledge. By contrast, what Dupuis discovers is that the secret he was looking for does not exist. There is no 'mystery' about women, at least in the sense of some secret information kept hidden from men. The widow's refusal to marry Dupuis does not warrant further investigation. It is simply a fact, with the implication that, properly understood, even such puzzles as Dupuis's mother preferring his brother are just facts as well. If this is true, then there is no cause for resentment, because a demand for explanation, legitimate enough in principle, is here simply misplaced.

In Challe's world, the demand for explanation springs both from natural human curiosity and, more fundamentally, from man's sense of his worth as a thinking human being who deserves respect. The mystery of women's desire is similar to that of divine will in that its solution has two aspects, corresponding to these two modes of relating to the world. The first kind of solution is to be sought in univocal concepts about nature applicable to all beings, the second to be secured by recognition of one's own dignity as an individual. The widow's conversation provided Dupuis with the first, and her subsequent relationship gave him the second. It is noteworthy that we never learn the widow's name: important as her role may be, it is only instrumental. Her function is to free Dupuis of his anger. Dupuis gets married, but he also stops railing at social hypocrisy. He is not Condamine. Moreover, it is he who narrates the story of Des Prez, the one character who remains excluded from the circle of friends. Des Prez's anger was as great as Dupuis's, and so only Dupuis can do it justice even as he exposes it to critique.

Les Illustres Françaises ends on this optimistic note. If a man such as Dupuis can be brought back into the fold, then surely anyone can. Still, we cannot forget that Silvie was sacrificed to Des Frans's unwillingness to be satisfied with anything less than a clear explanation of her infidelity, and that her lover, Gallouin, who was also Mme de Londé's brother and Dupuis's friend, was murdered. So it is appropriate that before they can be reconciled to society, both Dupuis and Des Frans must undergo a moment of trial. What is interesting, however, is that the emotional penalty for their excesses is not so much a precondition as the very means of their reintegration into society. When Des Frans learns from Dupuis that Silvie died an innocent woman, 'sa douleur pensa lui coûter la vie dans le moment' (he was near to dying of grief on the spot) (*IF* 620/*LLL* 550–1, tr. modified). The assembled company joins him in weeping for her: 'tout le monde le consola en s'affligeant avec lui' (everyone comforted him by grieving along with him) (*IF* 620/omitted in *LLL*).

Dupuis pays for his injustice in another way. He falls in love with Mme de Londé but is initially rejected by her. So cold is her behavior that first he attempts to rape her; later he tries to commit suicide, impaling himself on his sword in front of her. Confronted with this spectacle, Mme de Londé is moved to tenderness. Dupuis's own change of heart is not a matter of abandoning his angry self, but of acknowledging how in his heart love and hate are intertwined. When he explains his feelings in a letter to Mme de Londé, he writes: 'je vous aime jusques à l'adoration et jusqu'à la fureur' (I love you to the point of adoration and mad fury) (*IF* 642/*LLL* 571, tr. modified). This is not just conventional love rhetoric. Although he achieved an initial degree of liberation from his experience with the widow, Dupuis was not in love with her. Before he can enter into a deeper relationship with Mme de Londé, he must experience aggression and love as part of a single complex phenomenon. Up to this point he had kept these feelings entirely separate—an effort which had only exacerbated his anger and prevented him from feeling love with any depth. Challe may not be interested in portraying the inner struggles of his characters, but his depiction of their emotions through their actions is no less acute for all that. As we will see, a tendency to segregate aggression from love, this time for the sake of preserving a self-image of fundamental goodness, is a recurring feature in the life and career of Jean-Jacques Rousseau.

3

Reconnaissance in *La Vie de Marianne*

Marivaux's great achievement as a creative writer lies in the delicacy with which he dramatizes the interplay of self-consciousness, sociability, and sentiment in the lives of his characters. This interplay also informs the formal dynamic of his novels and plays, and it may be epitomized in the various actions covered by the French word *reconnaissance.* Acknowledging a child, a debt, or a truth; recognizing a person's true identity; feeling gratitude for benefits received, including that most precious benefit, an enhanced capacity to think or feel for oneself—in one combination or another these are the key moments in Marivaux's work as it rings many variations on the 'recognition scene'.[1]

By highlighting the relationship between different kinds of *reconnaissance,* such scenes also explore the interconnection of knowledge and gratitude that Challe, like other freethinking writers for whom intellectual independence had become an existential requirement, had put into question. The closeness of the link between cognition and emotion had traditionally been grounded in belief in God as the creator of the world and of humanity's ability to comprehend it. In the early seventeenth century, François de Sales could still use the phrase 'la connaissance engendre la reconnaissance' (knowledge begets gratitude) in an almost

[1] For an insightful study of the history of recognition scenes, see Terence Cave, *Recognitions: A Study in Poetics* (Oxford: Oxford University Press, 1988). See also Paul Ricœur, *Parcours de la reconnaissance* (Paris: Stock, 2004), a fascinating exploration of the semantic richness of the term that highlights the connections between epistemology and ethics. In the context of Marivaux scholarship, a study of *reconnaissance* may be helpful in rethinking the classic debate between Georges Poulet and Leo Spitzer about the relationship of mind and heart in Marivaux's characters. See Georges Poulet, 'Marivaux', in *Études sur le temps humain II: la distance intérieure* (Paris: Plon, 1952), 1–34, especially the remarks on 'se reconnaître', 11; and Leo Spitzer, 'À propos de *La Vie de Marianne* (Lettre à M. Georges Poulet)', *Romanic Review* 44 (1953), 102–26, especially 107 n.3. That *reconnaissance,* 'in every sense of the word', is a key to Marivaux's vision of happy social relationships has already been pointed out by Henri Coulet, *Marivaux romancier* (Paris: Armand Colin, 1975), 489, although Coulet does not study the uses of the term systematically.

proverbial manner.[2] Such a notion was put into question by the Enlightenment's focus on human autonomy and by the post-Cartesian preoccupation with the certainty of ideas originating in the operations of the mind. This questioning of epistemological dependence was not unrelated to a revolt against structures of political and social dependence that characterized the Enlightenment. At the same time, however, many writers saw in the ethic of sociability (of *politesse* and its *égards*) a defense against the exercise of arbitrary power and a crucial advance in humanity's moral refinement. The semantic density of *reconnaissance*, as it appears in the writings of authors such as Marivaux, provides a focus for exploring the tensions between autonomy and dependence, and between the knowledge that enhances the self and the gratitude that acknowledges the importance of the other.

In the drama, the classic example of such a scene appears in *Le Jeu de l'amour et du hasard* (Act II, scene 12), when the gallant servant Bourguignon reveals to the heroine Silvia that he is really the noble Dorante in disguise. To recognize Dorante's identity is for Silvia inseparable from acknowledging that she is in love: 'Ah! Je vois clair dans mon cœur' (Ah! I understand myself now). As the phrasing suggests, recognition also involves cognition, a greater awareness of self in relation to others. At the end of the scene, Silvia further acknowledges that 'j'avais bien besoin que ce fût là Dorante' (I truly needed that man to be Dorante), and it is possible to read this statement not only as a sigh of relief but as an expression of gratitude. The sense of vulnerability that had led Silvia to adopt a disguise of her own in order to test the husband her father had arranged for her, a vulnerability she has been experiencing more acutely since falling in love, has not led to humiliation but to reassurance.[3] In Marivaux's comic vision, the self-awareness produced by the recognition scene gives Silvia both a greater measure of self-possession and a willingness to view her attachment to Dorante as a gift rather than as a social or emotional constraint.[4]

[2] François de Sales, *Introduction à la vie dévote*, in *Œuvres*, ed. André Ravier (Bibliothèque de la Pléiade, Paris: Gallimard, 1969), 141. The specific objects of knowledge in question are forms of grace, but they are adduced as paradigmatic cases for knowledge in general.

[3] Marivaux, *Le Jeu de l'amour et du hasard*, in *Théâtre complet*, ed. Henri Coulet and Michel Gilot, 2 vols (Paris: Gallimard, 1993–4), i. 642. The translations are from Marivaux, *Up from the Country*, tr. Leonard Tancock, and *Infidelities* and *The Game of Love and Chance*, tr. David Cohen (Harmondsworth: Penguin, 1980).

[4] If Silvia does not express her gratitude in words, this is because the source of the favor is not a person but the structure of the play itself. Thus the gratitude would be more appropriately embodied in the tone and gesture of performance.

In the two major novels, *Le Paysan parvenu* and *La Vie de Marianne*, the workings of *reconnaissance* in its different aspects are complicated by two factors. First, Marivaux devises plots in which the acknowledgment by others of the hero or heroine's claims occurs not as a singular event; it is occasioned by repeated but always partial recognition scenes. Indeed, by leaving his novels unfinished, Marivaux refuses to equate recognition with the resolution of the plot. Recognition may ultimately be the end of the story—Jacob and Marianne, as narrators of their own lives, speak from a secure social position—but the story itself does not arrive at its conclusion.

Second, and again in contrast with the largely self-contained world of the plays, Marivaux foregrounds the equally open-ended relationship between the story and its readers. This is especially true of *La Vie de Marianne*, where we find three different kinds of recognition scene, each involving a different level of the text.[5] The first and most obvious examples involve Marianne herself. The story of an orphan whose noble birth is supported by uncertain evidence, the novel naturally focuses on the process by which her claim to identity and status comes to be acknowledged by others. Another form of recognition scene occurs in the later parts of the novel, in which Marianne's friend Tervire tells her story. On two occasions Tervire stages recognition scenes in order to reconcile other people to each other. In this capacity, she acts more as the author of a story than as a character. The activity of authorship appears again more explicitly in a third kind of recognition scene, one involving Marivaux's use of real-life models for two of the older female characters.[6] Marianne's adoptive 'mother', Mme de Miran, is modeled on Mme de Lambert, while Mme Dorsin recalls Mme de Tencin. Marivaux clearly expects his readers to recognize these women in the detailed portraits he has Marianne draw of their fictional counterparts. In each of these

[5] As Béatrice Didier remarks, 'recognition' is 'the paradigmatic sequence of *La Vie de Marianne*'. See *La Voix de Marianne: essai sur Marivaux* (Paris: Corti, 1987), 55. The stakes are less high in *Le Paysan parvenu*. In this comic novel closely linked to the picaresque tradition, 'recognition' is merely a matter of externals, that is, the acceptance by others of Jacob's social ascension. In contrast, Marianne needs others to certify that she has always been by nature (or birth) the gentlewoman she claims to be. In *Le Paysan parvenu*, those with the social power to award recognition are all morally compromised in one way or another, especially the women; in *La Vie de Marianne*, Mme de Miran and Mme Dorsin are models of virtue, and it is their opinion that counts most for Marianne. That Jacob is a man and Marianne a woman is also clearly an important difference.

[6] There is also a third character based on real life: a magistrate in whose portrait the reader is meant to recognize the real-life Cardinal de Fleury, the chief minister of France.

instances, I shall argue, Marivaux explores the relationship between *reconnaissance* as cognitive activity, as acknowledgment of someone's social or moral identity, and the sentiment of gratitude that may unblock recognition or flow from it. That Marivaux should posit a connection between the two kinds of *reconnaissance* shows that, as in his predilection for comic over tragic drama, his vision is one of ultimate reconciliation of head and heart. But in the disenchanted world of his mature novels that connection can by no means be taken for granted.

MARIANNE AND GRATITUDE AS SUCCESS STORY

The plot of the first few books of *La Vie de Marianne* consists largely of a series of incidents that give Marianne the opportunity to display a noble character, so that the people she meets will believe she must be of gentle birth, or at least that she should be treated as if that were the case. Yet, although she succeeds in winning the support of the influential Mme de Miran, in the absence of any documentary proof (or of the bodily evidence, scar or birthmark, that often plays a role in orphan stories) the social, if not the moral, recognition of Marianne can always be contested by those who for reasons of snobbery or self-interest deny her claim to consideration. Deferral of recognition was, of course, a characteristic device of earlier French novels, from *L'Astrée* to Marivaux's own *Les Effets surprenants de la sympathie*. But recognition there was a matter of removing a disguise, displaying a hidden but unmistakable sign, or curing the other person's moral blindness. Everything then fell into place. Marianne, by contrast, can only present herself in beauty and in tears, telling her story again and again in the hope of eliciting recognition of her refined sensibility. This strategy builds on the supposition, increasingly widespread in the polite society of the French *ancien régime*, that the nobility of Marianne's interlocutors is itself more than a matter of birth, that it is demonstrated by delicacy of discernment and by a generous sympathy that trumps material concerns.[7]

While recognition of her identity by others is a matter largely beyond Marianne's control, she does exercise some initiative in the mode of her

[7] See William Ray, *Story and History* (Boston: Blackwell, 1990), ch. 6, for a discussion of this dynamic.

response, and particularly in her expressions of gratitude. *Reconnaissance* is thus a two-sided process, and it involves moral and social considerations on both sides, as we can see from examining Marianne's experiences with the lecherous M. de Climal, her attitude toward respectable people of inferior social status, and, most importantly, her adoption as a surrogate daughter by Mme de Miran.

Soon after she arrives in Paris, Marianne loses the protection of the *curé*'s sister who had raised her and is entrusted by Père Saint-Vincent to the care of the hypocritical M. de Climal. The desperate Marianne explains how she justified accepting gifts from Climal by refusing to acknowledge, until forced to do so, the truth behind his kindness. 'Il se démasquait petit à petit, l'homme amoureux se montrait . . . mais j'avais conclu qu'il fallait que je le visse tout entier pour le reconnaître, sinon il était arrêté que je ne verrais rien' (Little by little he was removing his mask; the lover was beginning to appear . . . but I had concluded that I would have to see the whole of him before recognizing him for who he was, otherwise it was decided that I would see nothing).[8] This refusal to acknowledge the reality of Climal's intentions until she can no longer avoid doing so is made possible by the ambiguity of Climal's own language. For example, Climal is discovered kneeling at Marianne's feet by the handsome Valville, 'avec qui', Marianne exclaims in anger, 'j'ai eu un entretien de plus d'une heure et qui par conséquent me reconnaîtra!' (with whom I had a conversation for more than an hour and who as a result will recognize me!) (121). Climal takes offense at the idea that he was putting Marianne's innocence in jeopardy. He reminds her that all he asked for was 'un peu de reconnaissance' (a little gratitude), adding 'Ne sont-ce là mes termes?' (Are these not my words?) (122).

Equivocation about the meaning of *reconnaissance* in situations of sexual pressure is not in itself surprising. What distinguishes Marianne's narrative is the way the conflict between virtue and self-interest is colored by the emphasis on Marianne's struggle for intellectual self-possession. On the one hand, Marianne's lucidity as narrator of her own story reinforces the impression of calculation in the account of her conduct, a calculation that tempers some of the sympathy the eighteenth-century reader would normally have for a virtuous maiden in

[8] Marivaux, *La Vie de Marianne*, ed. Frédéric Deloffre (Paris: Garnier, 1963), 40. Subsequent references to this edition of the novel will be included in the text. Translations are my own.

distress. On the other, it forces us to become more aware that gratitude is not an unequivocally good thing. Marianne tells us that despite her initial reluctance to accept Climal's help, 'mes répugnances me quittèrent, un vif sentiment de reconnaissance en prit la place' (my loathing left me, a warm feeling of gratitude took its place) (35). Yet Marianne 'admits' to this gratitude with some embarrassment, since it shows that she had not given the implications of the gift much thought. In the absence of full awareness, it seems, her spontaneous outflow of gratitude in itself has no merit. The text belies any conventional notions about the value of unreflective sensibility. The point is brought home a few pages later when Marianne, taken aback by her landlady Mme Dutour's anger at seeing lingerie as well as a dress in Climal's gift package, says sarcastically of the servant Toinette that 'toute sage qu'elle était, quiconque lui en eût donné autant l'aurait rendue stupide de reconnaissance' (good girl though she was, anyone who had given her as much would have rendered her speechless with gratitude) (45). Toinette's lack of self-consciousness and calculation does not mean she is any more virtuous than Marianne. On the contrary, she is presented as someone who without thinking would give Climal whatever he wanted. When contrasted with Toinette's stupidity, Marianne's self-awareness appears less problematic, especially since Marivaux arranges events so that Marianne does not have to equivocate for long. She puts on Climal's finery just once, to go to church, but there a lucky fall precipitates the initial meeting with Valville. It is the later realization that Valville will recognize *her* in the young woman found in a compromising position with Climal that impels her to remove any ambiguity in her relationship with the older man.

Marivaux does not, however, leave the matter there. When Marianne as narrator, now in control of the story of her past, looks back on her relationship with Climal, she offers another, equally disenchanted view of the dynamic of recognition and gratitude in relation to him. In part five, Climal will make a deathbed confession of his sins and public amends to Marianne, but already in part two we find an anticipation of this turn of events.

> Je songe pourtant que je devrais rayer l'épithète de tartufe que je viens de lui donner; car je lui ai obligation, à ce tartufe-là. Sa mémoire me doit être chère; il devint un homme de bien pour moi. Ceci soit dit pour l'acquit de ma reconnaissance, et en réparation du tort que la vérité historique pourra lui faire encore. Cette vérité a ses droits, qu'il faut bien que M de Climal essuie. (88)

I remember however that I should strike out the epithet 'tartuffe' I have just given him; for I am obliged to that tartuffe. His memory should be dear to me; he became a good man as far I was concerned. Let this be said to discharge my debt of gratitude to him, and as compensation for the harm the truth of my history may yet do to him. This truth must be given its due, which after all M. de Climal must pay.

The passage is a curious one in that it casts Climal's perfidy of the moment in a different light, but without any sentimental effusion about his change of heart or any softening of the way his bad behavior is being portrayed. The reflections of Marianne as narrator may be read as counterparts to what her younger self thought in reacting to Climal's hypocrisy. Both cases highlight a disjunction between gratitude as emotional response and gratitude as obligation. In the earlier situation, it was Climal who expected a quid pro quo while Marianne acted as if gratitude were a matter of gratuitous feeling. Now it is Marianne who acquits herself of an obligation, at a point when the reader might expect a greater display of affect. Since the general tendency of this installment novel is to keep the reader in suspense as long as possible, one would think Marivaux would make an exception in this case only in order to soften the toughness of Marianne's attitude toward Climal and his gifts. Yet, the starkness of the passage shows us a Marianne even more down-to-earth than her younger self.

The key to this provocative statement lies in its concluding sentences. The harm done to Climal's reputation by Marianne's dwelling on his past misconduct may be repaired by gratitude for his return to virtue, but the truth, which includes the past as much as the future, cannot be denied. The expression *vérité historique* here means several things. It designates what actually happened, as opposed to idealized notions of behavior. In this sense, Marivaux is linking Marianne's story with the disenchanted fictions which came to be labeled *histoires* to distinguish them from the heroic and idealistic *romans* of the early seventeenth century.[9] But the narrative anticipation of a later event also underscores another contrast, one between present and future. 'Historical truth' thus tempers moral judgment (favorable or unfavorable) with awareness that human beings exist in time and display contradictory qualities at different moments. The anticipation of his redemption makes the reader aware that Marianne's mature gratitude is conditional on the

[9] Recall the full title of Prévost's most famous novel, the *Histoire du Chevalier des Grieux et de Manon Lescaut.*

recognition of this historical truth. This gratitude is vastly different from the spontaneous but blind feeling experienced by her younger self, and Marianne's use in the later passage of the language of economic exchange emphasizes that difference. But just as her earlier spontaneity was not a virtue, her later deliberation is not a vice. Her expression of gratitude is presented, not as a way of closing an uncomfortable moral gap opened up by the earlier narrative, but on the contrary as a way of underscoring her own freedom of agency, manifested in the narrative anticipation that shows us the contingent context of all gratitude.

The *vérité historique* of the young Marianne was that her only strategy for social survival was to play for time. Now, as narrator, she can play *with* time in order to be fair to Climal, but above all to be fair to herself. In their discussions of gratitude, Cicero, Seneca, and their successors among philosophers of sociability stress that one's obligation is not determined merely by the fact of a benefit.[10] Gratitude is part of a relationship in which both parties' moral standing is engaged, and so the ethos of the benefactor must be taken into account. While bestowing a favor creates a debt, what makes it a social rather than merely a commercial transaction is that in addition it is a demonstration of one person's freedom which enhances that of another person. That freedom includes a greater capacity to repay the obligation, but it is manifested primarily by the free recognition of the favor. The reciprocity of the relationship is undermined if the benefactor does not seek a genuine relationship with the recipient. As Charles Pinot-Duclos writes, in a popular mid-eighteenth-century book on French manners:

> Puisque les principes des bienfaits sont fort différents, la reconnaissance doit-elle toujours être de la même nature? Quels sentiments doit-on à celui qui par un mouvement de pitié passagère n'a pas cru devoir refuser une parcelle de son superflu à un besoin très pressant . . . On doit plus estimer les vertus par leurs principes que par leurs effets. Les services doivent se juger moins par l'avantage qu'en retire celui qui est obligé que par le sacrifice que fait celui qui oblige.[11]

[10] Seneca, *De beneficiis*, II.18–35. This issue is, naturally enough, absent from the Judeo-Christian tradition, where the benefactor is God, although in quarrels over the existence of evil and suffering in the theodicies of the late seventeenth century we see doubts emerging about whether God really deserves humanity's gratitude. It is also important to distinguish the discourse of benefits or favors from that of charity. In Marivaux's world, the latter is employed only by the naive (Père Saint-Vincent) or the hypocritical (the abbess of the convent where Marianne takes refuge).

[11] Charles Pinot-Duclos, *Considérations sur les mœurs* [1750, ed. F. C. Green (Cambridge: Cambridge University Press, 1939)], 200–1. Duclos's chapter 'Sur la reconnaissance et l'ingratitude' became the basis of de Jaucourt's article 'Reconnaissance (morale)' in the *Encyclopédie* xiii. 860A.

> Since the principles behind the favors are very different, must gratitude always be of the same kind? What feelings does one owe the one who by a momentary impulse of pity did not think he could refuse a smidgen of his excess to a very pressing need... One should evaluate virtues more by their principles than by their effects. Good offices should be judged less by the advantage gained by the one who is obliged than by the sacrifice made by the one who obliges.

The Climal story offers a negative illustration of this. Climal's gifts do not spring from free generosity but from his bondage to his own desire, and this constraint limits Marianne's scope of action in return. In this respect, Climal's advances contrast with those of a genuine lover, who places the beloved above himself, and even with the playful flirtation of the young people Marianne sees when she goes to church, wearing the finery Climal had given her. Since during the church service there is no opportunity for a conversation that would embarrass the orphan girl, she is free to accept the silent tribute the young men pay her. 'A l'égard des hommes, ils me demeurèrent constamment attachés; et j'en eus une reconnaissance qui ne resta pas oisive' (As far as the men were concerned, they remained faithfully attached to me; for which I felt a gratitude that did not stay idle) (62). Gratitude here is closely linked to the rise to self-consciousness of Marianne's instinctive awareness of how to see and be seen in good company. For Marivaux's heroine, gratitude is always linked to the enhancement of her agency.

As a consequence, Marianne is also reluctant to recognize any debt of gratitude to those whose own scope of action is limited by their inferior social status. This is less because she resents owing anything to someone below her than because, socially speaking, there is no benefit. Classical theories of gratitude did insist that a free man could owe gratitude even to a slave,[12] but there the focus was on whether it was possible for a slave to offer anything freely, rather than on the unquestioned agency of the free man. Marianne's situation as an orphan of uncertain social status makes her agency part of the problem, while the question about the inferior benefactor is not so much about the latter's freedom of will as about the refinement of his or her sensibility. A favor received from someone devoid of such refinement provides no scope for Marianne to discover and display the delicacy of sentiment that alone can prove, to herself and to others, that she is of good birth. However, Marivaux tempers the harshness of this truth by limiting Marianne's contact with

[12] Seneca, *De beneficiis*, III.18–22.

people of lower station and by introducing other factors that help justify Marianne's attitude. Thus, while Mme Dutour has her good side, she is dominated by material concerns. Even more important—because it shows lack of consideration rather than mere self-interest—she loses her temper in public, ostensibly on behalf of Marianne but in fact only embarrassing her.

The case of M. Villot, however, best illustrates the way social standing may limit the potential for grateful reciprocity. Villot is a man of modest means recruited by Mme de Miran's relatives to marry Marianne and thus remove the danger she poses to Valville. Villot's mother had served as wet-nurse to the wife of the powerful government minister who is supposed to enforce the family's decision. Villot unwittingly insults Marianne by revealing that he has been offered money to marry her, and then, less unconsciously, by suggesting she should be grateful that he is willing to marry someone without a family to vouch for her. Marianne rejects Villot's interpretation of her situation. But what clinches the issue for her, and shows that her refusal is not to be understood simply as a manifestation of her social pretensions, is Villot's own inability to see the scorn behind the mask of noble favor. In the course of the hearing before the minister, Mme de Miran arrives to save Marianne. The minister points to Villot and defends the suitability of the match. 'Là-dessus, Mme de Miran jeta les yeux sur M Villot, qui l'en remercia par une autre prosternation, quoique la façon dont on le regarda n'exigeât pas de reconnaissance' (Upon which, Mme de Miran cast her eyes on M. Villot, who thanked her for it by another low bow, although in the way she looked at him there was no expectation of gratitude) (333). Villot's failure to recognize when gratitude is warranted confirms that he cannot be the object of it himself.

By contrast, Marianne's meeting with Mme de Miran (and later Mme Dorsin) generates a gratitude that transforms the one paying the tribute. Part four of the novel begins with Marianne eager to paint the portrait of the lady 'à qui j'ai eu des obligations dignes d'une reconnaissance éternelle' (to whom I incurred obligations worthy of eternal gratitude) (166). The two women meet at the convent where Marianne has taken refuge, having resolved to break with Climal after being surprised by Valville. Not only does Mme de Miran offer to help Marianne, she transforms the relationship of benefaction by 'adopting' Marianne as a daughter. To complete the picture, when Mme de Miran learns that her son Valville is in love with Marianne, she declares her willingness to flout social propriety by allowing him to marry the orphan girl. 'Valville, à ce discours, pleurant de joie et de reconnaissance, embrassa ses genoux' (at this speech, Valville, weeping with joy and gratitude, embraced her knees) (206).

Mme de Miran's generosity liberates Marianne from shameful dependence on unworthy people. Yet, since in the novel as we have it the marriage never takes place and the opposition to Marianne's integration into the Miran household is not finally neutralized, we never do learn how that generosity enhances Marianne's agency in practical terms or enables her to recognize herself more fully through it. That it does so is evidenced by another kind of outcome: the very fact that Marianne, now a countess, has decided to write down her story, not to persuade or advance any cause, but simply in the confidence that her experiences are worth recounting. Her narration, in which she often stops to recall Mme de Miran's generosity and to ponder how best to depict her benefactor, is at once an act of gratitude and proof of Marianne's freedom of action. Indeed, the narrative shows the two elements to be inseparable.

In the short term, however, Marianne's most important expressions of gratitude must take the form of negative action. When Marianne's orphan identity is revealed to some of Mme de Miran's friends, Marianne determines to give up Valville to spare her adoptive mother any embarrassment. 'Ma reconnaissance pour vous est plus chère que mon amour' (My gratitude to you is dearer to me than my love [for him]) (281). This sacrifice is, in fact, the only one she can make, since she has no other possessions to offer. What makes her gesture special, however, is that it is done against the advice of Valville himself, who believes it possible to control the damage by saying nothing to his mother about the revelation of Marianne's secret. But 'cette mauvaise finesse dont on me conseillait d'user répugnait à mon cœur' (this unseemly ruse, which they advised me to adopt, was distasteful to my feelings), and so Marianne does not even try to temporize as she did with Climal. To underscore the uniqueness of the gesture, Marivaux makes Valville the one guilty of temporizing: not long after his mother consents to his marriage, he becomes infatuated with another woman but puts off telling Marianne. Instead, it is Marianne, mortified by signs of Valville's change of heart, who decides to engineer a revelation that goes against her own interests. She does so out of consideration for Mme de Miran's position. Still, while this incident shows us Marianne once again taking the initiative, she does so only in a limiting context.

In the event, Marianne's humiliation at being betrayed by Valville reinforces the bond of intimacy with her adoptive mother. Mme de Miran swears she will never abandon Marianne, but as the novel remains unfinished it remains unclear how the benefaction can produce any more concrete effects than did Marianne's gratitude. Perhaps Marivaux is trying to explore what such a relationship might mean when it transcends the realm of social or family obligation. The mother–daughter relationship between the two women means that Marianne's gratitude is not subject to the quantifications of social exchange, but at the same time the elective nature of the family tie means that gratitude is not a duty imposed by nature either. From the point of view of what we might call structural anthropology, the relationship plays the role normally allotted in novels and other forms of modern cultural imagination to romantic love. Even though it is hinted that Valville will return to Marianne (377), his fickleness casts doubt on love's potential as a foundation for an enduring form of gratitude that enhances the self as well as the other.

Taking the place of love is another sentiment that qualifies gratitude and provides a channel for the recognition of Marianne's noble identity. This is *tendresse.* The word appears frequently in *La Vie de Marianne* in various contexts, including that of love, to indicate delicacy of feeling, and at first glance it seems to form part of a conventional rhetoric of sensibility. For Marivaux, however, the term is marked by the *précieux* tradition as epitomized in Madeleine de Scudéry's *Clélie,* with its famous 'Carte de Tendre'. For Scudéry, *tendresse* makes possible an intimate form of friendship, but one that avoids the turbulence of passionate desire. It is not a sentiment accessible to just anyone. Rather, it is 'une certaine sensibilité de cœur, qui ne se trouve presque jamais souverainement, qu'en des personnes qui ont l'âme noble, les inclinations vertueuses, et l'esprit bien tourné' (a certain sensibility of the heart, which is almost never found with sovereign power except in persons of noble soul, virtuous inclinations, and well-turned wit).[13] As Roger Duchêne points out, this is not a large group. The capacity for *tendresse* is a gift given only to some even within the nobility. 'On naît tendre ou

[13] Madeleine de Scudéry, *Clélie, histoire romaine,* ed. Chantal Morlet (Paris: Champion, 2001–5), i. 118. For a general study of Marivaux's relationship to Scudéry, see Françoise Gevrey, 'Marivaux et Madeleine de Scudéry', in Delphine Denis and Anne-Elisabeth Spica, eds, *Madeleine de Scudéry: une femme de lettres au XVIIe siècle* (Arras: Artois Presses Université, 2002), 279–92.

incapable de l'être' (One is born tender or unable to be so).[14] This view is still implicit in *La Vie de Marianne*, where the word is never used to characterize persons of inferior social status, and where Marianne's claim to nobility rests primarily on her own sensibility. By appropriating the word *tendresse* to describe her own emotional relationships as if she had an unquestioned right to do so (there is no reflection on the use of *tendresse* in this otherwise most self-conscious narrative), Marianne simply places herself among those whose souls are noble.[15]

In the context of Marianne's romance with Valville or her later filial intimacy with Mme de Miran, it may seem that *tendresse* names a purely emotional state, a characteristic which belongs to an ideal world of feeling and bears no decisive social significance. Indeed, in the course of the eighteenth century the use of *tendresse* was 'democratized'. It came increasingly to describe the emotional bond among various members of the family, and its association with ordinary kinship made the notion potentially available to all. This broader use stood in contrast with the exclusivity of *tendresse* as a feature of romantic love or elitist *amitié amoureuse*. Within the family, *tendresse* also indicated a softening of the hierarchy of parents, spouses, and children.[16] We see something of this

[14] Roger Duchêne, *Les Précieuses, ou comment l'esprit vint aux femmes* (Paris: Fayard, 2001), 33.

[15] In the preface to *Les Effets surprenants de la sympathie*, Marivaux describes the lady to whom the story is addressed as having, like all 'the fair sex', 'ce sentiment intérieur presque toujours aussi noble que tendre, et qui fait juger sainement des faux ou des vrais sentiments qu'on donne au cœur' (that inner feeling, almost always as noble as it is tender, and which leads to sound judgments about the false or the true feelings stirred up in one's heart) (*Œuvres de jeunesse*, ed. Frédéric Deloffre and Claude Rigault (Paris: Gallimard, 1972), 3). He goes on to define tenderness in general as 'la trempe du cœur' (the tempering of the heart) that allows female readers to recognize real love in a story when they see it (*Œuvres*, 5). In this context, it is assumed that these are women of refinement. As in the dynamic of recognition, gender and literary genre are in fact crucial here. In *Le Paysan parvenu*, Jacob frequently uses the word 'tender' in describing his feelings and those of others, especially when he wishes to discriminate between love, tenderness, libertine desire. Yet, in his story 'tenderness' is not a marker of class; rather, it is associated with moral status, but only insofar as it is a (limited) sign of natural feeling for another person. The housemaid Geneviève, for example, may harbor tender feelings for Jacob, but she does not hesitate to prostitute herself to her master in order to secure his help for Jacob. The latter acknowledges the authenticity of the feeling but repudiates Geneviève nonetheless for her lack of virtue. Split judgments of this kind are foreign to the romance world of Marianne.

[16] In a suggestive but insufficiently noticed study, Maurice Daumas shows how the word *tendresse*, which originally was associated with purely physical softness (of meat, for example), came into widespread use after the middle of the seventeenth century as an expression of a higher level of emotional intimacy in family relationships as well as in descriptions of romantic love where it was important to get away from the lack of control

diffusion of meaning in the way Marianne's role as daughter to Mme de Miran becomes more important than the love relationship with Valville. Indeed, Valville's image as a lover is somewhat tarnished by Marianne's early observation that he was less *amoureux* than *tendre*, a more undifferentiated feeling that at once recognizes Marianne's worth and puts her in the same category as the other (noble) young women to whom he is drawn.

In *La Vie de Marianne*, which, despite Marivaux's contemporary allusions, is supposed to be set in the late seventeenth century, this evolution of feeling is presented as compatible with the maintenance of rigid social distinctions. But on at least two occasions, Marianne goes further by speaking of *tendresse* in connection with her gratitude. In part five, Marianne recalls Mme de Miran's 'bonté de cœur dont le mien est encore transporté quand j'y songe, et que je ne me rappelle jamais sans pleurer de tendresse et de reconnaissance' (goodness of heart which still takes my breath away when I think back on it, and which I never recall without weeping from tenderness and gratitude) (260). And in part six, after Mme de Miran reiterates her intention to allow the marriage to Valville to go forward despite the revelations of Mme Dutour, Marianne exclaims: 'Je pleurai d'aise, je criai de joie, je tombai dans des transports de tendresse, de reconnaissance' (I wept for relief, I cried for joy, I fell into transports of tenderness, of gratitude) (285).

We note that in each sentence *tendresse* precedes *reconnaisance*. The effect is to situate gratitude in a context that eliminates the element of humiliating dependence. *Tendresse* is a mark of freedom and equality; it is incompatible with any form of constraint or subjugation in one's relationship with the other, even when the superiority of the other is acknowledged. Indeed, that recognition flows first from *tendresse* as a manifestation of Marianne's delicacy of feeling and only then becomes awareness of obligation. Yet, while Marianne might well claim that her capacity for *tendresse* was inborn, its expression is inseparable from the initiative of Mme de Miran's generosity. *Tendresse*, therefore, is less a quality of the self than the medium through which generosity and gratitude interact in a way favorable to both parties. As Mme Dorsin,

associated with the word *amour* itself. Unlike *amour* also, *tendresse* is purely secular in its connotations, thus excluding at once the lowest and the highest forms of love. See Maurice Daumas, *La Tendresse amoureuse, XVIe siècle–XVIIIe siècle* (Paris: Perrin, 1996). Another suggestive analysis of the changes in emotional language beginning in Scudéry's time is Joan deJean, *Ancients against Moderns: Culture Wars and the Making of a Fin de Siècle* (Chicago: University of Chicago Press, 1997), ch. 3.

who is presented as the most perceptive character in the novel, remarks when Mme de Miran worries about how she will reconcile her affection for Marianne with concern for her son: 'C'est un bonheur que nous ayons affaire à [Marianne]: nous venons de voir un trait du caractère de son cœur qui prouve de quoi sa tendresse et sa reconnaissance la rendront capable pour une mère comme vous' (It is fortunate that we are dealing with Marianne. We have just seen a feature of her heart's character that shows what her tenderness and gratitude will enable her to do for a mother like you) (183).

In the emotional intensity of Marianne's 'transports' the implications of the way the two feelings are associated remain beneath the surface of the text, but they emerge more clearly in part eight, when Marianne, confined to a convent, is comforted by a nun who will turn out to be Mademoiselle de Tervire.

> Je la regardai alors, moitié vaincue par ses raisons et moitié attendrie de reconnaissance pour toute la peine que je lui voyais prendre afin de me persuader; et je laissai même tomber amicablement mon bras sur elle, d'un air qui signifiait: Je vous remercie, il est bien doux d'être entre vos mains. (384)
>
> I gazed at her then, in part convinced by her reasoning and in part touched with gratitude for all the trouble I saw her taking to persuade me; and I even let my arm fall fondly on her, in a way that signified: Thank you, how sweet it is to be in your care.

Here Marianne's tender gratitude appears in a new light, as if the experience of her relationship with Mme de Miran has given her a new poise and a new self-awareness about her actions. It manifests itself, indeed, almost as a kind of *noblesse oblige*, even before Marianne's right to such an attitude has been socially established. Tervire's noble birth is unquestioned, and her age and experience should claim Marianne's respect. Yet, as we shall see, Tervire has been shaped by a world very different from Marianne's, a world in which all forms of *reconnaissance* go awry.

TERVIRE'S FAILED DRAMATURGY OF RECOGNITION

Just at the point where there seems nothing left to discover about Marianne's identity except for the revelations of a final recognition scene, Marivaux shifts the narrative focus in part nine of the novel to the nun who has befriended Marianne in her convent. Mlle de Tervire is also an orphan, and her story is in its own way a tale of frustrated recognition. Tervire's identity is not in doubt, but deaths in her family, an evil stepmother, conniving matchmakers, and her own lack of native wit rob her of the status she deserves. By the end of book eleven, the last Marivaux wrote, Tervire has been reduced almost to anonymity. In a way that prefigures Sade's Justine, she is presented as a virtuous victim who rebounds from each humiliation no more savvy than before, ready to be exploited again. Just as we do not know how Marianne becomes the *comtesse de**** who writes the story, we do not learn how Tervire, whose distaste for forced vocations is made clear, comes to take the veil. Marivaux is in fact only interested in Tervire's past: although she has supposedly left her earthly identity behind, we are never given Tervire's religious name. She is identified first only as 'a nun' (271), and then by her family name—a small compensation, perhaps, for the earlier erasure of her social identity.

Interestingly, Tervire's two displays of initiative are connected with recognition scenes. Whereas the dynamic Marianne must adopt a passive role to be 'recognized' but is then enabled to display initiative in her gratitude, the passive Tervire is roused to action only when it comes to promoting the recognition of others. What these scenes show is that while Tervire is hindered by her own lack of benefactors, the crucial problem is that she does not know how to play the benefactor's role herself. In this respect, she follows in her mother's footsteps. The widowed Mme de Tervire had neglected her daughter after she remarried and had a son by her second, more socially prominent husband. She later gives away all her fortune to that son when he makes a good marriage. She counts on gratitude in return, but as the reader might expect from the pathetic context in which Tervire's story is set, the son turns against his mother. She has made the fatal mistake of transforming the free return of gratitude into an obligation, so that her self-sacrifice, instead of encouraging a generous emulation, becomes an irritation, a burden to be shaken off.

Meanwhile, the young Mlle de Tervire is more or less abandoned. After undergoing a humiliating series of trials, including a period of several years of living with a good-hearted tenant of her grandfather's as a kind of foster child, she is eventually taken in by her great-aunt. Mme Dursan had long ago disowned her own son for marrying a woman from a lower-class family of bad repute. She decides to make Tervire her heir. When Tervire protests against the harsh treatment of the son,

Mme Dursan, like Tervire's mother, manipulates the operation of gratitude in order to shift the burden of the relationship onto Tervire. 'Ta reconnaissance', she tells her, 'est une ressource que je lui laisse' (your gratitude is a resource I bequeath to him) (497). Not long afterward, the son, now ailing and destitute, appears out of the blue with his wife and his own son. Tervire schemes to bring the wife into Dursan's house under the guise of a maid, so that she can develop a bond with her mother-in-law. Tervire then plans a touching recognition scene between mother and son, and in order to maximize its impact she calls a priest to the man's bedside to give him the last rites. 'C'était au milieu de cette auguste et effrayante cérémonie que j'avais dessein de placer la reconnaissance entre la mère et le fils' (it was in the midst of this majestic and frightening ceremony that I was planning to stage the recognition scene between the mother and the son) (521).

The shock, however, is too great.

> Qui êtes-vous, monsieur? Votre victime, ma mère, répondit-il du ton d'un homme qui n'a plus qu'un souffle de vie.
>
> Mon fils! Ah! malheureux Dursan! je te reconnais assez pour en mourir de douleur, s'écria-t-elle en retombant dans le fauteuil, où nous la vîmes pâlir et rester comme évanouie. (527)
>
> Who are you, sir? Your victim, my mother, he replied, in the voice of a man who has only one more breath of life left.
>
> My son! Ah! unfortunate Dursan! I recognize you well enough to die of grief, she cried as she fell back into the armchair, where we saw her go pale and lie still as if she had fainted.

Mme Dursan's own death quickly follows that of her son. She does change her will in favor of her daughter-in-law but poisons the well of gratitude by making Tervire's financial security dependent on it. 'Vous ne sauriez, ni prouver mieux votre reconnaissance à mon égard, ni mieux honorer ma mémoire, qu'en exécutant fidèlement ce que j'exige de vous' (You could not find a better way to show your gratitude toward me, nor better honor my memory, than by faithfully carrying out what I demand of you) (531).

For no sooner is Mme Dursan in her grave than her daughter-in-law suddenly reveals a different character. She deprives Tervire of her income from the estate and destroys the budding romance between Tervire and her own son. This turn of events conforms to the melodramatic pattern of Tervire's story of victimization, yet it takes the reader aback, since at the moment Tervire first disclosed her plan to help the daughter-in-law, the latter was 'transportée de reconnaissance' (deeply moved by gratitude) (516). Tervire's imperceptiveness shades at this point into narrative unreliability, since the earlier account was clear and categorical. In Marivaux's other portrayals of hypocritical and malicious characters, there was always some indication that things were not what they seemed, but here the author gives us no clue that would have enabled us to predict the daughter-in-law's behavior.[17]

Or does he? Rereading the sentence just cited, we note the absence of the *tendresse* mentioned earlier by Marianne in a nearly identical situation. We should also recall the comment Tervire made earlier about the daughter-in-law's family. She was 'la fille d'un petit artisan' (the daughter of a lowly craftsman) of Saint-Malo, and although she was 'fort vertueuse et fort raisonnable, disait-on' she had 'une sœur qui ne lui ressemblait pas, une malheureuse . . . dont la conduite avait personnellement déshonoré le père et la mère qui la souffraient' (most virtuous and most reasonable, they said, [she had] a sister who was not like her, an unfortunate girl . . . whose conduct had brought personal dishonor upon the father and mother who tolerated it) (484). More important than the seed of doubt planted here about the daughter-in-law's own virtue is the detail about the family. Since Marivaux usually gives us only such detail about secondary characters as is required to advance the main story, and since we never see the sister or the parents, his intention seems to be to portray the sister-in-law against a background of ineradicable shame. If we keep this background in mind, the daughter-in-law's lack of genuine (or at least, lasting) gratitude becomes somewhat more understandable. She does not have the necessary freedom of social maneuver in which gratitude can flourish. Tervire can intercede for her with Mme Dursan, but she cannot erase the past. On the contrary, her scheme aggravates the problem because, in her determination to control every element of the plan, she leaves no room for improvisation or initiative by the beneficiary. It is surely significant that the daughter-in-law never gets the opportunity to tell her own story.

The device of introducing the daughter-in-law into the house as a maid and giving her the name 'Brunon' (the only one by which she is identified until, after the death of her mother-in-law, she becomes 'Mme

[17] According to Henri Coulet, Brunon's initial astonishment at Tervire's generosity was a bad omen: 'an astonishment like Brunon's . . . and a gratitude so ostentatious revealed a soul which was lacking in sincerity and a stranger to generosity.' See Coulet, *Marivaux romancier*, 235.

Dursan') bears some resemblance to the plot of one of Marivaux's comedies, but the device means something quite different in the novel as opposed to the play. In a work like *Le Jeu de l'amour et du hasard*, such disguises are linked to love rather than money, and the stooping-to-conquer experience provides an occasion for the character's moral growth. In addition, borrowed identities belong to an accepted tradition of theatrical masking, according to which normal conventions about social roles are suspended. In the more realistic context of the novel, Tervire can employ this stratagem only because 'Brunon' is in fact low-born. Even in her poverty, Tervire (and still less Marianne) would never consider being a maid herself or even passing for one. But Tervire does not stop to consider the effect of her plan on 'Brunon's' sensibility. She focuses exclusively on stage-managing the recognition scene. If the result is a disaster for her, it may be said to stem from Tervire's failure to understand the relationship between external and internal forms of recognition, when and how *connaissance* can generate *reconnaissance.*

Tervire's ineptitude is again displayed in the second of her recognition scenes. Arriving in Paris in search of help from her half-brother, she is shocked to learn that a destitute and gravely ill lady she meets at an inn is her own long-lost mother. In the last scene of the novel as we have it, we see Tervire, finally roused to anger on another's behalf, lecturing her half-brother in the middle of a party at his luxurious home. It is clear that if she was counting on the presence of spectators to work in her favor, she is mistaken. The brother had always been a snob, and there is no way he will change his ways in front of his friends just because a poorly dressed relative asks him to do so. Whereas Brunon cannot overcome her shame except by banishing the reminder of it in Tervire, the brother is simply immune to any shame at all.

I have suggested that Tervire does not know how to be a benefactor.[18] Given the emphasis on the ways she goes about arranging recognitions for others, one might put the matter another way: she does not know how to be a good author. If, as I have suggested, Marivaux's intention in telling Marianne's story was to dramatize occasions for gratitude, then Tervire is an anti-Marivaux as much as an anti-Marianne. Indeed, the

[18] For an insightful psychoanalytic interpretation of Tervire's behavior which offers an important complement to the one offered here, see René Démoris, 'Tervire ou la réparation impossible', in Françoise Gevrey, ed., *Marivaux et l'imagination* (Toulouse: Éditions universitaires du Sud, 2002), 213–27; and 'Aux frontières de l'impensé: Marivaux et la sexualité', in Franck Salaün, ed., *Pensée de Marivaux* (Amsterdam: Rodopi, 2002), 69–83.

whole Tervire narrative goes against what is most innovative in the first part of the book. The episodes involving Marianne and Mme de Miran, focused on improvised initiative, have an unpredictable quality. The reader is eager to read the next installment and to complain, as Marianne the narrator reports, when publication is delayed. By contrast, not only were the last three parts of the novel as we have it issued all at once, we see things coming as we read—there would have been little sense of anticipation between installments, only a familiar kind of foreboding. Tervire may be shocked to recognize her mother in the destitute lady languishing in the inn, but the reader is not at all surprised. Nor, despite the initial, and technically awkward, reversal of expectation in the Brunon episode, have we any trouble accepting that Tervire should become a victim once again. Marivaux's change of technique is difficult to explain unless we see it as a deliberate and ironic concession to the conventions of the type of lamentation narrative we find in the deterministic *histoires* of the late seventeenth century. Perhaps he wanted to show readers bemused by Marianne's provocative claims that recognition without surprise or complexity of emotional response is not a source of lasting pleasure, and thus of gratitude toward the writer who composed them.

GRATITUDE AND AUTHORSHIP

Marivaux's transaction with the reader dramatizes a third form of *reconnaissance* in the way he portrays his friends Mme de Lambert and Mme de Tencin in the characters of Mme de Miran and Mme Dorsin. In contrast to other *romans-à-clef*, such as those of Crébillon, the identity of the models is not in doubt. Since Marivaux's purpose is neither to titillate nor to advertise some secret knowledge, but rather to display his gratitude to two influential women, there is no teasing or ambiguity in his presentation. Yet, this clarity does not exclude all complexity of response. Marivaux's portraits are not conventional encomia. The very fact that he gives us two portraits, rather than select one woman for praise, shows that his interest is analytical as much as it is laudatory.[19] It is surely no coincidence that in comparing Mme de

[19] While Mme de Tencin was still alive at the time Marivaux wrote, Mme de Lambert had died in 1733, so from a practical point of view there was no need to give them equal treatment.

Miran with Mme Dorsin, Marivaux should focus on the kinds of gratitude their generosity elicits from other people. Once again the difference involves the complex relationship between head and heart.

The two characters are equally good-hearted, but they differ in their degree of intelligence. According to Marianne's disenchanted commentary, those who receive favors would prefer their benefactor not to be aware of the value of the favors they grant, and thus how great their own obligation. Thus, it is easier to feel grateful to Mme de Miran, whose intelligence is only of a 'raisonnable médiocrité' (reasonable middling sort) (219), than it is to Mme Dorsin, who appreciates all too clearly the value of what she does for others. With Mme Dorsin, 'ils ne sauraient plus manquer de reconnaissance sans en être honteux' (they could no longer fail to be grateful without being ashamed of it) (219), while with Mme de Miran, 'leur reconnaissance', since it shows the beneficiary's own intelligence, 'leur ferait presque autant d'honneur que s'ils étaient eux-mêmes généreux' (their gratitude would do them almost as much credit as if they were being generous themselves) (220). This paradoxical relationship between gratitude and the recognition of a debt is illustrated in Marianne's own dealings with the two women. Luckily, it is Mme de Miran who becomes Marianne's chief benefactor and thus allows the latter to combine gratitude with enhanced self-esteem.

In her portrait of Mme Dorsin, Marianne suggests that she later had many occasions to appreciate her generosity and even that they became friends—a close relationship, that is to say, but not as intimate as the one Marianne has with her adopted mother, Mme de Miran. However, in the novel as we have it, all Marianne actually owes Mme Dorsin are two invitations to dinner. Important as these are for introducing her to Paris society, these favors are not so extravagant as to make Marianne chafe under the obligation. Interestingly, in the one scene where Marianne speaks of her gratitude to Mme Dorsin, she does not link it to *tendresse*. On the contrary, when Mme Dorsin offers to shelter Marianne so that Mme de Miran need not feel any tension between wanting to help Marianne while protecting Valville from an unsuitable attachment, Marianne records a different reaction: 'je levai les yeux sur elle d'un air humble et reconnaissant, à quoi je joignis une très humble et très légère inclination de tête' (I raised my eyes to her with a humble and grateful air, to which I added a very humble and very slight nod of the head) (180). The repetition of 'humble' in this sentence (which shows Marianne's gesture to be as self-conscious as it is submissive) only underscores the absence of the uncomfortable notion of humility in

Marianne's description of her interactions with other benefactors. Of course, as Marianne explains, she does not want to display an enthusiasm that would imply that Mme Dorsin's gesture is enough to console her for having to separate from Mme de Miran (180), but the moment is suggestive nonetheless of the different kinds of response the two women inspire.

Yet, Marianne as narrator praises each woman equally. One might speculate that Mme Dorsin's lucidity can only truly be acknowledged after Marianne has become the clear-eyed narrator (and judge) of her own story. As for Marivaux, one might infer that what he himself appreciated most about the two women was the opportunity to compare their behavior. Doing so had the intellectual benefit of sharpening his insight into the complexities of human nature. Even more important, however, is the fact that these friendships enabled Marivaux to embody his insights in a successful work of art. That is why his benefactors deserve a place in *La Vie de Marianne*, whose structure is based on the contrasting stories of two heroines, Marianne and Tervire, but whose primary narration is the fruit of the help Marianne received from her patrons. The novel's success would be proof that in artistic creation critical insight, the acknowledgment of a debt, and the enhanced agency of the self can be mutually supportive. The reader's recognition of Marivaux's real-life models may in turn be understood, not as a formal identification merely, but as a step in the reader's own education, so that even though the reader may not have known the two women personally he or she will come to feel grateful for the benefit they receive through Marivaux's expression of his gratitude to them.

Like Tervire, then, Marivaux can thus be said to stage a recognition scene. But unlike Tervire, Marivaux understands that for recognition to work it must accommodate a more disenchanted, differentiated view of human motives. It is probably no coincidence that the Tervire part of the novel contains no references to real people and does not invite the reader's engagement with the narrative at any other level than that of the heroine's suffering. The literary transaction with the reader is thereby short-circuited, in a manner that recalls Tervire's appeals to her relatives. As a consequence, the narrative of Tervire's story peters out, even though the publication all at one time of the last three parts of the novel suggested that Marivaux was making a greater effort to bring her story to a conclusion. But perhaps this structural contradiction is only apparent. At the beginning of each of the novel's first installments, Marianne waxes ironic about the delays of publication and her failure to move the story forward as quickly as the reader would like. She seems to flout the unwritten contract between novelistic narrators and the reader's curiosity. But the contrasting conventionality of the Tervire story suggests that what is going on in the early installments is an attempt not to assume or to force the reader's gratitude for the gift of Marianne's story. It is Marivaux's repeated deferral of recognition that allows the reader to participate more actively in the working out of Marianne's initiatives. Whether the reader will be grateful for the opportunity is, as the author himself seems happy to accept, beyond his control. The more extravagant ambitions and anxieties of Rousseau offer a striking contrast to what might be called the confident diffidence of Marivaux.

4

Anger and Authorship in Rousseau

As a rhetorical stance, anger features prominently in Rousseau's writing, but the experience of anger is also an object for philosophical reflection. Indeed, the question of anger's moral value is closely linked to that of its usefulness in addressing moral questions generally. Yet, Rousseau's answers to those questions are not easy to determine, nor is it easy to see how they might form a coherent whole. At different times, his style conveys eloquent indignation and philosophical calm, even as he depicts with equal vividness human beings liberated from emotional disturbance and reacting passionately to insult and injustice. Since Rousseau, unlike Challe or Marivaux, claims to have developed a coherent and comprehensive philosophy, the complexities and apparent contradictions of his thought, expressed in a wide variety of discursive forms and styles, present a particular challenge to the critic.

One way of meeting that challenge is to look for a consistent fundamental concern beneath the surface variations of the arguments. One such concern is the search for a self free from internal contradiction. Anger and equanimity, for example, could then be judged good or bad insofar as emotional intensity fosters that freedom or aggravates the difficulties of preserving it in particular circumstances: the state of nature, modern European societies, or Rousseau's ideal republic.[1] The rhetorical complexities of Rousseau's texts are best understood as deliberate and coherent strategies for awakening from their dogmatic slumbers those readers able and willing to seek the truth behind the author's provocations. Such an approach avoids hasty accusations of incoherence, but the determination to take Rousseau 'seriously' may underestimate the extent to which his texts are themselves experimental in nature—that is to say, literary—by imposing on them too narrow

[1] A good recent example of this approach is Laurence Cooper, *Rousseau, Nature, and the Good Life* (University Park, Pa: Penn State University Press, 1999).

or idealized a conception of philosophical writing, or of intellectual coherence.[2]

From a literary standpoint, there is, or at least should be, no contradiction between respecting Rousseau's arguments as arguments and recognizing that he may be trying them out as part of a broader negotiation of the vocabularies and genres he inherits, or of the kind of cultural authority he may claim by their creative appropriation. A reflective distance from one's own ideas need not diminish the authenticity of one's convictions or undermine the arguments advanced in their support. On the contrary, it may be that disregarding the element of contingency and testability in one's arguments, or refusing to make room for such factors in one's rhetoric, is the real failure of seriousness. Certainly this is the case if one believes proper human actions or dispositions depend to some extent on context. Identifying a secure criterion for distinguishing 'good' from 'bad' anger, for example, does not eliminate the need for judgment calls in particular instances. Acknowledging the operation of such judgments within the text itself, even imperfectly or implicitly, also enables readers of different times and places to participate more fully in the author's quest for truth by testing their own convictions in a more self-conscious way. Such acknowledgment is especially vital when the nature and value of emotional transactions are at issue. In looking at the dynamic of anger and gratitude in Rousseau, I will be seeking the coherence behind the paradoxes and contradictions in the philosopher's arguments, but I will also be focusing on the ways Rousseau's works dramatize the writer's relationship to his own claims, and to others' claims on or against his writing. Before looking at his major published works in detail, it will be helpful to outline the general problematic of anger that subtends his writing career and to illustrate it with some key episodes from the autobiographical writings published only after his death.

ANGER GOOD AND BAD

According to Rousseau, human beings in society are completely dependent on other people for the satisfaction of their needs and the recognition of their worth. The competitiveness of a social system based on

[2] On this point, see Derek Attridge, *The Singularity of Literature* (London: Routledge, 2004).

private property and personal prestige nurtures vanity and a sense of entitlement in each individual. One result of this process is a susceptibility to frustration and slight so fundamental as to make us vulnerable to anger at every moment of our lives. A cure for anger would therefore do more than relieve an occasional disturbance of our inner balance. It would radically change our whole existence. In the midst of society, we would enjoy, at least to some extent, the inner peace of the state of nature.

Such a program recalls that of the later Stoics, who under the arbitrary violence of imperial Roman rule held out to slighted citizens the prospect of philosophical independence and tranquility. And so it is not surprising that Rousseau should open *Émile*, his book on education, with an epigraph from Seneca's essay *De ira*: 'The ills which ail us are curable; we were born to be upright, and nature itself, should we wish to be improved, will help us.'[3] We are not so cut off from nature that we cannot draw on its power to eliminate our susceptibility to anger, in which the destructive power of that dependence becomes manifest.

On the other hand, many of Rousseau's early works are infused with a tone of righteous indignation at the corrupting effects of social life.[4] The *Discours sur l'inégalité*, for example, denounces in the most energetic terms those who, precisely under the cover of philosophical equanimity, refuse to be moved by the suffering of others (*OC* iii. 156; G 1, 153). Tranquil self-possession is condemned as a culpable form of 'sleep'. Here, Rousseau's anger is not a symptom of disease but a healthy form of protest against complacency. Indignation is a sign of moral vigor, of commitment to truth. The contrast with the Senecan *Émile* is striking. Moreover, Rousseau adopted as his personal motto a line from another Roman writer for whom anger was a constant theme. First publicly announced in the *Lettre à d'Alembert*, four years before the publication of *Émile*, it is a phrase from Juvenal's fourth satire: *Vitam impendere vero*, 'to risk one's life for the truth' (*OC* v. 120 n.; *CW*

[3] Seneca, *De ira*, II.13. Rousseau, *Émile* (*OC* iv. 239; *E*, 31). The translation is taken from *Moral and Political Essays*, ed. John M. Cooper and J. F. Procopé (Cambridge: Cambridge University Press, 1995), 53.

[4] I use indignation as a synonym for anger since the two words are used that way in Rousseau's texts. We sometimes distinguish indignation, often modified by the adjective 'righteous', as a more worthy moral passion focused on injustice to others, from everyday anger over offenses to ourselves. This distinction, however, is not observed by many writers on the subject, and while Rousseau will sometimes want to differentiate between 'good' and 'bad' anger, he does not do so on the basis of terminology.

x. 348 n.).[5] The poems in Juvenal's first book vividly illustrate the angry attitudes Seneca had criticized fifty years earlier and explore the perverse use of Stoic principles to avoid confronting the corruptions of public life.[6]

The writer who tells the truth, however, may well find his readers becoming angry at him rather than with him. People at ease with current social arrangements may not want to be disturbed by inconvenient truths. Rousseau says he must tell the truth anyway, whatever the cost. He is willing to stand up to the powerful and to pay with his life, but what about the less fortunate or less secure among his readers? They might not want to hear more bad news, see their illusions destroyed, or be robbed of whatever tranquility they have managed to achieve. They may turn against the writer, attacking his motives as well as his arguments. Worst of all, in reacting to what they experience as a slight on their good faith, they may misunderstand, indeed distort, what the writer wanted to tell them; their resentment may have nothing to do with his actual message. If this happens, and the writer then finds himself anticipating a hostile reaction, his own righteous anger may turn into the resentful and self-destructive bitterness of the victim.[7] We

[5] Curiously, in their otherwise valuable notes, the editors do not reference the source, which is Juvenal, *Satires* IV.91. See *Juvenal and Persius*, ed. and tr. Susanna Morton Braund (Cambridge, Mass.: Harvard University Press, 2004), 204. Note that Rousseau is not donning the mantle of an ancient hero but doing what Juvenal's Crispinus, one of Domitian's fawning courtiers, does *not* do. 'He was not the kind of patriot', Juvenal writes, 'who could speak his mind's thoughts freely and risk his life for the truth.' The word *impendere* can also mean 'spend' or 'devote'. See Jacques Berchthold, '*Vitam impendere vero*', *Europe* 84.390 (October 2006), 141–60. For a study of Rousseau's relation to Juvenal, see M.-J. Villaverde, '*Vitam impendere vero*: de Juvénal à Rousseau', *Études Jean-Jacques Rousseau* 4 (1990), 53–70.

[6] W. S. Anderson, 'Anger in Juvenal and Seneca', *University of California Publications in Classical Philology* 19.3 (1964), 127–96. However, the question of Juvenal's overall relation to Stoicism is more complicated. According to Braund, the satires of book III present 'a shift away from the earlier angry personality'. Anger becomes a stage toward or a strategy aimed at 'Democritean tranquillity and ironic detachment' (*Juvenal and Persius*, 22–3). See also her more detailed study, S. H. Braund, *Beyond Anger: A Study of Juvenal's Third Book of Satires* (Cambridge: Cambridge University Press, 1988). Such a development may be relevant to Rousseau's use of the apparent contrast between Seneca and Juvenal, but it must be remembered that in Rousseau's day the more frequent literary contrast was between the satires of Juvenal and Horace, with the anger of the former opposed to the indulgence of the latter.

[7] For Rousseau's 'victimary' strategies, see Eric Gans, 'The Victim as Subject: The Esthetico-Ethical System of Rousseau's Rêveries', *Studies in Romanticism* 21.1 (Spring 1982), 3–32, and Jeremiah Alberg, in *A Reinterpretation of Rousseau: A Religious System* (New York: Palgrave, 2007).

have come full circle back to the corrosive moral disease for which Seneca designed his cure, and whose effects, so forcefully portrayed in the early Juvenal, led that satirist to adopt a more reflective attitude in his later poems.

Thus anger, just like peace of mind, may be good or bad. But how are the good forms of anger to be distinguished from the bad? In a corrupt society, in which even understanding and judgment are compromised, there is no clear, generally recognized method for making such distinctions. Can writers foster good anger without provoking the bad? When should they adopt an angrily provocative as opposed to a calmly therapeutic stance in their own writing, and can they themselves be clear about the motives for their choices?

The issues involved are not only psychological and epistemological, but institutional. What qualifies the writer to cure the reader's anger, or to stir it up? The criteria governing what Aristotle would call the *ethos* of speakers and the *pathos* of their rhetoric have always been a matter of contention,[8] but in eighteenth-century France the problem was particularly acute for independent *philosophes.* They did not occupy the kind of recognized office that defined and supported the discursive interventions of priests, magistrates, or royal ministers. Moreover, for occupants of such offices, the relation between public and private motivation, while no doubt questionable in particular cases, was not fundamentally problematic, since it was mediated by the structured practices of their profession. Thus, when d'Alembert claimed, in his *Encyclopédie* article 'Genève', that the city's pastors proclaimed from the pulpit a theology at variance with their more 'enlightened' beliefs, Rousseau can reply that consistency of private and public reasoning is irrelevant as long as they do their job of promoting virtuous behavior.[9] Rousseau will say something similar about the citizens of the *Contrat social*: as long as they obey the laws, their private beliefs or emotions do not affect their status or rights as citizens. This does not mean wise rulers should not encourage the citizens to 'love the laws' so as to make their obedience more authentic, but as long as they fulfill their duties, their inner convictions, and presumably their emotions, are not to be scrutinized.[10]

[8] Aristotle, *On Rhetoric: A Theory of Civic Discourse*, tr. George A. Kennedy (New York: Oxford University Press, 1991).

[9] See the *Lettre à d'Alembert* (*OC* v. 10–13; *CW* x. 258–60).

[10] See 'De la religion civile', *Du contrat social* IV.8 (*OC* iii. 460–9; G 2, 142–9). On this point, see Patrick Coleman, '"Aimer les lois": l'objet de l'éducation républicaine chez Rousseau', in Michael Böhler, Étienne Hofmann, Peter H. Reill, and Simone

Unlike the Genevan pastor, or the republican citizen, however, the early modern French philosopher had no official standing. In some other countries, notably Britain and (somewhat later) Germany, university professorships provided intellectuals with some institutional standing. In France, by contrast, no major philosopher in the *ancien régime* occupied a professorial chair. The seventeenth century saw instead the rise of the well-rounded *honnête homme*, who eschewed professional status and whose reputation was secured by the informal approbation of salon society. Over the course of the following century, election to a scientific or a literary academy acknowledged specialist achievement and bestowed some institutional prestige, but it was not the only path to cultural authority. The latter was gained from participation in the more informal activity of the republic of letters, whose members, of different sorts and conditions, distinguished themselves primarily through their ability to exploit the resources of print culture. As a consequence, the generic as well as the institutional boundaries of writing considered to be philosophical were blurred. In the absence of recognized institutional qualification, as Dinah Ribard has shown, seventeenth-century French writers who addressed matters of moral psychology or behavior authenticated their claims to public attention by projecting a persuasive persona within the texts themselves, or in closely associated paratexts (prefaces, frontispieces, detailed title pages, etc.). Direct or indirect biographical accounts or self-portraits, modeled on the lives of ancient sages or saints, offered evidence of the author's 'philosophical' way of life.[11] One should add that over the course of the period, another legitimizing factor was the writer's ability to foster a sense of philosophical competence in the reader as well, by casting serious moral reflection in such handy forms as the *maxime*, the informal letter, or the dictionary. The reader's empowerment served to vindicate the writer's authority.

Tensions within the system of informal norms for cultural authority created both opportunities and dangers for the unaffiliated writer. In the wake of his initial personal 'illumination', which led him to resign the

Zurbuchen, eds, *Republikanische Tugend: Ausbildung eines Schweizer Nationalbewusstseins und Erziehung eines neuen Bürgers. Contribution à une nouvelle approche des Lumières helvétiques* (Geneva: Slatkine, 2000), 459–70.

[11] Dinah Ribard, *Raconter, vivre, penser: histoires de philosophes 1650–1766* (Paris: Vrin, 2003). Writers did not necessarily have to speak about themselves. The ability to appreciate the characteristics of an exemplary philosophical life in the discussion of another person could also serve to illustrate one's own merits.

position as secretary to the Dupin family which had given him a first, fragile foothold in the intellectual world of Paris, Rousseau experienced these tensions in a particularly acute way. To be taken seriously by the 'enlightened' public of the mid-eighteenth century, he had to display that serene rationality which distinguished the true *philosophe* from the irrational irascibility of bigots and tyrants. At the same time, as a spokesperson for nature and humanity, he must also display a sensitive character acute and spontaneous enough to prove his own immediate relationship to nature, yet disciplined enough to enable an enlightened sympathy for others. Personal sympathies should nourish, not impede, reflection on the greater public good.

A final factor affecting the expression of anger and other vehement emotions in Rousseau's writing emerges from another direction. The absence, for good or ill, of secure institutional mediation extended to literature itself. The two discursive genres in which anger had a long-established critical role had lost much of their cultural authority. The first is the sermon. A writer such as Bossuet continued to be admired for the sublimity of his fulminations, but the cultural framework in which religious invective enjoyed a place of prestige was undermined by the rise of a more tolerant religion of sympathetic sensibility.[12] Rousseau's own 'Profession de foi du Vicaire savoyard' will be conspicuously irenic in its tone. The other genre is satire. Despite its long literary pedigree, the Juvenalian tradition especially was seen as too rude for an age of politeness and enlightened civility. Its use of personal invective (even if the targets named were fictionalized) was at odds with the decorum of French classicism and the ethos of *politesse*, as was its association with misogyny, a feature that spoiled Boileau's attempts to refine the genre. Angry personal satire was also at odds with the following century's ideal of universal and dispassionate reason. In his *Confessions*, Rousseau relates how in his early days in Paris he composed a satiric epistle against a colonel Godard who had mistreated him. Pleased as he was with the result, he maintains this little poem was 'le seul écrit satirique qui soit sorti de ma plume. J'ai le cœur trop peu haineux pour me prévaloir d'un pareil talent', even though had he done so, 'mes agresseurs auraient rarement eu les rieurs de leur côté' (the only piece of satirical writing ever to have come from my pen. I have too little hatred in my heart to

[12] On changes in sermon rhetoric, especially as regards the threat of divine punishment, see Bernard Groethuysen's classic study *Origines de l'esprit bourgeois en France* (Paris: Gallimard, 1927).

want to exploit this particular talent... my assailants would rarely have had the laughers on their side) (*OC* i. 162; *C*, 158).[13] It seems the mediating authority of literary genre was no longer sufficient to protect satire from the complaint that its anger could only be a vehicle for personal grievance, not for serious social or philosophical critique. Satirical writing did not of course disappear, but it took different forms, notably the less strident ironies and more flexible, less lyrical prose of Voltaire's *contes philosophiques*. With the important exception of Diderot (though his 'Satire seconde', *Le Neveu de Rameau*, remained unpublished), writers generally avoided labeling their works as satires.

Recognition of these shifts in literary expectations, along with a successful combination and self-validating display of 'philosophical' traits, is what characterizes many of the greatest texts of the French Enlightenment. Yet, even in the absence of institutional rules, not every writer of talent could secure recognition of his authorial qualification. Even as merit was beginning to be seen as its own legitimization it was still assumed that intellectual intervention had to be grounded to some extent in a social standing defined by other criteria. Voltaire managed his career with the closest attention to his status as a gentleman and later as a landowning patriarch. Montesquieu, Buffon, Helvétius, and d'Holbach all enjoyed privilege of this kind. In his own way Diderot did, too: he could not have written *Le Neveu de Rameau* if he had not already earned respectability as editor of the *Encyclopédie*. D'Alembert, who was born out of wedlock, was particularly conscious of, and attached to, his rights and privileges as a member of the French Academy. Marginal figures such as Challe could not hope to enjoy the same kind of recognition, even in the world of clandestine publication.

Rousseau distinguished himself from his contemporaries by resting his claim to social recognition on a different kind of qualification: freedom from any form of dependence on the very society to which he belonged. Similar claims to independence had been advanced by philosophers in antiquity, most radically by Diogenes, but independence was for them a road to the respect of the few, not to mass popularity. Rousseau made explicit and whole-hearted use of something

[13] In the *Lettre à d'Alembert*, Rousseau will likewise insist that the 'true' misanthrope detests satire (Rousseau uses the spelling 'satyre') (*OC* 5:41; *CW* 10:283). Even as caustic a writer as Bayle was at pains to denounce 'l'esprit de satire' as undignified and offensive. See Hubert Bost, *Pierre Bayle* (Paris: Fayard, 2007), 317. The contrast in this respect with the literary culture of Augustan England is striking.

that was already implicit in the print culture of his day: the notion of independence as in and of itself the ground for a philosophical authority recognized by the reading public as a whole. His success in making good on that claim, however, could never be entirely secure. Just as Marivaux's Marianne, as an orphan of uncertain status, constantly had to find new ways to transform expressions of obligation into self-enhancing displays of aristocratic disinterest, the self-made and anti-institutional Rousseau could rely only on continuing validation of his authorial persona to justify his attacks of social institutions. He struggled throughout his career to illustrate in and through each new book the sometimes contradictory ideals of the philosopher's detachment and the sensitive soul moved to anger by offenses to human dignity.

Looking back on his authorial career in the three autobiographical works he composed when he considered that career to have ended (and which were all published posthumously), Rousseau reflects on the relationship between anger and authorship at a number of points. We will briefly consider two examples from Rousseau's account of his early life in his *Confessions*, and one from his retrospective account of his career in *Rousseau Judge of Jean-Jacques*. Taken together, they illustrate two principal ways Rousseau sees anger as informing his writing and provide essential background to his transactions with the public in his published works.

ANGER AND THE WRITING SELF

The first of these autobiographical accounts is the most straightforward. In his early thirties, after an initial failure to make his fortune in Paris, Rousseau found a position as secretary to the comte de Montaigu, France's newly appointed ambassador to Venice. The snobbish and incompetent Montaigu constantly quarreled with his lowly but talented assistant, who resented being treated as a lackey rather than with the respect due a government official. After detailing a number of threats that provoked his 'anger and indignation' (*OC* i. 312; *C*, 303),[14] Rousseau declares: 'La justice et l'inutilité de mes plaintes me laissèrent dans l'âme un germe d'indignation contre nos sottes institutions civiles

[14] Here, Rousseau adds the word 'indignation' not just to intensify the expression but to introduce a dimension of righteousness and active judgment to the passion-word *colère*.

où le vrai bien public et la véritable justice sont toujours sacrifiés à je ne sais quel ordre apparent, destructif en effet de tout ordre, et qui ne fait qu'ajouter la sanction de l'autorité publique à l'oppression du faible et à l'iniquité du fort' (The justice yet futility of my complaints had planted in my mind a seed of indignation against our stupid civil institutions, in which true public good and true justice are always sacrificed to I know not what apparent order, destructive, in fact, of every order, and which only add the sanction of public authority to the oppression of the weak and the iniquity of the strong) (*OC* i. 327; *C*, 317–18).

This passage suggests that the philosophical critique of injustice in the *Discours sur l'inégalité* and the *Contrat social* originated in personal grievance. But what made Rousseau so ready to claim a right to anger in the first place? Another man in his position might well have felt more trepidation at offending his superior, and would have hesitated to view his personal experience as the basis for a sweeping social critique. One reason was that while Rousseau's position in the diplomatic service was a lowly one, it was nevertheless one that gave him, for the first time, official status. Yet even so, Rousseau's boldness is exceptional enough as to require further warrant.

Earlier in the *Confessions*, Rousseau had provided that warrant by relating a crucial boyhood experience: the unfair accusation that he broke a comb belonging to Mademoiselle Lambercier, the sister of the pastor who was tutoring Jean-Jacques and his cousin Bernard. Despite his continued denials, indeed in part because of them, Rousseau was severely punished for the crime. The physical pain, however, was overwhelmed by a feeling of indignation that would extend far beyond any wrong done to him personally.

> Ce premier sentiment de la violence et de l'injustice est resté si profondément gravé dans mon âme, que toutes les idées qui s'y rapportent me rendent ma première émotion; et ce sentiment, relatif à moi dans son origine, a pris une telle consistance en lui-même, et s'est tellement détaché de tout intérêt personnel, que mon cœur s'enflamme au spectacle ou au récit de toute action injuste, quel qu'en soit l'objet et en quelque lieu qu'elle se commette, comme si l'effet en retombait sur moi.
>
> This first experience of violence and injustice has remained so deeply ingrained in my heart that any idea that is at all associated with it brings back the emotions I felt at the time; and these feelings, originally excited on my own behalf, have acquired their own integrity, and have become so detached from any self-interest that my heart begins to burn with indignation whenever I hear

of any unjust action, whatever its object and wherever it occurs, quite as much as if I were myself to suffer its effects. (*OC* i. 20; *C*, 19)

Here Rousseau links individual slight and general injustice in a way that differs significantly from the account of the incident in Venice. His personal experience of injustice is not extended to include the experience of others like oneself. Rather, the initial anger is depersonalized, so that Rousseau's reaction to unjust actions, while passionate, is detached from his own interests. This gives his anger qualities that are associated with what Charles Taylor has called the 'disengaged reason' of the Enlightenment.[15] The anger is then re-personalized, not as an egotistical imperative but as a moral demand upon the self from outside. Anger no longer moves from the particular to the general but in the opposite direction: Rousseau makes injustice to others his personal cause.

Rousseau does not explain how this reversal came about, but the circumstances surrounding the comb story provide some clues. Rousseau did feel guilty in his relationship with Mademoiselle Lambercier, not for stealing the comb but for the erotic feelings she aroused in him. Since his own mother had died a few days after he was born, one can see how Rousseau might confuse self-assertive desire with destructive aggression, and then seek to repudiate that aggression and cling to a self-image of innocent vulnerability. Erotic initiative must therefore originate from an external source; it is something he undergoes rather than initiates. As a result, his early desire often took on masochistic expression, and he admits he enjoyed the spankings Mademoiselle Lambercier would give him as punishment for other infractions. Making things worse was the absence of the emotional support from other people needed to handle that guilt and even of the intellectual resources to understand it.[16]

Another consequence was that when Rousseau was accused of an aggressive or destructive act, he felt the accusation must be directed at someone else, not at the 'real' and innocent Jean-Jacques. He could make injustice to others his own because he had already been forced to do so in his own divided experience of self. One might say that he could be personally and passionately involved because responding to injustice to others was a way of discharging an inchoate debt of his own, owed to

[15] Charles Taylor, *Sources of the Self* (Cambridge, Mass.: Harvard University Press, 1989), and *A Secular Age* (Cambridge, Mass.: Harvard University Press, 2007).

[16] For the psychological complexities of this episode, which we cannot explore here, see Philippe Lejeune, 'Le Peigne cassé', *Poétique* 25 (1976), 1–29.

other people for the offense caused by his aggressive impulses. Yet, in another, paradoxical, sense one could argue Rousseau was also repaying a debt he owed himself. Finding an indirect way to name and answer an unspoken charge satisfied a legitimate need for clarity about the more obscure aspects of his experience. Because the society around him had not met *that* need, it was indeed at fault, and so Rousseau's self-defense was a way of acting on behalf of society, by compensating for that failure.[17] Thus, Rousseau's anger could be self-enhancing but not egotistical, detached from self-interest in its focus on the other and yet an expression of passionate identification with an 'other' who was not just a mirror of himself. Rousseau can see his anger as a justified, indeed, exemplary attitude because instead of collapsing the distinction between contingent personal slight and systematic injustice, it offers a space to mediate between them in a socially as well as personally beneficial way.[18]

Rousseau situates his anger in a very different kind of mediating context in the preface to his second autobiographical work, *Rousseau juge de Jean-Jacques*, commonly known as the *Dialogues* because of its form. Rousseau's former friend and now bitter enemy Mme d'Épinay, who feared what Rousseau might reveal about her personal relationships in *Confessions*, had persuaded the police to stop Rousseau from giving readings from his manuscript in a Paris salon. Rousseau now had to defend, not only his career, but his own assertiveness in defending it. The response he offers in the preface to the *Dialogues*, entitled 'Du sujet et de la forme de cet écrit' (On the subject and form of this writing), is a peculiar one. Whether or not anger had once been an energizing factor

[17] Alberg, *Reinterpretation*, makes the important point that Rousseau does not speak of the possibility of human failings being forgiven, rather than excused, veiled, or relocated within a context of non-culpability.

[18] One may ask how Rousseau's anger can have such positive effects when in most other people it reflects vanity and moral blindness. According to Christopher Kelly, the answer is that Rousseau's illumination was accidental. 'If [Rousseau's] system is correct in asserting that civilized humans are radically removed from naturalness, the rediscovery of nature must depend on a fortunate or fateful accident rather than systematic thought alone.' See Christopher Kelly, *Rousseau's Exemplary Life: The 'Confessions' as Political Philosophy* (Ithaca, NY: Cornell University Press, 1987), 246. The story told in the first books of the *Confessions* is in large part the story of how these accidents occurred and an attempt to universalize them into a new kind of 'phenomenology of mind' (ibid. 46; for the role of anger in this process, 129–31). For a discussion of Rousseau's indirect way of acknowledging the aggressive dimension of writing, see Patrick Coleman, *Reparative Realism: Mourning and Modernity in the French Novel 1730–1830* (Geneva: Droz, 1998), ch. 2.

in his work, he emphasizes that it is not a factor *now*. Rousseau does not write in the mode of penitential remorse, however, but of melancholy regret. He asks his readers' indulgence, not for any defects he may have displayed over the course of his life, but for those of the book he offers them now. He apologizes if his readers find his prose less energetic than they might expect from a man in his situation. 'Ce qui l'eût rendu vif et véhément sous la plume d'un autre', he writes, referring to the blackening of his reputation, 'est précisément ce qui l'a rendu tiède et languissant sous la mienne' (What would have made it lively and vehement coming from another's pen is precisely what has made it dull and slack coming from mine). And he adds, 'La colère anime quelquefois le talent, mais le dégoût et le serrement de cœur l'étouffent' (Anger sometimes stimulates talent, but disgust and heartbreak stifle it) (*OC* i. 664; *CW* i. 5).

What is curious about these formulations is that Rousseau is not comparing what he has written now with the books he himself had written earlier in his career. A vehement liveliness or a talent enlivened by anger—for Rousseau's readers this was precisely the quality they found in the *Discours* and other works that had established the reputation now being besmirched by his enemies. And yet, Rousseau does not claim that vehemence as an integral part of his own past, as a resource on which he himself once drew. That affective energy, he now writes, 'sometimes' energizes 'someone else's pen'. It is as if he wants to distance himself from his earlier books. Or perhaps, in his despondent state, he now feels those books were in fact written by someone else, a self with whom the connection has been broken. Yet, Rousseau is surely aware that people will read this preface with those earlier works in mind.

This shift from anger to melancholy opens a different kind of space for authorized speech than the one delineated in the comb episode. As a great reader of Petrarch, Rousseau understood how the experience of melancholy could provide writers with literary legitimacy, indeed with artistic prestige, precisely because of what it was they did not possess. If what was missing was not a material good but a transcendent one—an ideal object of love, a vital connection to God or the cosmic order—whose absence was also obscurely or inchoately felt by other people, then the writer's more acute and articulate experience of its loss provided evidence of a nobility of soul that warranted a claim to cultural recognition. Rousseau took this strategy a bold step further. He was the first writer to assert that the loss of *his own* energy was an experience of equivalent importance, placing him beyond everyday desire and interest, ennobling him through suffering, and endowing his writing with unique authority. What is even more provocative, the energy whose loss he mourns had been rooted, not in the transcendent power of love, but in his anger at being wronged. These moves would have a far-reaching effect on the conception of the artist's literary and cultural role as critical intellectual in the Romantic era and beyond.[19]

What is important here is that these moves gave Rousseau another way to reconcile emotional involvement with philosophical detachment. Anger becomes a vital force whose loss is to be mourned and yet is preserved in melancholy recollection. Authorship is now legitimized, or at least excused, by the pathos of loss. The writer's melancholy state combines detachment with pathos; 'philosophical' calm with an intensity of feeling elicits sympathy but also commands respect. Such a self-presentation, however, has its risks. I suggested earlier that adopting the rhetoric of angry critique may provoke the reader's own anger or a willful defensive distortion of the writer's intention that provokes in turn the latter's resentment. Presenting oneself as the melancholy victim is also risky. The reader's failure or refusal to sympathize with the author's loss could be experienced as an even greater offense than rejection of his criticism, since it would be a refusal to recognize his humanity. Yet, given the self-validating nature of that loss, it would be difficult to identify any recognized authorities to which Rousseau could appeal in defending himself against this ultimate slight. As in the case of the stolen comb, whatever resources he needs to deal with the problem will also have to be self-generated, and thus fundamentally questionable.

This brief review of the different ways Rousseau speaks of his anger in his autobiographies suggests that the dramatization of this emotion (or its transcendence) in his published work will be a complex and multilayered phenomenon, and indeed Rousseau's works highlight at various times all the broader cultural tensions about anger and authorship in eighteenth-century France.

FROM VINCENNES TO THE TWO *DISCOURS*

Rousseau's first political works, the *Discours sur les sciences et les arts* and the *Discours sur l'inégalité*, denounce the corrupting effects of civiliza-

[19] See Coleman, *Reparative Realism*, for discussion of this phenomenon in Staël, Constant, and Balzac.

tion in what Judith Shklar describes as 'an exercise in indignation'.[20] Curiously, however, neither *Discours* includes any reference to anger in the speaker, or to anger as an emotion he might provoke in his audience. Nor, in tracing humanity's alienation from the peaceful state of nature, does either *Discours* dwell on experiences of offense and anger of the kind that feature prominently in Rousseau's account of his own initiation into the fallen world of modern society.

Yet, in a letter to Mme de Warens dated a few months before he began the first *Discours*, Rousseau had spoken openly of anger as the animating force in his writing. He had been commissioned to write the articles on music for Diderot's *Encyclopédie*, and this gave him the opportunity to respond in print to all those who belittled his understanding of musical theory and his talent as a composer.[21] These critics included his patron Mme Dupin and above all the composer Jean-Philippe Rameau, whose scorn drove Rousseau to attack him with particular energy. 'Je tiens au cul et aux chausses des gens qui m'ont fait du mal', Rousseau writes, 'et la bile me donne des forces de même de [*sic*] l'esprit et de la science' (I have no hesitation in mistreating the people who have harmed me, and bile no less than wit or knowledge gives me strength). He goes on to cite a well-known line from Boileau's satires: 'La colère me suffit et vaut un Apollon' (Anger is enough for me and as good as an Apollo).[22] Righteous anger—backed up of course by appropriate display of the erudition that enables him to cite illustrious predecessors—provides Rousseau with all the qualifications he needs to intervene.

This is the kind of attitude one expects to find in a writer with a profile like Rousseau's: a poor but well-educated man from a provincial city struggling for recognition by the Parisian elite. It is the anger of the young diplomat stung by Montaigu's contempt. Indeed, so intemperate were Rousseau's articles for the *Encyclopédie* that Diderot and d'Alembert, who shared Rousseau's musical tastes, felt compelled as editors to

[20] Judith Shklar, *Men and Citizens: A Study of Rousseau's Social Theory* (Cambridge: Cambridge University Press, 1969), 28. The reference is to the second *Discours*, but it applies just as well to the first.

[21] In the *Confessions*, Rousseau speaks with undiminished resentment of Rameau's hostile reaction to *Les Muses galantes* when excerpts were performed at the home of M. de La Poupelinière, and to the revisions he was commissioned to make to Rameau and Voltaire's opera *Les Fêtes de Ramire* (*OC* i. 333–8; *C*, 325–9).

[22] Rousseau to Louise-Eléonore de La Tour, baronne de Warens, 27 January 1749, in *Correspondance complète*, ed. R. A. Leigh (Geneva: Institut et Musée Voltaire-Voltaire Foundation 1965–98), ii. 113; Boileau, *Satires* I.146.

soften their tone before publishing them. In contrast, Rousseau's vigorous attacks on social injustice in the *Discours* do not cite righteous anger as their inspiration. The reason is that after writing the letter to Mme de Warens cited above Rousseau did receive a visitation from Apollo, in the form of the so-called 'illumination' of Vincennes.[23]

The story is well known. On his way to visit Diderot, who was imprisoned in the military château of Vincennes for writing the subversive *Lettre sur les aveugles,* Rousseau came across the Dijon Academy's announcement of an essay competition in the *Mercure de France.* The question for debate was whether the progress of learning since the Renaissance had contributed to the corruption or purification of morals. All at once Rousseau experienced a 'violent palpitation' as his mind was filled with lively ideas which came to him 'avec une force et une confusion qui me jeta dans un trouble inexprimable' (with a strength and a confusion that threw me into an inexpressible perturbation) (*OC* i. 1135; *CW* v. 575).[24] Later he would write nostalgically about all the things he would have said had he been able to convey the magnitude of his experience.

> Oh Monsieur si j'avais jamais pu écrire le quart de ce que j'avais vu et senti sous cet arbre, avec quelle clarté j'aurais fait voir toutes les contradictions du système social, avec quelle force j'aurais exposé tous les abus de nos institutions, avec quelle simplicité j'aurais démontré que l'homme est bon naturellement et que c'est par ces institutions seules que les hommes deviennent méchants.
>
> Oh Sir, if I had ever been able to write a quarter of what I saw and felt under that tree, how clearly I would have made all the contradictions of the social system seen, with what strength I would have exposed all the abuses of our institutions, with what simplicity I would have demonstrated that man is naturally good and it is from these institutions alone that man becomes wicked. (*OC* i. 1135–6; *CW* v. 575)

Rousseau's vision of social injustice builds on the insight he gained from working in Venice with Montaigu, but it is not accompanied by feelings of indignation. Rather, any potential for anger in detailing social 'abuses' is neutralized by the insistence on man's natural goodness.

[23] Rousseau never seems to have spoken of his music or his musical writings as being inspired in this way. He is more concerned to assert his technical competence.

[24] See the second of the *Lettres à Malesherbes,* 12 January 1762 (*OC* i. 1135; *CW* v. 575). Another account appears in the *Confessions* (*OC* i. 351; *C,* 341–2), where Rousseau says that with the passage of time he has forgotten some of the details of the experience, and refers the reader to the earlier letter, whose account I follow here.

The *simplicité*, or unselfconscious straightforwardness, with which Rousseau would have communicated his vision, has its own energy, outstripping the force of satire's angry ironies and *ad hominem* diatribes. The experience at Vincennes differs from that in Venice in that it neither arises from nor provokes offense. Nor is Rousseau's solitary vision accompanied by any anxiety about the disparity between the way others judge Rousseau and the way he judges himself. As a consequence, Rousseau is free to denounce injustice in good conscience. Although he goes on to complain that what he calls his three principal books (the two *Discours* and *Émile*)[25] fail to do full justice to the insights he glimpsed that day, the 'effervescence' of his illumination, as he says in the *Confessions*, 'se soutint dans mon cœur durant plus de quatre ou cinq ans' (continued unabated in my heart for four or five years) (*OC* i. 351; *C*, 342). Despite 'les critiques des barbouilleurs' (the criticism of scribblers) that followed the publication of the first *Discours*, Rousseau was able to pursue a career as a philosophical writer with a self-confidence impervious to slight.[26]

Yet, if Rousseau was going to argue that intellectual and technological progress had corrupted morality, could he really reach the level of eloquence his judges expected without adopting an angry stance, which would provoke his audience and call into question the authenticity of his intervention? Here, the format of the invited essays provided a mediating context that reduced the potential for conflict. In many ways, the competition was an extension of those school exercises in which pupils imitated the orations they found in Cicero and Livy. These prestigious forebears provided a covering authorization for vehement critique, as long as the latter was cast in the forms of classical rhetoric. Invoking the same authorities and using the same language as one's opponents made it possible for original criticism to be heard, at least up to a point. And in forensic eloquence indignation was acceptable, even expected, as long as its expression was ennobled by sublimity of tone and transparent to the positive (if often conveniently abstract) ideal behind it.

[25] A number of critics have used this statement to establish a hierarchy among Rousseau's writings, but the Pléiade editors (*OC* i. 1136 n. 2) are right to explain the absence of *Julie* by the fact that it is a novel, and that of the *Contrat social* by the secrecy with which Rousseau was pursuing its publication at the time he wrote the letter.

[26] See Rousseau's second *Lettre à Malesherbes* (*OC* i. 1136; *CW* v. 575).

Unlike Voltaire or Montesquieu, Rousseau had not been educated in a Jesuit or Oratorian *collège*, but he had taught himself using the same classical models, so that it is not as ironic as it might seem to us that the first thing he wrote under the Vincennes tree was not a conversion narrative, but the so-called 'prosopopée de Fabricius' which became the nucleus of the first *Discours.* Rousseau makes the old Roman hero Fabricius speak from the grave to his own people, attacking the corruption of imperial Rome.[27]

O Fabricius! qu'eût pensé votre grande âme, si pour malheur rappellé à la vie, vous eussiez vu la face pompeuse de cette Rome sauvée par votre bras . . . 'Dieux! eussiez-vous dit, que sont devenus ces toits de chaume et ces foyers rustiques . . . Quelles sont ces mœurs efféminées? . . . Insensés, qu'avez-vous fait? . . . '

O Fabricius! what would your great soul have thought if, unhappily recalled to life, you had seen the pompous countenance of that Rome which your arm rescued . . . 'Gods!' you would have said, 'what has become of the thatch roofs and the rustic hearths . . . What are these effeminate morals? . . . Fools, what have you done? . . . ' (*OC* iii. 14; G 1, 13)

This rhetorical ventriloquism may seem to belie the ideal of straightforwardness. Yet, if we understand *simplicité* in subjective terms, not as the absence of rhetorical devices, but as the ability to employ these without anxious or resentful self-consciousness, then the contradiction disappears. Indeed, Fabricius' speech is notable for its lack of strain; it expresses indignation with real energy but without any bitter personal edge. It was no doubt Rousseau's achievement in striking this elusive note that led readers of his *Discours*, even those who disagreed with his thesis, to praise the Fabricius passage as a model of eloquence.[28]

Yet, although it conformed to cultural norms, Rousseau's first *Discours* was still a risky venture. It went far beyond the expected paradoxes and provocations of a debating exercise in advocating what readers took to be a wholesale rejection of science, and in restricting the privilege of philosophical inquiry to a few geniuses. So radical was Rousseau's critique, and so forceful the implication that it was not merely a sophisticated *jeu d'esprit*, that one might wonder on what basis he could claim access to the truths he proclaimed. In appropriating the authority of Fabricius'

[27] Gaius Fabricius Luscinus, whose austerity and incorruptibility were frequently praised in antiquity, notably by Cicero, *De officiis*, I.40, and Plutarch, *Life of Pyrrhus*.

[28] Jean Starobinski, 'La Prosopopée de Fabricius', *Revue des sciences humaines* 41 (1976), 83–96.

anger, Rousseau implied that his moral vision was not compromised by his own historical and discursive location.

Rousseau went some way toward forestalling the obvious objection to such a claim by making Fabricius a figure not just of righteous indignation but of heartfelt grief. Fabricius' anger is both heightened and distanced by lamentation for the virtue and simplicity that Rome has lost, and Rousseau's invocation of Fabricius' ghost is in turn tinged with melancholy that his like will not be found again. In other words, anticipating the move he would later make in the passage from the *Dialogues* cited earlier, Rousseau's authority is not so much grounded in any claim to possess virtue now as it is in the speaker's awareness of its loss. This mediated awareness is itself further mediated, for the loss most acutely felt is that of the authoritative figure who could name the loss directly. Authority can be claimed now only in the form of an acknowledgment of its absence. Rousseau implies that he feels this loss with exceptional sensitivity, but this is not the only warrant for his intervention. Or rather, the need for a warrant has now become less pressing. Unlike anger, grief is an emotion whose forceful expression does not require justification. Anger asserts the author's claim to a status that can be challenged, but while the capacity to feel grief acutely may also be used to distinguish oneself from others,[29] in itself grief is a feeling to which no one is denied the right. As a reaction to human weakness and vulnerability it carries its own authority, especially when it invites others to share in the experience. Rousseau can plausibly maintain that the fundamental *simplicité* of his initial vision has not been compromised, for a melancholy awareness that its fullness had receded beyond reach was part of what gave that vision its empowering force.

The *Discours sur l'inégalité* also originated as a submission to an Academy of Dijon competition, but the author's position was now very different. The success of the first *Discours* had made Rousseau something of a celebrity, validating the boldness of his intervention, but presenting him with new challenges. He had mounted an able defense against a number of writers who had challenged his sweeping assertions about the evils of progress, but he realized that his account of humanity's decline from its original goodness needed to be developed in a less schematic way. He also needed to locate the authority of his

[29] There are other instances in which grief can itself become an expression of pride ('no one experiences loss as much as I do') and Rousseau may exemplify this phenomenon elsewhere, in letters and in his autobiographies, but this is not the case here.

critical intervention more specifically in relation to that history. The second of these goals was met when Rousseau regained the Genevan citizenship he had lost when as a wandering youth he had converted to Catholicism in Turin. His return to Geneva's Reformed faith was certified by examiners who refrained from inquiring too closely into the actual beliefs of their newly famous compatriot, and so Rousseau could now add 'citizen of Geneva' to his name on the title page of his works. Citizenship of a republic whose sober virtue had enabled it to resist corruption qualified him to attack luxury and complacency elsewhere. However, it also brought with it an obligation to speak responsibly. Rousseau's attack on social corruption and his exaltation of virtue in the first *Discours* had been acclaimed, not just by philosophers or academicians, but by a broader public in France as well as in Geneva. He now had to decide whether to provoke his readers even further, and if so, how to channel their critical energy.

In the first *Discours*, Rousseau had not targeted any specific individual, class, or country. The corruption he described was universal; no one in particular was to blame. He did not seek to stir up political unrest in France, nor was it likely that the position he staked out would be taken as a call to arms. Things were different in Geneva. The city-state was small and the political situation more volatile. Although in theory all citizens were political equals, in practice Geneva was an oligarchy, ruled by the patrician families who controlled the Petit Conseil. There was an undercurrent of popular resentment that in the early eighteenth century had erupted into open strife. Rousseau was acutely aware of this, but he was not prepared to publicly acknowledge this fact, since it undermined his polemical contrast between republican equality and monarchical hierarchy. As Rousseau would show in the *Lettre à d'Alembert*, he accepted the argument that Geneva's strategic weakness in relation to its powerful neighbors demanded that internal conflict be kept to a minimum. Conforming to this demand, while insisting on redress for legitimate grievances, would require some rhetorical ingenuity. One device was to use theory to show up practice. According to the city's constitution, the 'magnifiques, très honorés, et souverains seigneurs' to whom he dedicated the *Discours sur l'inégalité* were the citizens themselves, not their rulers. In doing so, Rousseau was upholding their status against a history of encroachments by the oligarchy, but in such a idealizing way as to deflect any charge that he sought to foment resentment and political unrest.

Stirring up indignation would seem to be a less risky venture in France, where popular energy was stifled by the weight of monarchical institutions and where even those who enjoyed some freedom of action were more concerned to enjoy the seductions of polite civilization than to gird themselves for political struggle. Given the size and complexity of the country, an injection of critical energy would hardly threaten France's foundations. And yet, in the last part of the *Discours sur l'inégalité* Rousseau warns that if a people crushed by the weight of despotism should ever revolt, the consequences would be devastating. Oppression would have destroyed the moral virtues, and even the habit of prudential calculation, needed to hold violence in check. The French of Rousseau's day might not have reached that stage of degradation, but there was still danger in provoking their anger. Thus, while Rousseau's account of human socialization offers many reasons why readers should look with indignation at both past and present, it does so in such a way as to blunt the force of blame and to model forms of anger that are depersonalized and so less threatening to political stability.

Although Rousseau does not mention anger by name in describing the state of nature and humanity's fall from it, the absence or presence of perceived slight is an important differentiating factor in his depiction of early humanity. In their original condition, humans lack any self-consciousness or sense of intentionality. Any ill that befalls them is experienced simply as a physical event. Human encounters are rare. If someone grabs the apple you were going to eat, there is no reason to dwell on the disappointment or to pursue the offender. In the fertile climates that are humanity's first home, other apples hang within easy reach. There is no ego to feel slighted or anyone to blame, and so human beings enjoy peace of mind even when they suffer physical pain. Actually, it would be more correct to say it is the self-conscious contemporary reader who vicariously enjoys that peace; early humans did not know what they were feeling. By contrast, occasions for anger feature prominently in Rousseau's conception of humanity's historical development. Certainly, this is the conclusion the reader is invited to draw from Rousseau's insistence that alienation from the state of nature, even the rise of self-consciousness itself, seems at first to be the effect of external causes only. John Farrell goes so far as to claim that 'Rousseau's system . . . is a set of general hypotheses rather than an individual theory of persecution, but it licenses and, indeed, justifies each individual in the belief that he or she is the victim of powerful collective forces that have a direct effect upon his or her nature . . . with malicious intent.'[30]

Farrell draws attention to an important aspect of the *Discours*, but it is not the whole story. It is significant that Rousseau does not show people reacting with anger to the changes in their circumstances. The invention of private property is described as a trick played by a man clever enough to persuade others that a piece of land belongs to him, but although Rousseau alludes later on to the poor's resentment of the rich, we do not actually see anyone getting mad. The reader's anger may be stirred, but that emotion is not represented in the text itself, which depersonalizes the whole process. Second, Rousseau does discuss causes of change internal to human nature. When Rousseau moves from 'physical' to 'moral' anthropology, he emphasizes the restless freedom of human will. This faculty is associated with the 'perfectibility' of the species and is manifested in the development of language, reflective reasoning, and other skills which aggravate or distort the natural inequality of physical and intellectual endowment. While external changes in the earth's climate may have disrupted the harmonious balance between early humans and their environment, the evils of civilized society are also rooted in this perfectibility (*OC* iii. 162; G 1, 159).

This shift of focus does not, however, greatly affect the vectors of potential anger. In his determination to distinguish his account of human origins from that of the Bible, Rousseau avoids suggesting that the ambivalence of perfectibility calls us to self-examination and self-implication. The fall of Adam and Eve is one of those revealed 'facts' Rousseau deliberately sets aside in order to take the more scientific approach of developing a hypothetical but rationally plausible account of human origins (*OC* iii. 132; G 1, 132).[31] Rousseau illustrates the operation of free will at its most basic level by pointing out that people go on eating even after their hunger is satisfied (*OC* iii. 141; G 1, 140). Yet, he does not suggest they be blamed for that, or that they should blame themselves for their stomach ache. Nor does Rousseau picture

[30] John Farrell, *Paranoia and Modernity: Cervantes and Rousseau* (Ithaca, NY: Cornell University Press, 2006), 263.

[31] Like the natural right theorists before him, Rousseau does not directly attack the biblical account of human origins but claims to be offering a story on which rational people of any religious background can agree as a basis for social laws. See Richard Tuck, *Natural Rights Theories* (Cambridge: Cambridge University Press, 1979). For a brief discussion, see the introduction to Rousseau, *Discourse on Inequality*, tr. Franklin Philip and ed. Patrick Coleman (Oxford: Oxford University Press, 1994).

those who suffer the effects of economic inequality wondering why their ancestors allowed the institution of private property to take hold, or considering what their own responsibility might be. Instead, his account focuses on the unfolding of an impersonal pattern of development. Just as Rousseau does not depict people angry at the world, he does not show them angry at themselves or at each other.

The one exception to this pattern may prove the rule. Anger is named, and its expression described, in Rousseau's discussion of that stage of history when human beings had formed extended families or clans and complex social relations first emerged. This is when self-consciousness in the reflective form of self-love (*amour-propre*) becomes enduringly distinct from the natural sense of one's own being (*amour de soi*). Anger is an inevitable result of this development.

Sitôt que les hommes eurent commencé à s'apprécier mutuellement et que l'idée de la considération fut formée dans leur esprit, chacun prétendit y avoir droit; et il ne fut plus possible d'en manquer impunément pour personne... tout tort volontaire devint un outrage, parce qu'avec le mal qui résultait de l'injure, l'offensé y voyait le mépris de sa personne souvent plus insupportable que le mal même.

As soon as men had begun to appreciate one another and the idea of consideration had taken shape in their mind, everyone claimed a right to it, and one could no longer deprive anyone of it with impunity... any intentional wrong became an affront because, together with the harm resulting from the injury, the offended party saw in it contempt for his person, often more unbearable than the harm itself. (*OC* iii. 170; G 1, 166)

Reparation for these offenses took the form of personal vengeance, and men became 'bloodthirsty and cruel'. Rousseau writes in such a way that the reader cannot identify with the offended party. The violent reaction to slight is not dignified as a reaction to injustice; it stems from a wounded vanity the reader is invited to judge from the outside with distaste.[32]

[32] One difference between the *Essai sur l'origine des langues* and the second *Discours* is that it gives anger a greater role in early human development. Anger belongs to the passions that give rise to languages as they do to love and other social relationships. 'Ce n'est ni la faim ni la soif, mais l'amour la haine la pitié la colère qui ont arraché les premières voix' (Not hunger nor thirst, but love, hate, pity, anger wrung their first voices from them) (*OC* v. 380; G 1, 253). In the *Essai*, however, anger also arises from the difficulty of surviving in colder climates. Northern peoples are characterized by their irascible temperament because 'des hommes soumis à tant de besoins sont faciles à irriter' (men subject to so many needs are easily irritated) (*OC* v. 408; G 1, 280). The harshness of the environment is reflected in the sounds they make, which are harsh and noisy, less pleasing to the ear than those that arise in the gentler environment of the south. 'La colère

And yet, Rousseau does not introduce this distancing strategy because he wants his readers to look inward at their own temptations to vanity and violence, or to see their primitive forebears as sinners to be condemned. On the contrary, that era when humanity had no law but that of immediate revenge Rousseau calls a 'golden age'. There was a happy balance between primitive indolence and the 'petulant activity of our amour propre' (*OC* iii. 171; G 1, 167). Since these early families still for the most part led self-sufficient lives, enjoying the benefits of both independence and loving companionship, offense and revenge were only passing occurrences. They may be the products of wounded *amour-propre*, but from a psychological point of view their destructive effect does not extend very far. When revenge is immediate, there is no grudge to bear. When the operation of self-love is limited to momentary comparison and self-examination, there is no room for guilt or any other inner conflict to fester, for resentment to develop over time and lead to more insidious forms of violence.

It is true, of course, that revenge duels have fatal consequences. But in the golden age, it seems, the prospect of one's own death generates no anxiety, and that of another no sadistic anticipation. All that matters is immediate action to remove what is *insupportable*. In the state of nature, human beings did not fear death, because their imaginations had not yet been awakened, and one must suppose that in the golden age any such fear was still minimal. Perhaps Rousseau called this the golden age because one could fall passionately in love and get violently angry but still enjoy (albeit unreflectively) the benefits of that freedom from the anxiety about mortality preached by so many ancient and modern philosophers. It is significant in this respect that Rousseau should be concerned in the *Discours* to differentiate himself from Hobbes, for whom fear of death is the key factor in the creation of political associations.

arrache des cris menaçants que la langue et le palais articulent; mais la voix de la tendresse est plus douce, c'est la glotte qui la modifie, et cette voix devient un son' (Anger wrests [from us] threatening cries which the tongue and the palate articulate; but the voice of tenderness is gentler, it is modified by the glottis, and this voice becomes a sound) (*OC* v. 410; G 1, 282). Since the people of the *Discourse*'s golden age are preoccupied with love, can we infer that their anger does not express itself in harsh, angry language of northern need but in the softer tones of southern passion? This would fit Rousseau's portrait of their life as idyllic in spite of its violence, but there are problems in interpreting the typology of north and south in the unpublished *Essai* that cannot be pursued here.

The interpretation of golden age humanity presented here may be somewhat speculative, but what does seem clear is that golden age anger is free from anxiety and guilt. Anger may arise from self-love and issue in violence, but the emotion in itself, in line with Rousseau's overall attitude toward this stage of humanity, is still a straightforward one, in the positive sense Rousseau gives to *simplicité*. I believe this is because Rousseau wishes to contrast the anger of early humanity with the deep-seated and long-lasting resentments that appear at a later stage of social development, when reflective moral or religious norms of conduct are internalized. By projecting themselves back into an earlier stage of emotional history, readers may be able to shake off some of this burden. If their own anger can be freed from guilt and resentment, if they can recover something of the simplicity of the golden age (while retaining the refined sensibility that recoils from its more violent manifestations), then in a paradoxical way appropriating anger would be a way of achieving philosophical detachment. One begins to see the logic in Rousseau's otherwise curious procedure in the *Discours* of laying the groundwork for justified anger at social institutions and the mistakes of one's own forebears while avoiding any dramatization of that emotion itself in anything other than the golden age. To portray anger in the degraded context of historical reality would do nothing to liberate socialized humanity from its sad condition; on the contrary, it would only accelerate its further decline into self-defeating resentment.

While Rousseau ends the *Discours sur l'inégalité* on an indignant note, denouncing contemporary societies in which a handful of people enjoy an excess of goods while the multitude goes hungry, the contrast with the rhetoric of the first *Discours* is striking. Instead of apostrophizing the indignant spirit of a Fabricius in order to galvanize his readers, he uses an extended simile to evoke a figure of primitive freedom who does not speak at all.

Comme un coursier indompté hérisse ses crins, frappe la terre du pied et se débat impétueusement à la seule approche du mors, tandis qu'un cheval souffre patiemment la verge et l'éperon, l'homme barbare ne plie point sa tête au joug que l'homme civilisé porte sans murmure, et il préfère la plus orageuse liberté à un assujettissement tranquille.

As an untamed steed bristles its mane, stamps the ground with its hoof, and struggles impetuously at the very sight of the bit, while a trained horse patiently suffers whip and spur, so barbarous man will not bend his head to the yoke which civilized man bears without a murmur, and he prefers the most tempestuous freedom to a tranquil subjection. (*OC* iii. 181; G 1, 177)

Even more than golden age man, the horse is a figure of simple (as well as innocent) anger. Yet, while Rousseau's wild horse is a stirring rhetorical image, it invites neither intimate emotional identification nor emulation on the part of the reader. The image communicates energy, but does not determine any particular course of action. As critics have long recognized, the purpose of the *Discours sur l'inégalité* is to raise the reader's consciousness, not to map a road to reform. On the emotional level, too, the implied reader is provoked more to a generalized recalcitrance than to the kind of anger that demands specific redress.

Yet, this is not Rousseau's final word. More specific lessons are to be found in the emotionally charged dedication Rousseau added to his second *Discours*, in which he addresses a specific group of readers, the citizens of Geneva. The work's indignant but general conclusion was designed primarily for the inhabitants of advanced and complex modern societies like France, where it is difficult to imagine serious change taking place without violent disruption. The dedication gives that prudence a bolder edge by focusing on readers whose way of life is less corrupted, and who may thus be able to recover something of the golden age's simplicity of anger. Those French readers who have something of a republican soul in them are invited to read over their shoulders.

In her study of Rousseau's Geneva, Helena Rosenblatt suggests that the originality of Rousseau's dedication lies in the way it redefines the contrast between the republican ideal of virtue and the ethic of polished sociability. The austere simplicity of the former was contrasted by many political thinkers with the luxury and laxity of large commercial societies. Admirers of the ancient republics denounced the corrupting influence of money and credit in modern life, but a number of influential writers in eighteenth-century England and France had begun to argue that commercial societies fostered a *douceur* or refinement of manners, notably an increasing aversion for violent or rude behavior and a greater appreciation for the civilizing influence of women. Rosenblatt astutely remarks that Rousseau redefined the terms of the debate by claiming that Geneva, not Paris, was the home of genuine *douceur*. He 'turned the language of *doux commerce* against itself in order to further a classical republican as well as Genevan and Calvinist ideal'.[33] The word *douceur* (gentleness) appears in fact no fewer than four times in the dedication.

[33] Helena Rosenblatt, *Rousseau and Geneva: From the 'First Discourse' to the 'Social Contract', 1749–1762* (Cambridge: Cambridge University Press, 1997), 87.

Rousseau argues that, far from undermining the republic, Geneva's development into a hub of international trade gave other countries good reason to respect its political independence. Within the city itself, women play an important role in making life agreeable, but they also ensure that the (male) citizens do not lose their patriotic vigor. By making virtue attractive, Genevan women are able to rescue young men from the bad habits they adopt when they travel to other countries; they keep them from preferring the 'frivoles dédommagements de la servitude' to the 'auguste liberté' of the republic.

Rousseau's depiction of Genevan harmony sits oddly with his challenge to the usurpation of political power by the city's patrician elite. The careful reader will notice, however, that in the *Discours* itself Rousseau cites the 'douceurs d'un commerce indépendant' (gentleness of independent dealings) as one of the characteristics of humanity's golden age—that same age in which men responded violently to any slighting of the *considération* they believed was their due (*OC* iii. 171; G 1, 167). Rousseau certainly does not advocate any violent revolution in Geneva, but he is suggesting that, when their rights are slighted, the city's ordinary citizens can be energized by an indignation that is not culpable but innocent. Rather than represent a threat to the city's *douceur*, a readiness to get angry can be a factor in its preservation. In the second *Discourse*, the sweetness of the golden age was in fact inseparable from a sensitivity to slight. This is because the demand for *considération* stemmed from the very same drive to compare and judge the relative merits of persons that gave rise to romantic love. In the state of nature, physical desire is an undifferentiated need that can be satisfied by any mate. What gave the golden age its name were the charming songs and dances of courtship, in which lovers expressed a more refined preference for one potential partner over another and sought to be preferred and idealized in return (*OC* iii. 169–70; G 1, 165–6). Of course, romantic love is a source of violence among rivals for the same woman, but in the pastoral setting of early humanity it still retains the goodness of *simplicité*. In republican Geneva also, Rousseau implies, republican patriotism, the passionate preference for one's own country above all others, is compatible with, and is reinforced by, the refinements of love that unite the citizens to their wives. A key factor is that for Rousseau love of country manifests itself not primarily in identification with the state or in respectful *considération* for its political leaders, but most fundamentally in love of the citizens for each other.

Every citizen is worthy of *considération* and entitled to demand it in return.

This demand for recognition and respect can, of course, be corrupted by an excess of *amour-propre*. The solution is to channel the energy of self-love in ways that combine republican vigor and polite *douceur* in a manner analogous to the happy balance between love and honor in the golden age. Cultivating a readiness to anger should be part of this effort. Anger cannot be allowed to disturb the peace, but it must be available in moments of crisis for the defense of the city or one's own rights. When oppressors without and within know that the citizens are ready to respond forcefully to slight, they will be more likely to give them the *considération* they claim. Instead of fomenting violence, the potential for anger deters it.

Thus in the dedication Rousseau fosters a sense of frustrated entitlement in his fellow citizens, who have been slighted by Geneva's ruling elite, while at the same time idealizing the internal harmony of his native city. These two gestures can be combined because, as in his depiction of the golden age and in the *Discours* more generally, the energizing claim to redress does not involve any ascription of blame, either to the ruling elite for usurping power or to the citizens for relaxing their vigilance. No one bears any personal responsibility. The implication is that the writer's own indignation is not something for which he should be reproached. It, too, is a legitimate expression of his virtuous citizenship. Of course, as a writer with easy access to publication and a burgeoning international reputation, Rousseau is no ordinary citizen. If in theory all citizens deserve the same consideration, it is hard to imagine any society functioning unless some people take on the role of representing society to itself. In the *Contrat social*, Rousseau will maintain that no individuals can represent others in asserting the general will. Yet, some people must be authorized, explicitly or informally, to articulate, reinforce, or reinterpret social values, to model for others, through their life or their art, what public and private virtue looks like. Can the presence and prestige of such agents foster the vigor of republican pride without generating the socially corrosive anger of resentment—including a resentful backlash on the agent, or in Rousseau's case, author himself? This is one of the questions Rousseau addresses in the *Lettre à d'Alembert sur les spectacles*.

LETTRE À D'ALEMBERT: COMIC, TRAGIC, AND MELANCHOLY ANGER

In his *Encyclopédie* article 'Genève', d'Alembert recommended that Geneva end its puritanical ban on theatrical performances. A well-regulated theater, he argued, would provide moral edification and enlightenment as well as innocent entertainment. Dramatic heroes would provide useful models of virtuous conduct. D'Alembert did not have to add that the plays he had in mind were those of Voltaire, the most celebrated dramatist of the age, who now lived just outside Geneva and hoped to have his works staged in that city. Rousseau reacted with indignation to this campaign to install Voltaire as the city's cultural mentor and more generally to the challenge to his own views about civic virtue as expressed in his two *Discours*. Yet, he could not easily justify his anger. Voltaire was a freethinker and a Frenchman, not a confessing citizen of Geneva like Rousseau, but he could not attack him on these grounds without raising awkward questions. As d'Alembert had insinuated in his article, many of Geneva's pastors privately espoused a rational Christianity closer to deism than to Reformed orthodoxy, and these beliefs were not very different from Rousseau's own. If Voltaire was an outsider, so too, for all practical purposes, was Rousseau. Despite his fervent declaration of Genevan loyalty, Rousseau lived just outside Paris, whereas Voltaire's estate at Ferney, though still in France, was within commuting distance of Geneva. Finally, since in 1752 he had published a drama of his own, *Narcisse*, Rousseau was poorly placed to criticize the theater as such. He had defended his recourse to dramatic writing in the long preface to the published version of his play, but he could only make his case by introducing distinctions and qualifications incompatible with angry *simplicité*.

In replying to d'Alembert, Rousseau needed to do several different things. He had to rebut the arguments about the cultural value of the theater in terms that would appear plausible to sophisticated French readers. He needed to propose alternative means of shoring up civic spirit in Geneva in ways that would demonstrate his identification with the moral world of his fellow citizens. Most important, Rousseau had to defend his personal authenticity to readers from both countries. A detached and patiently rational response to d'Alembert would fail to meet what he took to be an attack on his integrity. On the other hand, since d'Alembert's article was written in a calm and reasonable tone, it would be difficult for Rousseau to adopt an angry stance in reply without exposing himself to accusations of hypocrisy, self-contradiction, or to the supreme error of *ridicule.*

If Rousseau took d'Alembert's article so personally, it was because it seemed to cap a series of challenges to his own public image. As part of the moral 'reform' he undertook to align his conduct more closely with the ideas of the first *Discours*, he had given up a job with the wealthy Dupin family to live in the country on the income from his writing and music copying. However, this did not prevent him from accepting the hospitality of another wealthy patron, Mme d'Épinay, who lent him a house on her country estate. As long as Rousseau could argue that his relationship with his hostess was one of free and egalitarian friendship, rather than patronage, he could claim that he had not compromised his republican independence. But a crisis arose when Mme d'Épinay asked him to accompany her on a trip to Geneva, and he refused. His friends, including Diderot, accused him of ingratitude. He thought the charge unfair: he had no duty to perform any specific task; gratitude, like the generosity that inspires it, must be freely given. Moreover, Rousseau believed Mme d'Épinay was going away to conceal the fact that she was pregnant by her lover Grimm, and he did not want to be entangled in her private affairs. In the *Confessions*, Rousseau recalls the 'tremblement de colère' (fit of anger) he felt when he read a note from Diderot reproaching him for not volunteering to escort his patron to his own native city (*OC* i. 476; *C*, 466).

This anger was all the more acute because it was difficult to justify to those around him. He could not reveal the immediate reason for his refusal, nor could he easily defend his more general position that his independence was compatible with receipt of a favor, and that gratitude to the lady did not entail any actual obligations. Such arguments would have seemed incomprehensible to his French contemporaries, imbued with the rules and constraints of polite sociability.[34] Rousseau found himself striking out in blind haste. 'Quand le premier transport de mon indignation me permit d'écrire, je lui traçai précipitamment la réponse suivante, que je portai sur le champ ... pour la montrer à Mme d'Épinay, à qui dans mon aveugle colère je la voulus lire moi-même ... (When my first transport of indignation had subsided sufficiently for me to be

[34] See Chapter 5 below.

able to write, I hastily scribbled the following reply which I took straight round...to show it to Mme d'Épinay, to whom in my blind fury, I wanted to read it myself...) (*OC* i. 477; *C*, 466). Rousseau describes his anger as blind because he did not yet know how to give it a more articulate and persuasive form.

Unable to defend his position without being misunderstood, Rousseau broke off all relations with Mme d'Épinay, and with Diderot, who until then had been his closest friend.[35] He rented a small house at Montmorency, some distance away. It was there that he received the volume of the *Encyclopédie* that contained d'Alembert's article. In his last conversation with Diderot before his move, he had heard about the piece, and convinced that it was a plan devised in tandem with high-placed Genevans to establish a theater in the city, he became 'indigné de tout ce manège de séduction dans ma patrie' (indignant at this whole machinery for seduction in my native city) (*OC* i. 495; *C*, 483). Now that he had extricated himself from a compromising situation, he saw an opportunity to regain the moral high ground by defending the city's ordinary citizens from the insidious pressure of its false friends. 'L'amour du bien public', he declares in the *Lettre à d'Alembert*, 'est la seule passion qui me fait parler au public, je sais alors m'oublier moi-même, et si quelqu'un m'offense je me tais sur son compte de peur que la colère ne me rende injuste' (Love of the public good is the only passion which causes me to speak to the public; I can then forget myself, and if someone offends me, I keep quiet about him for fear that anger make me unjust) (*OC* v. 120n.; *CW* x. 348).

Given the vehement tone of the *Lettre*, which includes an open announcement of his break with Diderot, Rousseau's declaration cannot be taken at face value. The fact that in this same note about the public good Rousseau also publicly adopts his motto from Juvenal, *vitam impendere vero* (*OC* v. 120n.), suggests that the stance he is taking in the *Lettre* is not simply one of philosophical calm. As we saw in the concluding remarks of the *Confessions* passage about the theft of Mademoiselle Lambercier's comb, for Rousseau impartiality and detachment could be compatible with anger. His experience enabled him to experience injustice to others as an offense to himself, but in such a way that

[35] Rousseau was also angry at Diderot for revealing to their friend Saint-Lambert what Rousseau had told him in confidence: that he had fallen in love with Sophie d'Houdetot, Saint-Lambert's mistress—another 'betrayal' Rousseau could not discuss openly without condemning himself in others' eyes.

the resulting anger was disinterested, in the sense that it was not about him. Nevertheless, it was genuinely his own, not an abstract or borrowed rhetorical stance. The appeal to Juvenal is an attempt to convey the same idea. In the poem, staking their lives on the truth is what the fawning courtiers who are the targets of Juvenal's anger do not do. By adopting the phrase as his motto, however, Rousseau also distinguishes himself from the poem's speaker, who never spells out the extent of his own commitment. As is often the case in classical satire, the reader of Juvenal is invited to ask to what extent the speaker meets his own standards, or whether he compromises by reserving his anger for safe targets.[36] The implication is that the satirist stands at an ironic remove from the indignation he dramatizes. But Rousseau is not appropriating Juvenal's irony. To do so would be to embrace a duality of consciousness open to further suspicion. Rather, he is identifying himself more closely with the expression of indignation itself. He sacrifices his life to the truthful *simplicité* of his reaction to injustice. In the preface to the *Lettre*, Rousseau declares that because of the persecution he has suffered, he is 'rentré dans le néant' (gone back to nothingness) (*OC* v. 7; *CW* x. 256). In other words, Rousseau's commitment to the truth, as manifested in his anger, has already led to a kind of death. The subject who speaks in the *Lettre*, he says, 'outlives himself'.

If there is ironic distance here, it lies in the difficulty of showing how this selfless anger could be embodied in a plausible character and expressed convincingly in a polemical text. Under the pressure of personal challenge, Rousseau could no longer adopt the persona of the philosopher speaking in the public square, as he had done in the more academic *Discours*. His audience was no longer an assembly of 'men' in the abstract. On the other hand, the speaker of Juvenalian satire was too closely entangled with individualized agents and objects of attack. Rousseau's discursive situation here is more like that of the theater, where the spectators constitute a 'public', but one conditioned by national and cultural identity and the prejudices of the day, and are addressed by an author whose convictions can only be expressed through characters who belong to the same world as that of the audience.

[36] Juvenal's attacks on Domitian's court were composed after the emperor's death. In the *Lettre*'s discussion of theater (*OC* v. 32; *CW* x. 276), Rousseau will cite Juvenal himself on this point to sharpen his denunciation of the comic dramatists of his own day: *Dat veniam corvis, vexat censura columbas* ('that's a judgment that acquits the ravens and condemns the doves'), Sat. II.63. See *Juvenal and Persius*, 154–5.

The rambling structure of the *Lettre à d'Alembert* reflects the constant interweaving of Rousseau's critique of the theater as a literary and social institution with a dramatization of the difficulties of his own discursive stance—and particularly of his anger—in relation to the two main theatrical genres: comedy and tragedy. The former is associated primarily with Rousseau's relationship to his French, the latter with his Genevan, audience.[37]

According to critical tradition, comedy reforms morals by provoking laughter at vice. On the contrary, argues Rousseau, the truth is that 'rien n'est moins plaisant et risible que l'indignation de la vertu' (nothing is less funny or laughable than virtue's indignation) (*OC* v. 24–5: *CW* x. 270). Characters whose anger was not itself made comical by their egoism or some other foible would be as boring as a preacher giving a sermon (*OC* v. 43; *CW* x. 285). But why should the critical anger of the comedy be represented by a figure in the comedy, where he will be necessarily exposed to judgment himself? Why couldn't the faults of the various characters be brought out through comic interactions among themselves, or through interaction with a central figure of unpretentious virtue? Rousseau's answer is that while spectators might laugh at seeing their own minor foibles portrayed on stage, what allows them to enjoy the play is the opportunity to laugh at characters in whose foolishness they do not see a reflection of themselves and who allow them to enjoy a feeling of moral superiority. The consequence for dramatic form is that the secondary characters' foolishness must be outweighed by that of the comedy's central figure, onto whom the spectators can project the contradictions and inner conflicts they cannot face in themselves. The indignation of virtue cannot therefore be conveyed by a controlling dramatic perspective but must be represented by a character within the world of the play, and one characterized by a *passion dominante* that puts him in contradiction with himself.

The fact that Molière's *Misanthrope* could have become an exception to this rule, were it not for the force of convention, justifies both the vehemence of Rousseau's attack on the French theater and his despairing sense that his own anger will be misunderstood. The great dramatist could have made Alceste just ridiculous enough to be funny (making this paragon of old-fashioned sincerity fall in love with the coquette

[37] For a full discussion of the *Lettre* as a whole, see Patrick Coleman, *Rousseau's Political Imagination: Rule and Representation in the 'Lettre à d'Alembert'* (Geneva: Droz, 1984).

Célimène was a nice touch, Rousseau says) without sacrificing the integrity of his anger at the corruption and complacency of the characters around him. Yet, Rousseau also maintains that the play only really succeeded because Molière 'betrayed' his character and his own genius by reducing his hero to a mere figure of fun. The notion that Molière's play is split between a conventional comic depiction of Alceste as the self-centered victim of his angry temperament, and a more thoughtful portrayal of a heroic loner driven to anger by the corrupt complacency of those around him, is rightly taken to be a projection of Rousseau's own anxiety about the way other people saw him. But Rousseau's 'Romantic' interpretation of *The Misanthrope* would not have resonated as it did without some basis in the original material. Two elements in Molière's portrayal of anger provide some basis for Rousseau's charge that righteous anger cannot be heard without mockery in the France of his day.

The first involves the social status of Molière's hero. The foolishly angry person in traditional comedy usually belongs to a class of persons whose anger exceeds their entitlement to take offense: impotent old men who still want the privileges of social or erotic power, peasants or vulgar *nouveaux-riches* who claim more honor than their station warrants, and women generally (with the important exception of virtuous ladies spurned or betrayed in love). Unlike the impotent *senex* of Roman comedy, or the pathetic Arnolphe of Molière's *École des femmes,* Alceste is a young and attractive man. He is also high-born, not a servant such as Sganarelle or a social climber like *Le Bourgeois gentilhomme.* Nor, finally, is Alceste a prude, resentful of other people's pleasures. If even the indignation of a character free from such flaws can be made the subject of mockery, can anyone expect their anger to be taken seriously?

Molière's play may in fact be read as a reflection on the tendency in seventeenth-century French culture to delegitimize all claims to anger on the social stage. The ideal of *politesse* and mutual *égards* may be distorted by a hypocritical concern for appearances, but rudeness, even from someone like Alceste, will no longer be tolerated. From one point of view, this represents a move toward greater equality of status. No longer could an elite minority claim entitlement to anger as its privilege, including the violent action that might result from it. In the *Lettre à d'Alembert,* Rousseau himself refers to this progress in civilization when he endorses the French monarchy's ban on dueling. He also cites with approval an incident in which Louis XIV threw his cane out the window rather than strike a courtier who offended him (*OC* v. 66; *CW* x. 304).

At the same time, to delegitimize anger in a society still based to a large degree on personal standing may be to remove one of the few opportunities available for resisting oppression. Increasingly unable to define the expansion of the absolute monarchy in terms of personal slight, noblemen were deprived of the only basis on which they could respond to encroachments on their independence. Under such a regime, a comedy about anger would have to depict everyone's anger as foolish. Now, only the king enjoyed an uncontested right to take offense, and he could not himself be represented on stage and thus subjected to dramatic critique.[38]

Rousseau was not wrong, therefore, in seeing Alceste's outrage as a response to the very impossibility of taking offense at the way of his world from a position within that world. The real problem is that Rousseau refuses to consider the possibility that this aspect of the play might constitute only one layer of meaning within a complex work of art, which is also, and primarily, a comedy about self-regard. His view also seems to be that a dramatist cannot leave any tension or ambivalence unresolved in his play without jeopardizing his claim to moral esteem. Since Molière was both a great artist and a popular entertainer, Rousseau has to conclude that Molière intuited the 'real' character of his misanthrope and then betrayed his own creation. Alceste cannot be a man of deep contradictions; rather, he must be a figure of simple integrity, one whose behavior had to be set at odds with his essence in order to make the audience laugh at him. In comic drama, Rousseau is saying, the author cannot embody righteous anger in a character without undermining either the moral authority or the social acceptability of that emotion.

Reflection on this dilemma introduces a melancholy note into Rousseau's conception of artistic agency, a note echoed and amplified in the preface to the *Lettre*. As we will see in a moment, however, he does not present that melancholy as evidence only of his own wounded sensibility. Rather, it becomes a token of his authenticity as an author, transcending any tensions or contradictions that might emerge in his own discourse. As in the preface to the *Dialogues*, melancholy is more than an internalized response to slight; it is an emotional claim on others designed to forestall further slight. Here, Rousseau builds on a second undercurrent in Molière's *Misanthrope*. The play's subtitle

[38] On comedy and absolutism, see Jean-Marie Apostolides, *Le Prince sacrifié: théâtre et politique au temps de Louis XIV* (Paris: Minuit, 1985), ch. 5.

describes Alceste as *atrabilaire*, that is, as suffering from black bile. As Pierre Naudin has shown, traditional humoral medicine defined this condition as an 'adust' or burnt form of choler. It is anger shading off into melancholy.[39] Whether Molière intended the spectators to think of Alceste as a melancholy man and, if so, how this would affect their reaction to his anger may be disputed. Yet, however foolish his anger is judged to be, the general delegitimization of that emotion is cause enough for melancholy.

The shift to the language of melancholy is also a response to the impossibility of conveying righteous anger in tragedy. Near the end of the *Lettre* Rousseau considers the suggestion that one could foster public spirit in the citizens of Geneva by depicting in dramatic form the 'great souls' of the city's ancestors as they confronted the misfortunes of the past (*OC* v. 110; *CW* x. 339). In France, Voltaire had already expanded the range of 'classical' tragedy to include inspiring incidents from national history in *Adélaïde du Guesclin* (1734), and his example would be followed in the second half of the century in such plays as Belloy's *Siège de Calais* (1765). Historical tragedy would later play an important nation-building role in Germany when it was taken up by Goethe and Schiller. The development of a repertoire of national plays would at first sight seem to fulfill the wish expressed in the dedication of the *Discours sur l'inégalité*, that of representing to the citizens the heartening image of their own civic energy, but in the *Lettre à d'Alembert* Rousseau raises two objections to such a plan. The first is prudential. If the authors of such plays succeed in stirring the citizens' patriotic fervor, by recalling, for example, the day in 1602 when Geneva successfully repelled an invasion by neighboring Savoy, they may reawaken hostility toward a people with which the city now lives in peace. Rousseau does not add that the citizens' patriotic anger might also turn against those within the city who have been guilty of colluding, politically or culturally, with foreign powers. Given Geneva's recent history of civil unrest, notably a popular revolt in 1737 that had been settled by the mediation of France, Rousseau did not need to spell out the local implications of what he was saying. As an alternative to national tragedy, he proposes the establishment of peaceful civic

[39] Pierre Naudin, *L'Expérience et le sentiment de la solitude de l'aube des Lumières à la Révolution* (Paris: Klincksieck, 1995), 220–1. Naudin's analysis refines and corrects the earlier interpretation of René Jasinski, who saw Alceste as a straightforward melancholic in *Molière et le Misanthrope* (Paris: Armand Colin, 1951).

festivals in which 'nothing' is represented other than the citizens' love for each other (*OC* v. 115; *CW* x. 344). Any outbursts of martial spirit would then quickly be neutralized by the enchantments of domestic bliss (*OC* v. 123n.; *CW* x. 351).

In any case, Rousseau assumes that dramas drawn from Geneva's history would have little popular appeal. So colonized are the Genevans by the prestige of foreign literary tradition that they would consider a dramatic hero who was not of royal blood or mythical prestige unworthy of their attention. Apostrophizing the 'worthy citizens' of the past, Rousseau expresses his indignation. 'Ah, dignes Citoyens! Vous fûtes des Héros, sans doute; mais votre obscurité vous avilit, vos noms communs déshonorent vos grandes âmes, et nous ne sommes plus assez grands nous-mêmes pour vous savoir admirer' (Ah, worthy citizens, you were, doubtless, heroes but your obscurity abases you, your common names dishonor your great souls, and we are no longer great enough ourselves to admire you) (*OC* v. 110; *CW* x. 339–40). The implication is that Rousseau, too, cannot influence the citizens' collective self-representation from within the cultural horizon of Geneva. Neither in a comic nor in a tragic mode can his indignation be deployed without distortion; at best, it is useless. Indeed, whatever influence he might hope to exercise will be an indirect and negative one, through the dramatization of anger's futility. This is matter for regret, but not entirely. For a consequence of Rousseau's argument is that the charge against him, that despite his identification with Geneva he does not live there, loses its point. If it is impossible to represent the city to itself authentically and effectively from within, he cannot be reproached for taking his distance.

In reflecting on his authorial role in the *Lettre*, Rousseau does not justify his anger, but neither does he claim to have transcended it. Instead, he adopts the persona of the melancholy misanthrope as his own. Since he has abandoned the corruptions of Paris life to live in solitude, he writes in the preface, his angry passion has calmed down. 'Loin des vices qui nous irritent, on en parle avec moins d'indignation' (Far from the vices that irritate us, we speak of them with less indignation) (*OC* v. 7; *CW* x. 255). This newfound equanimity is not entirely a good thing, however. Rousseau is now called upon to defend his honor as a Genevan citizen by showing that, despite his association with the *Encyclopédie*, he shares the civic and religious convictions of his compatriots (*OC* v. 6; *CW* x. 255). Too calm a response would be inadequate to the occasion, for the more rational and dispassionate his reply, the more Rousseau would appear to value philosophy over patriotic 'zeal'. Zeal is a passion Rousseau would normally want to temper, as in his discussion of Genevan drama, because of its potentially destructive power. That is not the problem here, for while his zeal, and the indignation that goes with it, is as heartfelt as ever, its assertive energy has been sapped. Illness has robbed it of its vigor, while the betrayal of his 'Aristarque' (his friend and counselor Diderot) has deprived him of crucial intellectual support.[40] Without the 'talent' needed to give it discursive form, zeal is too weak to be harmful. Rousseau can therefore be zealous in good conscience; his patriotism is nothing other than praiseworthy.

Like a speaker's claims to speak 'more in sorrow than in anger', anticipations of futility are a familiar feature of political rhetoric. They disarm any suspicion that the speaker is blinded by his emotion or deluded about the extent of his power. In Rousseau's writing, however, the pathos of this lament has an additional function: it gives retrospective validation to the anger Rousseau says he no longer feels. In Rousseau, 'talent' signifies something more than intellectual endowment; it is also a form of will, since its function is to husband the energy of passion, the better to give it articulate expression. Rousseau's lament for the loss of his talent in the preface to the *Lettre à d'Alembert* encourages the reader to feel just how valuable and powerful that talent must have been. Rousseau also declares that he would not now be writing about such sensitive subjects as Genevan religion and social peace if he had not already written on other, less vital topics (*OC* v. 5). The very fact that he had been willing to intervene on less important matters creates, he claims, an obligation to speak now, but this obligation is at the same time an authorization, since what really created the obligation was the success of those interventions. Were Rousseau not already famous, no one would care whether he said anything now, and readers must acknowledge that it was the animating energy of anger in his writing that made it successful. In terms he will later repeat in the preface to his *Dialogues*, Rousseau hopes his readers will not find in the *Lettre à d'Alembert* 'cette âpreté qu'on me reprochait, mais qui me faisait lire . . . ' (that bitterness . . . for which I was reproached but which caused me to be read) (*OC* v. 7; *CW* x. 256). The 'but' here is crucial.

[40] Aristarchos was considered to be the greatest literary critic of antiquity. He was credited with establishing the text of Homer's poems as we now have them. To flatter Diderot with this name, therefore, is also a way for Rousseau to flatter himself.

The contradictions of which he is accused are thrown back onto the reading public. By contrast, even as he complains of illness and mourns the loss of that short period of 'fermentation' that allowed his talent to shine Rousseau can claim to be at one with himself. Any guilt his anger might have caused him can be allayed, since with the loss of his talent he has paid a steep price for his earlier boldness. Rousseau's melancholy thus preserves the integrity of his anger through the mourning of its loss. It is still his voice, after all, which is heard throughout the work. According to its author, the *Lettre* consists largely of 'digressions' into which he has 'thrown' himself in order to find the stimulation he no longer draws from within (*OC* v. 6–7; *CW* x. 255). If adopting the motto from Juvenal indicated a desire to die into an anger that was as pure, uncompromising, and straightforward as Alceste's, the actual dynamic of the text is presented as a constant compensatory movement away from an anger he can no more successfully embody in his own feeble self than can the commonplace heroes of Geneva's past. The writer's dramatization of his indignation reworks the compromised objectivity of comedy and the failed dignity of tragic pathos into a claim for a melancholy authority, located in the empty space left by the failure of the two theatrical genres to make good on their promises.

JULIE AND THE CONTAINMENT OF ANGER

Rousseau wrote the *Lettre à d'Alembert* in the midst of composing his novel *Julie, ou la nouvelle Héloïse*. In the *Lettre*, he suggested that Richardson's *Clarissa* represented a 'sublime' exception to the general perniciousness of literature, and that under certain conditions, as in England, could provide opportunities for the kind of contemplative readings conducive to true happiness (*OC* v. 75; *CW* x. 311). The religious connotations of the expression are significant; they point to a relationship between the exemplary character and the 'world' very different from what we have seen in Rousseau's critique of comedy and tragedy. That relationship is characterized by a more productive form of alienation, one which can be incorporated within the dynamic of the work itself. This claim is not grounded in contemporary theories of fiction; rather, it is made a posteriori, as Rousseau takes stock of what he had accomplished in his own novel. In the 'second', post-publication preface to *Julie*, Rousseau reflects on the way readers become convinced of his heroine's reality—that is to say, her status as a figure distinct from and resistant to their imaginative identification and appropriation—by the experience of mourning her death. They are also surprised to find Julie's personal failings do not undermine the moral authority she has for them by the end of the book.[41] Rereading the novel, Rousseau experiences the same complex reaction to his own work. It is his creation, an expression of his intimate self, and so he can justly take as addressed to him all the letters grateful readers wrote to the author of a book that comforted and consoled them. At the same time, the novel has its own independent integrity. As 'editor' of the letters that make up this epistolary fiction, he acknowledges responsibility for it (*OC* ii. 26; *CW* vi. 19), but with the confident feeling that the book's goodness is unaffected by any defect in his own sensibility. Most notably, while the novel may challenge conventional notions about feminine virtue, it cannot provoke in its readers any legitimate anger. In the novel's first preface, Rousseau says he can see how someone who only read the first part of the book might throw the book down in anger, but he could not respect anyone who could do the same after reading the whole novel (*OC* ii. 6; *CW* vi. 4). He would not be angry at them, however. Anyone who responds in this way is too lacking in sensibility for their opinion to affect him.

Yet, anger is by no means absent from the novel itself. In its 'good' and 'bad' forms, it appears throughout the story. Any story of star-crossed lovers will of course include some angry protest at the fate that keeps them apart. The hero, known only by the chivalric nickname St Preux,[42] expresses justified indignation at the social prejudices invoked by Julie's father, Baron d'Étange, when he forbids her from marrying a commoner of modest means, while Julie experiences the 'premier mouvement de colère que j'éprouvai de ma vie' when St Preux doubts her love (the first angry reaction I have ever experienced) (ii, 7; *OC* ii. 211; *CW* vi. 172).[43] Later, when he has accepted Julie's marriage to Wolmar, St Preux can still be provoked to anger when Julie's father alludes mockingly to the past (v, 7; *OC* ii. 606; *CW* vi. 496). He cannot renounce that emotion entirely without betraying the love that defines

[41] See Coleman, *Reparative Realism*, ch. 2.

[42] Philip Stewart has argued convincingly for retaining Rousseau's spelling of the hero's name, or rather the pseudonym by which he is known, rather than Saint-Preux, as in many modern editions, on the grounds that '"Saint-Preux" is a name and "St Preux" is a saint, albeit a playfully fictive one' (*CW* vi. xvii).

[43] References to the body of the novel are to the part and letter number, then to the pages of the edition and translation.

his identity. On the other hand, St Preux deserves reproach for 'l'aveugle colère' that prompts him to challenge Édouard to a duel when he thinks his friend has insulted that love (i, 60: *OC* ii. 163; *CW* vi. 132).

In all these cases, the character's anger is limited in scope and effect. The duel never takes place, nor does the lovers' anger challenge the social order as such. Not that Rousseau downplays the element of violence and injustice in that order. When Julie's father promises his daughter to M. de Wolmar, the man who had saved his life in battle, he does not think of asking her consent. On the contrary, he himself gets angry when Julie balks at becoming the instrument of her father's gratitude (iii, 18; *OC* ii. 348; *CW* vi. 286). In what becomes a major turning-point in the story, the Baron's anger becomes so violent that he strikes Julie with a force that precipitates the miscarriage of the child she is carrying. This child represented Julie's last hope for changing her father's mind, but the moment is so traumatic that Julie cannot experience any anger herself. Indeed, she only names the father's anger after it has been replaced by sudden concern for her welfare. 'Ici finit le triomphe de la colère et commence celui de la nature' (Here ended the triumph of anger and began that of nature) (ii, 68; *OC* ii. 175; *CW* vi. 143). That Rousseau does not have her meet anger with anger helps him redeem the morally 'fallen' Julie in the eyes of his readers. Rousseau has a sense for how far he can challenge their prejudices. The offense to Julie is avenged only on the literary level: in this epistolary novel the Baron is quoted by other characters, but he writes no letters of his own.[44]

In contrast with the Baron, M. de Wolmar, the man Julie is forced to marry, never gets angry. His equanimity is initially a source of puzzlement—why would a man of so little emotion want to get married?—and then of admiration in the other characters. He is 'un maître équitable et sans colère' (an equitable and dispassionate master) (iv, 10; *OC* ii. 448; *CW* vi. 368) who commands universal respect even from those he disciplines. He does not require others to stifle their emotions, however, and creates such an atmosphere of confidence that even St Preux finds himself at home on his rival's estate. And yet, the absence of anger in Wolmar eventually becomes a source of a discomfort more subtle but no less disturbing than excess of anger in the Baron. Praiseworthy as it may be, it also suggests a crucial defect of sensibility. Julie

[44] The one short note he writes (iii, 10; ii. 325) serves only to prove the rule.

and St Preux do their best to transform their passion into a more disinterested platonic love, but the value of that struggle depends on the resistance they meet, and on maintaining the continuity of their emotional identity. The difficulty of the enterprise is suggested by the hidden resentments still harbored by St Preux. Julie's cousin Claire relates how he reacted when one day she teased him too far: 'Tu ne vis de tes jours pareille colère' (You never in all your days saw such anger) (vi, 2; *OC* ii. 643; *CW* vi. 529). This anger, clearly disproportionate to the occasion, signals that all is not well beneath the apparent calm of the Clarens community. The fact that Wolmar shows no sign of jealousy only makes matters worse. How can St Preux insist on the reality of the wrong he suffered (and thereby begin truly to deal with it) when Wolmar does not know what it means to be wronged? Wolmar cannot offer forgiveness, only indulgence for feelings he cannot comprehend.

Julie keeps her own thoughts a secret, but she is the one who finally identifies a reason to be angry at Wolmar: his atheism. What St Preux calls Wolmar's 'tristes aveux' (sad admissions) about his inability to believe in the existence of God 'donnent bien plus d'affliction que de colère à Julie' (cause Julie more sorrow than anger) (v, 5; *OC* ii. 594; *CW* vi. 487). But why should Julie be angry at all? Wolmar's atheism, we are told, is not the 'ironique fierté des esprits forts', who reject divine truth out of arrogant pride. He simply has no religious faith, and for this he is not to blame. On one level, therefore, Rousseau only mentions anger to emphasize the difference between Julie's reaction and that of the intolerant religious authorities of his day. Julie's distress stems instead from compassion: Wolmar lacks the consolations of faith she herself needs so much. Still, from a dramatic point of view, the fact that the idea of anger is raised at all in St Preux's report of Julie's feelings suggests that she experiences Wolmar's atheism at least to some extent as a refusal to acknowledge his participation in the essential incompletion and dependence of the human condition that she herself experiences so painfully. However considerate his behavior might be, Wolmar's failure of imaginative identification with her suffering becomes a source of hurt.

At the end of the novel, Rousseau hints that Julie's edifying death will lead to Wolmar's religious conversion, but he refrains from turning his novel into an apologetic, just as he refrained from presenting too forceful a critique of the patriarchal social order. As 'editor' of the letters, he does not need to take a stand; it is enough to have achieved a delicate and dynamic balance between the unruly imperatives of passion and the constraints of social order. By making room for, and then containing, the dynamic of anger within its imaginative world, the novel, as Rousseau sees it, legitimizes its own cultural authority. The book's phenomenal success vindicated Rousseau's confidence that it would not provoke any lasting anger in its readers. On the contrary, as we shall see in the next chapter, they responded to it with unprecedented expressions of gratitude for the ways the novel created a space in which they could articulate their own conflicted feelings. This space is that of the heroine's felt absence, and therefore reflects, and reflects on, the turn in the *Lettre à d'Alembert* away from the impossible social space of the comic or tragic stage to the psychological space opened up by the author's melancholy withdrawal. The double paradox of *Julie* is that the heroine became more present, more real, through her death, and that the author also became more present and real to his readers by removing himself from the novel and letting it speak for itself. The problem with Rousseau's last great work, *Émile*, is that the author turns this paradox inside out: he wants to reinsert himself into the center of the work while preserving the benefits of granting it its own independent dynamic. This problem will become apparent in *Émile*'s treatment of anger.

ÉMILE AND THE 'PROFESSION DE FOI'

The success of *Julie* vindicated Rousseau's ambition to produce a book a book that would at once articulate strong social critique, create a space for imaginative play, and offer his readers moral and psychological help. His educational treatise *Émile* suffered a very different fate. While it was enthusiastically received by many readers, it was condemned by religious and political authorities in both Paris and Geneva. Rousseau was forced to flee to rural Switzerland to avoid arrest. Even before the work appeared, however, Rousseau exhibited a strange combination of emotions. The non-dogmatic and only nominally Christian theism of the 'Profession de foi du Vicaire savoyard' included in the book was bound to attract the censors' ire, but Rousseau's apprehension about the fate of his work went beyond any reasonable anxiety. He suspected everyone involved in its publication—publishers, printers, even the sympathetic Malesherbes, the French official in charge of the book industry—of hostile intentions. The possibility that the book's exceptional intellectual and practical value might not be recognized was apparently so threatening a prospect to Rousseau's sense of himself that he could not maintain the kind of equanimity he depicted in the book itself. Indeed, the intensity of Rousseau's anxiety suggests that while the severity of the official reactions to *Émile* may have been unexpected, they confirmed some underlying unease in the author about how self-evident the book's cultural value really was.[45]

Some of this unease may be related to the way the author's relationship to his material evolves over the course of the text. The tutor, who at first is mostly a mouthpiece for Rousseau's educational principles, becomes more of a character within the text, just as Émile changes from an allegorical exemplar into a more rounded character. The tutor's interactions with his pupil become episodes in a story whose coherence is more novelistic than philosophical in the theoretical sense.[46] If the tutor is a character within the story, then, as in a novel, we look for the critical perspectives the author might be bringing to bear in dramatizing the character's actions for us. At the same time, however, the tutor's voice becomes more and more identified with that of the author, who thereby brings the text into a more intimate personal connection with himself. Especially in the sections devoted to Émile's courtship of Sophie, the woman of his dreams, the tutor seems to be staging the drama of Émile's emotional education as much for his own satisfaction (and that of the author) as for the reader's benefit. One might say that Rousseau wants to be the first to enjoy the positive contribution his

[45] In this respect, *Émile* offers a striking contrast with the *Contrat social*, in some ways an even more radical work, but about which Rousseau had much less anxiety, perhaps because he did not see it as having the same popular appeal. Unusually for Rousseau, the *Contrat social* does not express much concern about the authority it claims or the reactions it might provoke. Nor does it consider anger as a factor in human interactions within its ideal republic. In one of its most famous passages, for example, Rousseau underscores the paradox that the citizen's political freedom is inseparable from his commitment to obey the general will by saying that the political body may legitimately force him to be free. Yet, there is no hint that, as a person, the citizen may react with anger to such constraint, or that the political authorities may themselves be moved to anger at any defiance. Hobbes, by contrast, expected individuals to resent being punished for their disobedience, even by a legitimate sovereign (*Leviathan*, ch. 21, para. 22). Such emotional considerations play no role in Rousseau's discussion, which merely explicates what he calls 'l'artifice et le jeu de la machine politique' (the device . . . and the operation of the political machine (I.7; *OC* iii. 364; G 2, 53). The largely technical focus of the *Contrat social* on the mechanics of political will and the mathematics of its measurement, in which the claims the author makes stand or fall on their own internal cogency, no doubt explains the difference.

[46] The best discussion of the genre of *Émile* is that of Laurence Mall, *Émile ou les figures de la fiction* (Oxford: Voltaire Foundation, 2002).

book is offering the world. As a consequence, despite the book's use of the tutor or the Vicaire as mediating figures, a critique of *Émile*'s ideas becomes hard to distinguish from criticism of the authorial agency at work in and behind the book.[47] This personalized authorial agency is all the more vulnerable to attack in that the boldness of its interventions is not mitigated, as in the *Discours sur l'inégalité* and the *Lettre à d'Alembert*, by reference to the exile or illness that distances the author from his discourse. Nor is this agency mediated, as in *Julie*, by a literary form in which the destructive potential latent even in the most positive ideal is acknowledged and contained. *Émile*'s justification lies in its postulation of an essential goodness that makes it safe for the author to enter its world whole-heartedly and find his own reflection in it. A study of the way anger is discussed and dramatized within *Émile* will show that this move comes at a price.

In the first books of *Émile*, anger is viewed as a disease to be avoided. 'Tant que les enfants ne trouveront de résistance que dans les choses et jamais dans les volontés, ils ne deviendront ni mutins ni colères et se conserveront mieux en santé' (As long as children find resistance only in things and never in wills, they will become neither rebellious nor irascible and will preserve their health better) (*OC* iv. 287; *E*, 66). Like the Stoics and their early modern admirers, Rousseau views anger as the result of a judgment we make about the world, and rational judgment tells us not to be angry when we trip over a stone. Since no offense is being given, there is no cause for anger, and if we can look at everything bad that happens to us as the expression of impersonal necessity rather than malignant intention, we will never get angry at all. Following this advice, however, was generally considered to be difficult; a long course of philosophical therapy might be required to adjust our worldview along these lines. Rousseau, by contrast, believes that with proper foresight one can raise children whose potential for anger will never need to be tamed. The wise tutor creates an environment in which the child can learn on his own, without interference from other people. He (the paradigmatic child is a boy) will not do or get whatever he wants, but since the obstacles he encounters will appear to arise only from his material environment, his frustration will exhaust

[47] I am indebted on this point to Michael Bell, *Open Secrets: Literature, Education, and Authority from J.-J. Rousseau to J. M. Coetzee* (Cambridge: Cambridge University Press, 2007).

itself in physiological reactions of no lasting consequence. Free from the pressure or projection of a hostile will, Émile cannot himself be willful.

When, at a subsequent stage of his education, the boy does enter the world of human interaction, he will see that other people do get angry, and he may be tempted to imitate them. Here again, the solution does not lie in striving for mastery. Rather, anger is presented as a disease whose ugly effects the child will naturally want to avoid.

Laissez venir l'enfant: étonné du spectacle, il ne manquera pas de vous questionner . . . Il voit un visage enflammé, des yeux étincelants, un geste menaçant, il entend des cris; tous signes que le corps n'est pas dans son assiette. Dites-lui posément, sans affectation, sans mystère: Ce pauvre homme est malade, il est dans un accès de fièvre. Vous pouvez de là tirer occasion de lui donner, mais en peu de mots, une idée des maladies et de leurs effets: car cela est aussi de la nature, et c'est un des liens de la nécessité auxquels il se doit sentir assujetti.

Let the child come; surprised at the spectacle, he will not fail to question you . . . He sees an inflamed face, glittering eyes, threatening gestures; he hears shouts—all signs that the body is out of kilter. Tell him calmly, without affectation, and without mystery, 'This poor man is sick; he is in a fit of fever.' On this basis you can find occasions to give him, but in a few words, an idea of illnesses and their effects, for that, too, belongs to nature and is one of the bonds of necessity to which he should feel himself subjected. (*OC* iv. 328; *E*, 96)

In presenting anger as an unattractive, even repulsive, physical disturbance, Rousseau follows Seneca and Plutarch, but with an important difference. For the ancient writers, anger was to be avoided because its ugliness marred the beauty of the noble soul.[48] It was an argument that appealed to human self-regard. Men of worth and status would not want to sully their dignity with unseemly displays of ungoverned feeling. For Rousseau, it is important that freedom from anger should not itself become a source of pride. It is precisely man's tendency to imagine himself the center of the universe that feeds his propensity to anger and leads him to see injustice everywhere he looks: 'il voit partout de la mauvaise volonté: le sentiment d'une injustice prétendue aigrissant son naturel, il prend tout le monde en haine, et sans jamais savoir gré de la complaisance il s'indigne de toute opposition' (He sees ill will everywhere. The feeling of an alleged injustice souring his nature, he develops

[48] Plutarch, 'On the Avoidance of Anger' 458a–459b, in Plutarch, *Essays*, tr. Robin Waterfield and ed. Ian Kidd (Harmondsworth: Penguin, 1992), 188–90. Note that this concern is present even when one is beating one's slave. See also Paul Veyne's introduction to Sénèque, *Entretiens, Lettres à Lucilius* (Paris: Laffont, 1993).

hatred toward everyone; and, without ever being grateful for helpfulness, he is indignant at every opposition) (*OC* iv. 314; *E*, 87). What Émile finds in this spectacle is a lesson about his own weakness. In comparing anger to an illness, Seneca had focused on the prospects for a cure. Here, Rousseau emphasizes instead that all human beings are subject to disease. All Émile can do is minimize his risk of contagion by distancing himself in distaste from the afflicted party. The point seems to be that if Émile himself becomes angry he will lose, not the respect, but the sympathy of other people. He will be shunned just when he is beginning to enjoy the pleasures of sociability.

In the first book of *Émile*, however, just before his recommendation that children be made to obey 'things' rather than 'wills', Rousseau presents a very different image of anger. He remembers seeing a child hit by a nurse exhausted by his constant crying:

Je le crus intimidé. Je me disais: ce sera une âme servile dont on n'obtiendra rien que par la rigueur. Je me trompais; le malheureux suffoquait de colère, il avait perdu la respiration, je le vis devenir violet. Un moment après vinrent les cris aigus, tous les signes du ressentiment, de la fureur, du désespoir de cet âge étaient dans ses accents. Je craignis qu'il n'expirât dans cette agitation. Quand j'aurais douté que le sentiment du juste et de l'injuste fût inné dans le cœur de l'homme, cet exemple seul m'aurait convaincu. Je suis sûr qu'un tison ardent tombé par hasard sur la main de cet enfant lui eût été moins sensible que ce coup assez léger, mais donné dans l'intention manifeste de l'offenser.

I believed he was intimidated. I said to myself, 'This will be a servile soul from which one will get nothing except by severity.' I was mistaken. The unfortunate was suffocating with anger; he had lost his breath; I saw him become violet. A moment after came sharp screams; all the signs of the resentment, fury, and despair of this age were in his accents. I feared he would expire in this agitation. If I had doubted that the sentiment of the just and the unjust were innate in the heart of man, this example alone would have convinced me. I am sure that a live ember fallen by chance on this child's hand would have made less of an impression than this blow, rather light but given in the manifest intention of offending him. (*OC* iv. 286–7; *E*, 65–6)

To see malevolent intentions everywhere is a mistake born of diseased self-love, but failing to react when one is wronged is the mark of a 'servile soul'. The proud child may need a lesson in humility, but the child who cannot distinguish injustice from necessity cannot be educated at all. He can only be trained. Not that his lack of spirit makes him more docile. On the contrary, if he cannot recognize injustice he cannot recognize justice either. Only the person who has a sense of the respect owed to him can acknowledge what he owes to other people, that is to say, become a true moral agent.

The two elements of pride and humility are combined in the story of Émile's initiation into the world of private property. The tutor encourages Émile to learn about agriculture by sowing some beans on a small patch of land on the estate where he is living. The boy is thrilled when the young plants start to grow but is outraged when one day he finds his beans plowed under (*OC* iv. 331; *E*, 98).[49] Émile's righteous indignation is short-lived. He discovers that Robert, the gardener of the estate, had previously sown melon seeds on that same plot of land. Angry at seeing his work gone to waste, Robert has taken his revenge by destroying Émile's beans. The reader then learns the whole incident has been staged by the tutor. Émile's right to the fruit of his labor is limited by the prior rights of others. It is important that Émile feel the anger of dispossession, but then that anger must give way to the recognition that his personal claim to property exists only as part of a larger social system. The tutor arranges a compromise by which Robert grants Émile use of part of the land in return for a share of the crop (*OC* iv. 332; *E*, 99).

On one level, the story simply illustrates sound Lockean doctrine. Yet, considered in the context of the larger story of Émile's relationship to anger, the story is equally important for what it omits. Once the immediate shock of dispossession has gone, Émile and Robert do not transfer their anger onto any third party. There is no suggestion here that one might be justified in getting angry at those persons or institutions that created the potential for conflict by inventing the notion of private property in the first place, or by allowing unequal distribution of property to be enshrined in law. Instead of leading to political unrest, anger is absorbed into a sense of shared vulnerability to forces beyond one's control. In this respect, the scene recalls the depiction of pity in the *Discours sur l'inégalité*. The primary and most natural form of solidarity is a shared awareness of human weakness, in which the primitive sense of one's due is replaced by compassion.[50]

[49] For a more extensive discussion of this episode in relation to Rousseau's ideas about property, see Patrick Coleman, 'Property, Politics, and Personality in Rousseau', in Susan Staves and John Brewer, eds, *Early Modern Conceptions of Property* (London: Routledge, 1995), 254–74.

[50] Similarly, the Vicaire savoyard praises anger at social injustice while counseling prudence in its exercise: 'Voit-on dans une rue ou sur un chemin quelque acte de violence et d'injustice? à l'instant un mouvement de colère et d'indignation s'élève au fond du cœur, et nous porte à prendre la défense de l'opprimé' (One sees some act of violence and

The second point is one that has important implications for the aesthetics of the book as a whole. In contrast with Rousseau's earlier examples of the indignant baby and the 'diseased' angry man, we are not shown what Émile or Robert look like in their anger. The two characters do not react to each other's anger as if to a disease, nor is the reader invited to contemplate their distorted features in distaste. The only physical expressions Rousseau describes are Émile's tears and pathetic cries when he finds his beans destroyed. The implication is that Rousseau wants his characters to react sympathetically to each other's emotion, and the reader to identify with them both. The effect complements that of the earlier story about the indignant infant. The spectacle of the infant's anger commanded a certain respect, but it was not an agreeable sight. His physiological response distorts his appearance just as much as does the angry man's 'illness'. The infant may be innocent, but he is unlikely to inspire the kind of identification that might encourage readers to indulge their own vehement emotions. By giving the infant a slightly off-putting appearance, Rousseau manages to endorse the righteousness of his anger without encouraging anger in his readers.

Curiously though, Rousseau insulates Émile from contact with such ambivalent spectacles as that of the angry child. That child, it must be pointed out, is not the baby Émile but an anonymous boy introduced for a moment into the book from the reality outside the text. Émile is later shown recoiling from the ugliness of the angry man, but he is not made to witness, nor is he invited to share, the infant's indignation at injustice. Of course, Émile is no 'servile soul', but he never faces any challenge to his dignity, at least, not the kind of slight that normally demands a forceful riposte and therefore puts either his equanimity or his honor at risk. Indeed, his natural spiritedness is never channeled into interactions with others with the potential to generate gratitude or resentment.

injustice in the street or on the road. Instantly an emotion of anger and indignation is aroused in the depths of the heart, and it leads us to take up the defense of the oppressed). Yet, he immediately goes on to add: 'mais un devoir plus puissant nous retient, et les lois nous ôtent le droit de protéger l'innocence' (but a more powerful duty restrains us, and the laws take from us the right of protecting innocence) (*OC* iv. 596–7; *E*, 287–8). The Vicaire does not specify what these laws might be. Presumably they are those that prohibit private retaliatory violence. Whatever the case, Rousseau's point seems to be similar to the one implicit in the Robert story: the capacity for anger is a crucial good, but one without practical application. For more on pity in the *Discours*, see Chapter 5.

The situation changes when Émile reaches what Rousseau calls the 'age of the passions'. The expression is somewhat misleading, since Émile has been subject to passion before, as his anger in the garden story demonstrates. What Rousseau means by passions here are those feelings which cannot be sublimated by redirecting them to the transcendent general idea or value behind the specific object of desire. A passion in this strong sense can only be satisfied by a particular object. The most important of these passions is the desire for a sexual partner.[51] Despite the Platonizing overtones with which Rousseau colors his discussion, he realizes such passions are not fully amenable to philosophical therapy. If all goes well, Émile's preference will not be a blind one, but even an informed choice is still a decision based on comparison and affective preference. However controlled the process or considered the decision, it implicates the self in ways that are at odds with either the Stoic or the pathetic acceptance of impersonal necessity. A similar issue will arise in the 'Profession de foi du Vicaire savoyard'. One reason this text provoked such a scandal was that for all Rousseau's talk about a universal and 'natural' religion, he makes it clear that the Vicaire's adherence to a particular religious worldview involved a choice, one that could have gone another way. Those who based their claims for and against religion on evidence that demanded unequivocal assent could only protest at such an account of belief.[52]

In contrast with *Julie*, however, where the contingencies and negative side-effects of even the best choices can be openly thematized within the dramatic framework of the epistolary narrative and integrated into the larger dynamic of an elegiac novel, the educational treatise cannot countenance any real negativity. This is because Rousseau insists that the ideal of equanimity must be embodied in the characters (who therefore can never be deeply at odds with themselves) and not just in the overall point of view of the work. This strategy seems to be crucial to achieving *Émile*'s constructive purpose. But despite Rousseau's determination to present the relationship between Émile and Sophie, the tutor and Émile, the Vicaire and God, and ultimately the implied

[51] The only other example Rousseau gives is hunting, which may be seen as the passionate version of the natural search for food. To distract Émile from the pursuit of women, the tutor encourages him to hunt game instead.

[52] One could say something similar about Émile's choice of a country to inhabit at the end of his political education. In this instance, however, Rousseau does not deem it necessary for him to make any specific comparisons or decide on a specific place. Émile can live anywhere he is left alone.

author with his reader, as entirely conflict-free, these relationships, if they are to be more than allegorical, must include a personal dimension, manifested in contingent and contestable action. The consequences can be seen in the curious role anger, or its avoidance, plays in the dynamic of love and religious faith in books four and five of *Émile.*

Rousseau's treatment of women's right to get angry begins in conventional fashion. Women are made to obey men, he writes. A young girl 'doit apprendre de bonne heure à souffrir même l'injustice, et à supporter les torts d'un mari sans se plaindre' (ought to learn early to endure even injustice and to bear a husband's wrongs without complaining). She should learn that nature did not give women 'des traits si délicats pour les défigurer par la colère' (delicate features to be disfigured by anger) (*OC* iv. 710–11; *E*, 370). And yet, one of the features that distinguish Sophie from ordinary girls is a praiseworthy capacity for anger. She listens with 'indignation' to suitors who flatter her with empty gallantry, and even though she doesn't let her anger show, she greets them with 'un ironique applaudissement qui déconcerte, ou d'un ton froid auquel on ne s'attend point' (a disconcerting, ironic approval or an unexpectedly cold tone) (*OC* iv. 754; *E*, 399). She is right in believing she deserves better recognition of her worth. Even Émile will become a legitimate target of her anger when one day he fails to appear at her home as he had promised (*OC* iv. 810–13). Sophie's moral dignity as a human being gives her a legitimate expectation that promises made to her will be kept. Of course, when Sophie learns why Émile was late—he was helping a peasant who had broken his leg falling from a horse—her anger dissolves. Indeed, the idea that Émile had responded to a higher duty so increases her love for him that she abandons her modest reserve and openly declares her willingness to be his wife. On another level, Sophie can also identify with the poor peasant, since both of them live in a state of dependency. As in the story of Robert's garden, the acknowledgment of shared weakness helps limit that sense of being wronged which gives anger its force.

Whether Émile could ever legitimately or appropriately be angry with Sophie is another matter. When he arrives late after helping the peasant, he is taken aback by her anger. Instead of reacting with indignation of his own, he tries to read her real feelings in her eyes. He can't believe she really means what she says. 'Sophie, plus irritée de sa confiance lui lance un regard qui lui ôte l'envie d'en solliciter un second. Émile interdit, tremblant, n'ose plus, très heureusement pour lui, ni lui parler, ni la regarder: car n'eût-il pas été coupable, s'il eût pu supporter sa colère, elle ne lui eût jamais pardonné' (Sophie is further irritated by his confidence and casts a glance at him which takes away his desire to solicit a second one. Taken aback and trembling, Emile no longer dares—very fortunately for him—to speak or look at her; for even if he were not guilty, she would never have pardoned him if he had been able to bear her anger) (*OC* iv. 811; *E*, 440). The logic here is puzzling. Rousseau is saying that Sophie could not respect an innocent man who would not respond to her angry attack with anger of his own. Émile's silence thus implies he is guilty, but of what? He has a good reason for being late, and the Rousseau who rails at gallantry can hardly be suggesting that Sophie is really being slighted. The subjunctive tense of the verbs in the second part of the sentence remind us that Émile must be ready to respond in anger to any insult to his manly dignity, but such an eventuality can only exist as a counterfactual hypothesis. In the actual situation, Émile would no longer deserve to marry Sophie if he got mad.

One explanation for this tortured logic is that while Émile must be ready to defend his dignity against slight, any actual anger would suggest an unseemly degree of emotional dependence on Sophie. This interpretation is supported by another incident the tutor stages to test Émile's mettle. One morning, he enters Émile's room and asks him what he would do if someone told him Sophie was dead. The calm with which the tutor considers the possibility provokes Émile to anger. 'Il s'approche, les yeux enflammés de colère, et s'arrrêtant dans une attitude presque menaçante: ce que je ferais . . . je n'en sais rien; mais ce que je sais, c'est que je ne reverrais de ma vie celui qui me l'aurait appris' (Emile approaches, his eyes inflamed with anger, and stops in an almost threatening posture: 'What would I do . . . I don't know. But what I do know is that I would never again in my life see the man who had informed me') (*OC* iv. 814; *E*, 442). On one level, this challenge is a dramatic way of discovering whether Émile has preserved his independence after falling in love. The tutor follows up with a long speech about clinging only to the beauty of virtue, which does not perish. 'Étends la loi de la nécessité aux choses morales', he advises. 'Apprends à perdre ce qui peut t'être enlevé; apprends à tout quitter quand la vertu l'ordonne . . . ' (extend the law of necessity to moral things. Learn to lose what can be taken from you; learn to abandon everything when virtue decrees it . . .) (*OC* iv. 820; *E*, 446). Émile shows he is on the way to self-mastery by the way he tempers his immediate reaction. But it is still crucial that he *begin* by getting angry. Otherwise the strength of the attachment he must transcend, and thus the power of his virtue, would be in doubt. Since strength (*force*) is the basis of virtue (*OC* iv. 817; *E*, 444), equanimity too easily attained is moral weakness. If Émile had failed to get angry, he would have forfeited the tutor's as well as Sophie's respect.

It is significant, however, that we do not see Émile expressing any anger to Sophie herself, even if only to show her how he masters his emotion. The explanation seems to be that Émile had come to expect something from the tutor he never expects from Sophie: a guarantee that things will go well in his quest for love. Prior to beginning the search for a marriage partner, the tutor had secured his hold on Émile by giving their relationship a more personal quality. He asked his pupil to trust him (*OC* iv. 651; *E*, 325). Trust had not been a factor in Émile's early education, when reliability was defined in terms of nature's impersonal laws. Émile initially reacts to the announcement of Sophie's 'death' as a betrayal of that trust. His feeling is so strong that even after he conquers his attachment he cannot imagine forgiving the person who brought him the bad news. By the same token, however, Émile's lack of anger at Sophie suggests that he does not see her as a person in whom he can place his trust, and who could therefore betray that trust. As an ideal figure, she is endowed with a virtue and beauty that justifies a sublimated generalized attachment, even, as we have just seen in the spectacle of her anger, a submission without humiliation. Yet, if Sophie is also supposed to be a real woman, how can their relationship not involve some degree of personal trust, along with the expectations and emotional vulnerability that accompany it?

Rousseau does not address this question, probably because he has framed his portrayal of Sophie in such a way as to forestall it. Unlike the women in his literary model, Fénelon's *Télémaque*, Sophie is not just an allegorical object of love.[53] While continuing to portray her as an ideal figure, Rousseau gives her a more fully embodied character; her realistic traits, including her foibles, are supposed to add to her charm. But this duality puts Émile in a bind. To get angry with her is impossible, for how can one be angry with perfection? Yet, to the extent that she is only human, to be angry would be ungallant, since it would be unmanly to take advantage of female weakness. Still, as a trusting lover, Émile must surely care about the way Sophie treats him, and thus it should be possible to imagine him getting angry at her. One must conclude that as

[53] For an extended analysis of *Émile*'s relation to *Télémaque*, see Mall, *Émile, ou les figures de la fiction*, ch. 8.

a person Sophie ultimately does not in fact really matter to Émile once she has played her role in his erotic education.

This interpretation is confirmed by what we have of the educational treatise's abortive sequel, *Émile et Sophie, ou les solitaires*. In the opening pages of what was to have been Rousseau's second epistolary novel, Émile and Sophie's marriage has already broken down. Depressed by a miscarriage, Sophie has allowed herself to be seduced by another man. When he discovers the truth, the enraged Émile demands a separation, insisting on taking custody of their son in order to 'satisfy' his anger. But he soon changes his mind. 'Laissons-lui l'enfant, de peur qu'il ne lui ramène à la fin le père' (Leave her the child, lest he bring the father back to her) (*OC* iv. 909). Émile wants to ensure the break will be definitive. Sophie herself is so full of self-loathing that she welcomes her abandonment, leaving Émile free to face life alone and independent once more. Whether the couple would eventually reunite remains an open question, but the pages Rousseau did write make it clear that not only in the exemplary story of a philosophical treatise but in the realistic plot of a novel Émile's personal connection to Sophie is a thin one.[54]

The character in the treatise most anxious to keep Émile's trust is the tutor. He cannot bear to see his pupil go, just as the author, increasingly identified with the tutor, finds it difficult to grant his book its own dramatic integrity. Even as he encourages the newly married Émile and Sophie to begin an independent life together, the tutor cannot help drawing them back into his orbit. At the very end of the book, Rousseau imagines a scene in which Sophie decides to show her sway over her husband by forcing him to sleep in a separate room. The frustrated Émile is described as on the verge of an angry fit (*OC* iv. 865; *E*, 478). Yet, the purpose of the scene is not to dramatize the resolution of his anger, or to reveal any possible resentment motivating Sophie's behavior. Rather, it is to give the tutor the opportunity to lecture the couple at length on how to manage the economy of desire. The characters' success in that enterprise is oriented toward the erotic satisfaction of their creator. The author's voice merges with that of the tutor when the latter exclaims at the end of the book: 'Combien de fois contemplant en eux

[54] There is some secondhand testimony suggesting that Rousseau did plan to reunite the couple at the end of the novel, but since Émile, despite his protestations, does not seem to miss his 'lost' wife, there is room for doubt. In contrast to Prévost's *Cleveland*, the literary model for *Émile et Sophie*, the hero is not haunted by the sense of incompletion that would provide an inner impetus for such a reunion.

mon ouvrage, je me sens saisi d'un ravissement qui fait palpiter mon cœur' (How many times, as I contemplate my work in them, I feel myself seized by a rapture that makes my heart palpitate) (*OC* iv. 867; *E*, 480). The happy tutor is untroubled by any worry that his charges might chafe under his authority. On the contrary, Émile announces that, while he will raise his own son, he wants the tutor to remain 'the master of the young masters'.

Similarly, the author does not appear to be worried about how his book might affect his readers. Although *Émile* offers Rousseau's most sustained thematic treatment of anger, good and bad, it differs from his earlier works in not taking any measures at the rhetorical level to anticipate and contain responses to its representation of that anger. Of course, since Rousseau considered *Émile* to be a positive book, concerned with construction, not critique, there did not seem to be any need for defensive measures. But precisely because the text evolves from a philosophical allegory grounded in a long tradition of pedagogical treatises into a personalized statement whose warrant is a goodness to be taken on trust, it is vulnerable, as the tutor is, to charges of presumption and manipulation. Rousseau was unwilling to anticipate the possibility of a negative response, and so was unable to protect himself by making enough room for it in the elaboration of the work itself. When *Émile* was in fact condemned, Rousseau was devastated and disoriented; above all, he felt his trust in the public's trust in him had been betrayed. Rousseau would recover sufficiently from the shock to write further books, but he would be careful to stipulate that he no longer did so as an 'author'. That is to say, he disclaimed any authority other than that of his own suffering as a victim of persecution.

Ironically, the episode of *Émile* that provoked the most outrage was the one in which Rousseau did make a conscious effort to give his convictions a dramatic framework and thereby establish a mediating space between the writer and his work. Unlike the relationship of man and man, or man and woman, the relationship between man and God is explored in 'Profession de foi du Vicaire savoyard' by a character who does not claim any authority other than the authenticity of his own personal quest. The 'Profession de foi' exhibits the same ambivalent attitude toward anger found elsewhere in *Émile*, but it reconfigures it in such a way as to leave more room for the possibility of an equally ambivalent response on the part of the reader.

In accordance with the principles of negative education, the young Émile is not taught anything about religion. The child could only parrot words whose meaning he can't understand. He should concern himself with grand metaphysical questions only when 'le progrès de ses lumières porte ses recherches de ce côté-là' (when the progress of his enlightenment leads his researches in that direction) (*OC* iv. 557; *E*, 259). Rousseau does not tell us, however, how a boy like Émile might come to conduct such investigations. Instead, he introduces another character into the book, a boy very much like the adolescent Jean-Jacques of the later *Confessions*. This nameless character, we are told, found himself in Italy, alienated and alone. Mistreated by the priests who sought to convert him from Calvinism to Catholicism, he reacted with an anger whose physical symptoms recall those of the angry infant described earlier in *Émile*: 'des larmes de rage coulaient de ses yeux, l'indignation l'étouffait' (tears of rage flowed from his eyes; indignation choked him) (*OC* iv. 559; *E*, 262). Yet, instead of driving him to seek justice, his emotion only aggravated his alienation by leading him into self-destructive delinquent behavior.[55] Fortunately, he was rescued by a kindly priest, himself a victim of ecclesiastical persecution and now serving in nearby Savoy as a humble Vicaire (that is to say, he never was appointed to a parish of his own). The Vicaire offers the boy an uplifting vision of an orderly and beautiful cosmos in which each individual holds a place of dignity in the eyes of a just and benevolent God. While the Vicaire's speech includes a substantial amount of philosophical exposition, its purpose is as much therapeutic as it is intellectual. The fact that it is not addressed to Émile underscores this point. Despite his momentary experience of injustice in the garden episode, Émile never experiences this kind of distress (at least, not in this book),[56] and so he is not in a position to appreciate the value of what the Vicaire has to say.

One might think that by addressing the 'Profession de foi' to a character much like himself, and not to Émile, Rousseau diminishes both the philosophical integrity and the universal applicability of its doctrine. In fact, the opposite is true. To preserve his equanimity, the fictional Émile had to be insulated from the ugly and depressing aspects of life. At best he could contemplate them from afar, from the outside, as in the episode of the angry man. His 'objective' view of the man as sick precludes not only identification—the immediate goal at the

[55] It is important, however, that the boy does not direct his anger outward in aggression against others. He may be ashamed, but he is not guilty of anything.

[56] Whether or not Émile would undergo a similar psychological trial in the novelistic sequel is unclear.

time—but any insight into the human condition beyond what could be provided by abstract enlightenment. The fact that Rousseau never describes Émile's religious education has also led many critics to view the 'Profession de foi' as a 'detachable metaphysics' to which Rousseau is not committed. The Vicaire's God is a comforting fiction, implicitly acknowledged by Rousseau as such.[57] But the fact that Rousseau dramatizes the articulation of religious convictions instead of arguing for them directly does not mean he is not committed to those convictions (though it does not mean he is fully committed to them, either). Rather, in contrast to *philosophes* past and present who have sought to prove religious truth by demonstrative argument, Rousseau wants to suggest that convictions of this kind are best presented dramatically. Whether or not they are demonstrably true is less important than whether they project a coherent and habitable point of view. This question requires a shift in the discursive mode of the book even more decisive than the one which marked Émile's initiation into romantic love, which was still dominated by an allegorical conception of the book's characters.[58]

A key element in the Vicaire's religious therapy is his insistence that the angry God of the Bible is a distortion of the real God of 'natural religion'. The biblical warning against false prophets whose teaching stems from desire for gain or misplaced zeal applies to the Bible itself. The true God is not angry but 'clement and good', making allowance for human weakness (*OC* iv. 613–14; *E*, 299–300). The logic of the Vicaire's argument leads him to conclude, contrary to dominant Christian opinion, that if truly bad people do exist, they do not go to hell; they simply cease to exist when they die. People who have made mistakes but whose intentions were good are assured of eternal life. The evidence for this assurance is internal; it does not come from any special revelation, mediated by other people's interpretations or agendas. It is the Vicaire's exercise of his own capacity to apprehend the cosmic order of creation and feel himself in harmony with it that convinces him he is fundamentally good, and that God must recognize the goodness of his creation in him.

[57] See Roger D. Masters, *The Political Philosophy of Rousseau* (Princeton: Princeton University Press, 1968).

[58] On this point, see the important methodological reflections, inspired in part by Mikhail Bakhtin, of Rowan Williams, *Dostoevsky: Language, Faith, and Fiction* (Waco, Tex.: Baylor University Press, 2008).

The Vicaire's God is an unorthodox one from a Christian point of view, but differs just as much from the impersonal divinity of the Enlightenment deists, who (or which) rewards law-abiding behavior rather than individual persons as such. The Vicaire avoids the vocabulary of sin and salvation, but he does speak of personal assurance, and it is the Vicaire's communication of this experience of being recognized to a young man too long deprived of it that is crucial to curing him of his anger. But if God has a personal relationship with human beings such that he looks compassionately on their weakness of will, does this not imply he is also capable of taking offense at their willfulness or presumption? The Vicaire deflects the question by offering as his one example of such presumption the claim that God favors particular people or nations over others. Rousseau rejects the biblical idea of election because he believes it implies that the rest of the human race, to whom God has not revealed himself or whose reason fails to convince them of his existence, is predestined to damnation. If God ever gets angry, it can only be with those who offend his goodness by imputing such an attitude to him. 'Le Dieu que j'adore n'est point un Dieu de ténèbres, il ne m'a point doté d'un entendement pour m'en interdire l'usage; me dire de soumettre ma raison c'est outrager son auteur' (The God I worship is not a god of darkness. He did not endow me with an understanding in order to forbid me its use. To tell me to subject my reason is an insult to its author) (*OC* iv. 614; *E*, 300, tr. modified). The Vicaire's God is just personal enough to get angry with those who believe he can get angry (and by implication look kindly on those who do not), but not so personal as to impose on human beings the burden of any response other than what should come naturally to all rational and sentient beings.

Conversely, one may ask whether from the Vicaire's point of view it is ever legitimate, or whether it even makes sense, for human beings to get angry at God. Again, Rousseau avoids addressing this question. Despite his mistreatment by the priests of Turin, the young man of Rousseau's story is never said to be angry at God. Nor does the Vicaire express any anger at the God who allowed him to suffer at the hands of church authorities. Ironically, he is much less 'biblical' in his thinking than Voltaire, who saw in the angry Job a kindred spirit, protesting against the wrongs done to him, and even more for God's failure to respect his need at least to make sense of them.[59] In this respect, however,

[59] See Voltaire's article 'Job', in his *Dictionnaire philosophique.* For the general context, see Bronislaw Baczko, *Job, mon ami: promesses du bonheur et fatalité du mal* (Paris: Gallimard, 1997).

he mirrors the attitude of his creator. It is in fact curious, given Rousseau's susceptibility to anger, that, like the Vicaire, he never expresses any resentment toward God. Although he is aware of the difficulty of devising a convincing theodicy, he is much less vexed by the problem than many of his contemporaries.[60] In the second of his *Rêveries*, for example, written after the persecutions brought on by the condemnation of *Émile*, Rousseau is content to say that 'Dieu est juste; il veut que je souffre; et il sait que je suis innocent' (God is just; he wills that I suffer; and he knows that I am innocent) (*OC* i. 1010; *CW* vi. 16). It is possible his refusal to see himself as being wronged by God reflects a deeper refusal to countenance the possibility that he might do something to offend God. And yet, while Rousseau is confident that, as he says in the same passage of the *Rêveries*, his turn will come sooner or later, he does not speak of God as owing him that reward. Indeed, Rousseau might well agree with Pascal that God owes us nothing.[61] But he gives that phrase a meaning very different from Pascal's. The Vicaire's God owes him nothing, not because divine sovereignty cannot be constrained by human expectations, but because the whole vocabulary of obligation, and consequently of offense, mischaracterizes humanity's interaction with the divine. Far from feeling abandoned and anxious about his election, the Vicaire finds relief in being freed from any concern about God as a possible source of hostile intention.

In this respect, the Vicaire's religious teaching accords with the negative education practiced in the early books of *Émile*. It proposes a therapy for anger centered on the elimination of any reason or occasion for taking offense. God is not even obligated to justify himself to human reason, as demanded by Challe. It is enough that the Vicaire can inhabit, without logical or existential contradiction, the world delineated by his religious speculations. It is an important sign of his confidence in the integrity of the text that, in contrast with the tutor's

[60] In his *Lettre à Voltaire sur la providence* (1756), Rousseau had already rejected the idea that God was responsible for the evil in the world. Consideration of his arguments lies beyond the scope of this discussion. For a good presentation of the interpretive difficulties involved, see Victor Gourevitch, 'The Religious Thought', in Patrick Riley, ed., *The Cambridge Companion to Rousseau* (Cambridge: Cambridge University Press, 2001), 193–246.

[61] See the provocative commentary in Leszek Kolakowski, *God Owes Us Nothing: A Brief Remark on Pascal's Religion and the Spirit of Jansenism* (Chicago: University of Chicago Press, 1995). Kolakowski, however, misleadingly conflates all anti-Jansenist readings of Augustine as reflecting a heretical ('semi-pelagian') overestimation of human merits.

anxious quest to secure Émile's continued allegiance, Rousseau does not have the Vicaire push for a response from the young man to whom he speaks (*OC* iv. 635; *E*, 313). The author is content to offer a teaching that is at once personal in tone yet free, like the God it depicts, from the entanglements of personalized intention or expectation. In the event, the Vicaire's speech struck a deep responsive chord in his contemporary readers, even among those who disagreed with particular points in its theology. Unfortunately, Rousseau's rhetorical strategies did not—and probably could not, given the sensitivity of the subject at the time—protect *Émile* from official condemnation. Nor did they offset the all-too-insistent demand for a grateful response that elsewhere in the book the tutor, and the author behind him, seems to make on the reader. One wonders if the two issues are not somehow related. Rousseau's ambivalence about anger, in social relations and in the relationship between author and reader, is matched by an equivalent difficulty with gratitude.

5

Rousseau's Quarrel with Gratitude

One of Rousseau's complaints about modern society was that it collapsed the distinction between gratitude and other, more compulsory forms of obligation. Ingratitude would be rarer, he declared in *Émile*, if *bienfaits à usure* (favors done at an extortionate interest rate) were less common (*OC* iv. 521; *E*, 234, tr. modified). In the *Confessions*, Rousseau maintains that a disposition to gratitude was an important part of his personality, but he does so, significantly, in relation to an episode in which free reciprocity has broken down. Upon his return to Madame de Warens after seeking medical help at Montpellier, Rousseau finds that his place as her favorite has been taken by a young man named Wintzenried, who acts as if he owes her nothing. The young Jean-Jacques had earlier had no problem sharing Maman's affections with his own predecessor, Claude Anet, whose appreciation for her favors matched his own, but he cannot be as patient with Wintzenried as Anet was with him. This is because 'la parité manquait entre les personnes' (there was no similarity between the persons involved). 'Je trouvai encore moins dans ce jeune homme les qualités qu'Anet avait trouvé en moi: la docilité, l'attachement, la reconnaissance' (still less did I find in this young man the qualities that Anet had found in me: docility, affection, gratitude) (*OC* i. 265; *C*, 258). In his autobiography, he pays a tribute of gratitude to the unassuming kindness he often encountered in his youth from people like M. Simon in Annecy or the Lausanne innkeeper who gave him credit. Of the latter, he writes, characteristically: 'Des services plus importants sans doute, mais rendus avec plus d'ostentation, ne m'ont pas paru si dignes de reconnaissance que l'humanité simple et sans éclat de cet honnête homme' (I have often been rendered other, doubtless more important services, but which, more ostentatiously performed, have never seemed to me as deserving of gratitude as the simple and unaffected humanity of that honest man) (*OC* i. 147; *C*, 143). Later in the same work, however, he recounts with undiminished agitation how he bristled when his high-minded friends offered pointed reminders of his obligation to his patrons and attempted to dictate the form his gratitude should take. We saw in the last chapter how the pressure exerted on him by Grimm and Diderot to accompany Madame d'Épinay on her trip to Geneva provoked Rousseau's resentment. 'Tout bienfait exige reconnaissance', he admitted in one of his autobiographical letters to Malesherbes, and 'je me sens le cœur ingrat par cela seul que la reconnaissance est un devoir' (every benefit demands gratitude; and I feel my heart to be ungrateful from the very fact alone that gratitude is a duty) (*OC* i. 1132; *CW* v. 573).

Rousseau was just as uncomfortable about being a benefactor. A memorable passage of the sixth of his *Rêveries du promeneur solitaire* tells the story of a young lame boy Rousseau used to see on the streets of Paris. The first few times they met, he would cheerfully give the boy a coin, but 'ce plaisir devenu par degrés habitude se trouva je ne sais comment transformé dans une espèce de devoir dont je sentis bientôt la gêne' (this pleasure, having gradually become a habit, was inexplicably transformed into a kind of duty I soon felt to be annoying) (*OC* i. 1050; *CW* viii. 49). So constrained did Rousseau feel that he finally avoided that street altogether. 'Je sais', he writes, 'qu'il y a une espèce de contrat et même le plus saint de tous entre le bienfaiteur et l'obligé' (I know that there is a kind of contract, and even the holiest of all, between the benefactor and the beneficiary) by which the latter commits himself to be grateful and the former commits to renewing his generosity as much as he can. To break this contract is unjust, but nonetheless it is 'l'effet d'une indépendance que le cœur aime, et à laquelle il ne renonce pas sans effort' (the effect of an independence the heart loves and renounces only with effort) (*OC* i. 1053–4; *CW* viii. 52). In the sixth *promenade*, he imagines what it would be like instead to possess the magic ring of Gyges, which made its wearer invisible. With such a ring, he could be as 'beneficent and good' as God while escaping 'dependence on men' (*OC* i. 1057–8; *CW* viii. 55)—except that he might be tempted to take advantage of the ring to become a voyeur.[1]

[1] For Gyges' ring, see Plato, *Republic* 2.359a–360d. Rousseau's text suggests that the evil of voyeurism lies less in the violation of other people's privacy than in creating, through erotic pleasure, another form of dependence on them. For an analysis of this passage in relation to the problem of beneficence, especially in its implications for gender relations in Rousseau, see Judith Still, *Justice and Difference in the Works of Rousseau: 'Bienfaisance' and 'Pudeur'* (Cambridge: Cambridge University Press, 1993), 120–1.

Rousseau's discomfort with gratitude[2] (and other dispositions such as trust which involve relationships where the emotional intersects with the social, and in which the reciprocity of gift-giving shades off into contractual exchange[3]) points to a broader tension in early modern French discussions of civility. Is it possible to imagine a society in which gratitude was wholly disentangled from an oppressive sense of dependence? In classical discussions of the theme such as Cicero's or Seneca's, that question did not arise. While the ancients emphasized that gratitude must not be compelled, in general they were not concerned with drawing a clear line between customary, political, and religious obligation. Their focus was more on instilling in well-born souls the values of honor and magnanimity. In early modern Europe, however, when with the rise of nation-states political rule began to be defined around a new notion of sovereignty, and when religious divisions were forcing theologians to rethink the role of both church and state in mediating humanity's relationship to God, distinguishing the exact scope and form of different kinds of obligation became a matter of pressing concern. One might say that the development of polite sociability in the *salons* and other unofficial sites of social exchange in seventeenth-century France reflected a desire to disentangle gratitude from the domain of political obligation, where it was becoming superfluous, and to reconstitute it as part of a new dynamic of civil sociability distinct from the rationalized, absolutist politics of monarchy and court.[4]

Indeed, changing ideas about the basis of human cognition and interaction suggested that gratitude might no longer have a role to play in the acknowledgment of the authority of natural and political laws. In the area of epistemology, it is instructive to compare two famous texts of the early seventeenth century. In his *Introduction à la vie dévote*,

[2] Today, we do not think of gratitude as a 'passion', but Descartes does list it as such in his *Les Passions de l'âme* (art. 193). As Carole Talon-Hugon has reminded us in *Les Passions rêvées par la raison: essai sur la théorie des passions de Descartes et de quelques-uns de ses contemporains* (Paris: Vrin, 2002), Descartes's work stands at the intersection of different languages about the emotions—medical, Thomist, Stoic, and Augustinian—and this discursive complexity continues into the eighteenth century, when the scope of the terms 'passion', 'affection', and 'sentiment' often overlaps or is hard to distinguish. I will use the word 'emotion' here because I wish to focus on the relational aspect of feeling and because in today's speech it allows for a range of meanings from the physiological to the cognitive.

[3] The distinction between gift and contractual exchange is a difficult one and the subject of an important contemporary debate that cannot be summarized here.

[4] Daniel Gordon, *Citizens without Sovereignty: Equality and Sociability in French Thought 1670–1789* (Princeton: Princeton University Press, 1994).

François de Sales advances as a generally accepted principle, even a proverbial expression of obvious wisdom, that knowledge begets gratitude (*la connaissance engendre la reconnaissance*).[5] Knowledge is a gift, and the more you know, the more aware you are that it is a gift. In Descartes's *Meditations*, the philosopher who has put everything in doubt, on the supposition that an evil genius might be fooling him, arrives at the idea of a God who anchors all knowledge in his infinite and perfect being. He takes a moment at the end of the third meditation to contemplate and adore this God, but says nothing about being grateful.[6] No doubt this is because Descartes himself has done the epistemological work. Gratitude has no place in a conception of knowledge based on clear and distinct ideas. Certainty comes from method, not from mercy, and the acquisition of knowledge diminishes rather than underscores man's dependence on things outside himself.

In political philosophy, too, gratitude was becoming an increasingly irrelevant concept. Hobbes and other natural right thinkers sought to develop an idea of obligation that, however absolute, was based on a conception of the human being as an individual unto himself. Political obedience was to be ensured by the calculations of reason and the threat of external force, not by the education of virtuous feeling: acknowledging the sovereign's authority is a matter of behavior, and even as they constrain themselves, the subjects continue to enjoy psychological independence. Eighteenth-century French *philosophes*, especially those of materialist bent, carried this trend forward by exalting the rule of law in all areas of life. It might seem to us that grounding all human relationships in an impersonal system of laws implies a deterministic, or at least instrumental, view of human nature at odds with the Enlightenment emphasis on freedom, but we need to appreciate how this discourse could hold an emotional appeal for those who felt the oppression of arbitrary human will. It is in fact remarkable how much faith many writers of the French Enlightenment placed in the rule of law (the expression *les lois* was

[5] François de Sales, *Introduction à la vie dévote*, in *Œuvres*, ed. André Ravier (Paris: Gallimard, 1969), 141. The book was first published in 1609, with a final revised edition in 1619.

[6] Descartes, *Meditations métaphysiques*, ed. Jean-Marie Beyssade and Michelle Beyssade (Paris: Flammarion, 1992), 131; *Meditations on First Philosophy, with Selections from the Objections and Replies*, tr. Michael Moriarty (Oxford: Oxford University Press, 2008), 37. The work was first published in 1641. This is not to say, however, that gratitude has no place in Descartes's moral, as opposed to strictly epistemological, thinking. On this point, see Michael Moriarty, *Fallen Nature, Fallen Selves: Early Modern French Thought II* (Oxford: Oxford University Press, 2006), 44.

sometimes invoked in an absolute sense) as not only a necessary but a sufficient answer to the problems of social interaction.

This outlook stood in tension with the equally influential but deliberately anti-systematic discourse of polite sociability inherited from the *salons* of the seventeenth century. The creation of an unofficial public sphere governed by personal *égards* also promised liberation from oppressive constraint. In different degrees and combinations, both currents of thought contributed to the Enlightenment's confidence about social reform, and yet neither could be adopted wholesale by the leading *philosophes*. The idealization and homogenization of law might offer relief from the chaos of conflicting arbitrary rules, but it might, as Montesquieu recognized, also appear dangerously reductive as a model of social interaction if it ignored the importance of the informal realm of tradition, custom, and social ecology encapsulated in the word *mœurs*. Conversely, while the extension of the flexible rules of politeness to social life might provide an alternative to the rigidity of law, such a move could also be experienced as unduly personalizing obligation in domains better governed by abstract rights. If only everybody got what they deserved by right, then one could do away with the burden of gratitude—and the burden of being a benefactor, as in the story about the beggar boy. Yet, would a society in which gratitude has no role to play really be a place in which human sensibility, and the expressive potential associated with it, could develop to its fullest extent? Rousseau's persistent ambivalence on this point, expressed in different ways throughout his works, illustrates some profound and under-appreciated tensions in early modern thinking about the ordering of human relationships.

DISCOURS SUR L'INÉGALITÉ

A striking fact about humanity's natural state, as Rousseau depicts it in the *Discours sur l'inégalité*, is that emotion of any kind is entirely absent. Men are solitary and independent: they are strong enough to survive without assistance, and when they lose their strength, they die without fuss.[7] Living entirely in the moment, without memory and reflection,

[7] I use 'men' rather than 'human beings' because Rousseau's focus is on males. He speaks very little of women in the state of nature, and minimizes mothers' attachment to their children, a bond which according to his theory lasts only a short time.

they have no occasion to regret the past or worry about the future. While they are subject to sudden fright, they have no fear. Nor are they prone to what have been called the 'vehement passions' of anger, rashness, or intense grief.[8] Since nature provides for their physical needs, there is no need to compete for resources. Should someone steal your apple, it is easier to pick another apple than to fight for the stolen one. Rousseau agrees that 'plus les passions sont violentes, plus les lois sont nécessaires pour les contenir: mais . . . il serait encore bon d'examiner si ces désordres ne sont point nés avec les lois mêmes' (the more violent the passions, the more necessary are laws to contain them: but . . . it would still be worth enquiring whether these disorders did not arise with the laws themselves) (*OC* iii. 157; G 1, 155).

It is well known that by conceptualizing the state of nature in this way, Rousseau was taking issue with modern natural law thinkers on the origins of political association. For Hobbes, for example, gratitude, along with benevolence or trust, is one of the 'laws of nature' reason tells us we should follow to preserve the peace and ensure our self-preservation amidst the violence of the state of nature.[9] Scholars of Hobbes dispute whether these laws are moral in character or are merely out-workings of self-interest, but either way they presuppose a reflective

[8] Philip Fisher, *The Vehement Passions* (Princeton: Princeton University Press, 2002).

[9] 'As justice dependeth on antecedent covenant; so does gratitude depend on antecedent grace; that is to say, antecedent free gift; and is the fourth law of nature, which may be conceived in this form: that a man which receiveth benefit from another of mere grace endeavour that he which giveth it have no reasonable cause to repent him of his good will. For no man giveth but with intention of good to himself . . . of which if men see they shall be frustrated, there will be no beginning of benevolence or trust, nor consequently of mutual help, nor of reconciliation of one man to another; and therefore they are to remain still in the condition of war, which is contrary to the first and fundamental law of nature which commandeth men to seek peace.' Hobbes, *Leviathan*, ch. 15, para. 16. I have used the edition of Edwin Curley (Indianapolis: Hackett, 1994), 95. See also *De cive* III.8, where gratitude is the third 'law of nature'. Note that in Samuel Sorbière's 1649 French translation of this text, Hobbes's Latin *fiducia*, translated by Michael Silverthorne as 'good faith' (Hobbes, *On the Citizen*, ed. and tr. Richard Tuck and Michael Silverthorne (Cambridge: Cambridge University Press, 1998), 47) is rendered as *reconnaissance*. Since it is likely that if Rousseau read Hobbes directly, it would have been in Sorbière's translation, the passage is worth quoting in the French text: 'La troisième loi de nature est qu'on ne permette point que celui qui, s'assurant de notre reconnaissance, a commencé le premier à nous bien faire, reçoive de l'incommodité de sa franchise, et qu'on n'accepte un bienfait qu'avec une disposition intérieure de faire en sorte que le bienfaiteur n'ait jamais un juste sujet de se repentir de sa bénéficence.' See Thomas Hobbes, *Le Citoyen, ou les fondements de la politique*, ed. Simone Goyard-Fabre (Paris: GF-Flammarion, 1982), 117.

self-consciousness human beings do not possess in the state of nature, rigorously conceived.

Rousseau is equally concerned to reject the argument that sociability finds its source in the natural weakness of human nature.[10] In his widely read compendium of natural law, Pufendorf writes: 'Man is an animal with an intense concern for his own preservation, needy by himself, incapable of protection without the help of his fellows, and very well fitted for the mutual provision of benefits.'[11] It follows that gratitude is one of the 'common duties of humanity' underpinning the 'common sociality'.[12] For Pufendorf this duty is owed 'by every man to every man': the system of favors recognizes and promotes the equal dignity of all men. It is not tied to a hierarchical, oppressive system of feudal obligation. According to James Tully, Pufendorf's discussion of gratitude is meant to show the reader how the performance of duties is 'advantageous to each party'.[13] Yet, the author's obsequious dedication of the work to 'the most illustrious and exalted hero, Lord Gustavus Otto Steenbock', stresses the subservience of one to the other: 'I might be rightly criticized for ingratitude if I neglected any opportunity, however slight it might be, at least to declare the extent of my obligation to you.'[14]

The dedication of the *Discours sur l'inégalité* also pays 'public homage', in this case to the Republic of Geneva, but Rousseau's rhetoric stands in sharp contrast to Pufendorf's. Although he speaks of the duties he owes to his country, the emotion that informs them is not gratitude, but 'zeal' (*OC* iii. 111; G 1, 114).[15] As a citizen, and thus as a member of the very General Council he is addressing, he need not legitimize his writing by referring to a patron, or to a relationship with any particular individual. Zeal is a response to ideas, in this case to republican political principles, rather than to persons. The city's patrician elite, which in practice ruled the republic, was quite aware of the difference. It rightly discerned the subversive potential of the work, for despite the

[10] Catherine Larrère, 'Rousseau', in Philippe Raynaud and Stéphane Rials, eds, *Dictionnaire de philosophie politique* (Paris: Presses universitaires de France, 1996), 590.

[11] Samuel Pufendorf, *On the Duties of Man and Citizen*, tr. Michael Silverthorne, ed. James Tully (Cambridge: Cambridge University Press, 1991), 35.

[12] Ibid. 64.

[13] Ibid. xxi.

[14] Ibid. 3.

[15] Rousseau had in fact lost his Genevan citizenship because he had converted to Catholicism as a young man. At the time of writing, however, he was preparing to recover his status and adopts the stance of a loyal Genevan.

extravagant praise Rousseau lavishes on the ruling magistrates, the *Discours* implicitly encourages the citizenry to measure the government's conduct against those principles. Thus, while Rousseau's state of nature is radically pre-social, the relationships between citizens evoked in the dedication are not social ones either, in the sense that they are viewed as a result of the pattern of human development set out in the *Discours* itself. Rather, they rest on a political foundation which, in Rousseau's presentation, seems to be immune to the corruption that comes with 'progress'. The republic fosters in its citizens a spirit of independence unknown to men living under other regimes.

Still, Rousseau is more than ready to acknowledge the personal dimension of his relationship to the city that nurtured him. Above all, he recalls the lessons in republican virtue he learned from his father, an independent craftsman proud of his status as a citizen equal (in theory, at least) to any other. Yet, although he writes wistfully about 'les tendres instructions du meilleur des pères' (the tender teachings of the best of fathers) (*OC* iii. 118; G 1, 128) he does not say anything about being grateful to him. On the biographical level, this omission may be explained by the fact that the elder Rousseau left his 10-year-old son behind when, after a swordfight in the street, he exiled himself from Geneva rather than make amends to the authorities. Rousseau was torn between a need to idealize his father and a reluctant recognition that the man had abandoned him. On the textual level, this ambivalence takes the form of an apparently contradictory but all the more seductive portrayal of his homeland. In the happy world of the Genevan republic, the transmission of republican values is personalized but without creating any personal obligation. Rather, in proving that the author's zeal for the city's well-being is pure and uncorrupted, it serves to enhance his claim to independence.[16]

This zeal is not only compatible with a denial of personal debt; it may even be nourished by resistance to such an idea. This is another lesson Rousseau learned from his father. The latter, who liked to have his 'Tacite, Plutarque et Grotius, mêlés devant lui avec les instruments de son métier' (Tacitus, Plutarch, and Grotius before him amidst the tools of his trade) (*OC* iii. 118; G 1, 120), was in fact, as his decision to leave Geneva would demonstrate, more a potential dissident than a submissive son of the republic himself. The one and only mention of gratitude

[16] For a different but related self-enhancing use of 'zeal', see the preface to the *Lettre à d'Alembert* (*OC* v. 6; *CW* x. 255).

in the body of the *Discours* confirms this idea in a different way. In part two, Rousseau reminds the reader of the traditional principle that 'la reconnaissance est bien un devoir qu'il faut rendre, mais pas un droit qu'on puisse exiger' (gratitude is indeed a duty that ought to be performed, but it is not a right that can be exacted) (*OC* iii. 182; G 1, 177). He does so in order to refute the thesis that political authority derives from the model of paternal authority.[17]

The neediness of men abandoned to their own devices may not be a factor in the state of nature or in an idealized republic, but it certainly plays a role in the historical world. As Rousseau tells the story, once human population spread beyond the bounds of naturally fertile areas, people were forced to cooperate with each other. The institution of private property, however, reinforced the power of the strong and the lucky over the rest. Like the political contract that eventually followed, it provided security for the weak only by allowing the powerful to oppress them in a more orderly way. Since the thrust of Rousseau's hypothetical history is to demystify social relationships by unmasking their origin in violence and trickery, any reference to the softer side of human reciprocity, including the notion of gratitude, would spoil the argument. There is, however, one place in the *Discours* where neediness, instead of providing an opportunity for oppression, becomes the occasion for an emotional connection, one that Rousseau views as beneficial, and that he calls pity.

Pity, for Rousseau, creates sympathy for another human being through identification with his suffering. This imaginative bridge between one person and another lays the foundation for a first, fragile kind of social bond.[18] However, while pity introduces the idea of human vulnerability hitherto absent from Rousseau's analysis of human nature, it does so from the position of a spectator who is not needy himself. This spectator is vulnerable to the experience of the other's vulnerability, not his own. One might explain this dissymmetry by arguing that Rousseau's aim in the *Discours* is to restore to his readers a sense of power and initiative stifled by modern society. To focus on the subject's vulnerability would be counterproductive. Pierre Force suggests very plausibly that Rousseau also wants to emphasize, in opposition to Augustinian and Epicurean traditions, that pity is not self-interested, in the bad sense

17 Rousseau cites Locke and Sidney for support on this point.

18 *OC* iii. 154–6; *CW* x. 152–4. The role of pity in Rousseau's philosophical system has been the subject of an extensive debate that cannot be addressed here.

of a self-love exclusive and exploitative of others.[19] As Rousseau describes it, pity expects no return. And yet, the compassionate man is not presented as detached or disinterested. Even if it does not lead to an exchange of favors, pity does forge a kind of relationship—if it did not, then it could not function as a catalyst for sociability. At the same time, however, Rousseau says nothing about the other person's response to the spectator's compassion.[20]

What Rousseau is doing, I believe, is dramatizing neediness in such a way as to avoid provoking in his readers a feeling of dependence on others. The description of the compassionate man, like Rousseau's description of the zealous citizen, models a mediated form of solidarity. The subject Rousseau dramatizes is not invulnerable, an impersonal analyst looking down on humanity from above. He is vulnerable to others' vulnerability, but not in such a way as to create a relationship of dependence. He can imagine himself as the sufferer, who becomes an object of a spontaneous compassion that is all the more precious in that no gratitude is expected, just as he can imagine himself as compassionate without becoming bound, like Rousseau himself in the sixth *promenade*, to the object of his compassion. If self-interest is what stifles pity, what triggers the defensiveness of self-interest is the feeling of being stifled by constraint.

Rousseau's reader is involved in the scene of pity, one might say, but not absorbed into it—and so less likely to recoil in a self-protective way from the spectacle Rousseau stages for him.[21] It would be easy to criticize this strategy as fostering a facile sentimentality. But Rousseau wants to prevent the self from scrutinizing its own compassion, since reflection (with the attendant activity of self-judgment) is another form of constraint, generating the self-interest that causes one person to be alienated from another. Rousseau's critique of tragedy in the *Lettre à d'Alembert*—it encourages spectators to congratulate themselves for shedding tears over imaginary victims, and so to excuse themselves

[19] Pierre Force, *Self-Interest before Adam Smith* (Cambridge: Cambridge University Press, 2003), 24–5.

[20] It has been claimed that the omission only shows how Rousseau always focuses on the self at the expense of any real acknowledgment of the other's reality. See John Charvet, *The Social Problem in the Philosophy of Rousseau* (Cambridge: Cambridge University Press, 1974). Given Rousseau's anxious awareness of the other's gaze, this otherwise shrewd explanation falls short of the mark.

[21] On the aesthetics of absorption, see Michael Fried, *Absorption and Theatricality: Painting and Beholder in the Age of Diderot* (Berkeley and Los Angeles: University of California Press, 1980).

from helping victims in the real world—shows him to be aware that any attempt to balance involvement and detachment can easily be distorted by the ruses of self-love.[22]

It is precisely the ease with which compassion can be distorted that makes it impossible for Rousseau to make sympathy the basis of an ethical system, in the manner of his contemporaries Hume and Smith. The figure of the impartial but sympathetic spectator offers those philosophers another way of reconciling personal connection with a salutary distance. For Rousseau, however, a restless will and a vivid imagination are more fundamental to human nature than reason, and so the dynamic of sympathy can never be kept free from corruption. In any case, these British thinkers do not appear on the intellectual horizon of the *Discours sur l'inégalité*. In the foreground instead are those rationalist *philosophes* in France who integrate relationships of gratitude all too smoothly into their 'codes' or 'systems' of nature. Rousseau was already acquainted with this line of thinking through writers such as Mandeville. Through his friendship with Diderot, he was also acquainted with some of the more radical thinkers such as Helvétius and Holbach. Although the major works in this tradition postdate the *Discours*, a brief look at the latter's *Système social* will illustrate the kind of thinking Rousseau opposes.

According to Holbach, 'la justice veut que l'homme se rende utile à la société, parce qu'elle lui est utile et nécessaire à lui-même. La reconnaissance est un acte de justice' (justice wills that man make himself useful to society, because it is useful and necessary to himself. Gratitude is an act of justice).[23] Justice and utility are conflated, and from this perspective there is no difference between the traditionally free obligation of gratitude and enforceable obligations as defined by law. Moreover, Holbach takes a view of compassion that while superficially similar to Rousseau's is in fact decisively different. He tells us, for example, that misanthropy is bad, but not because it is a denial of fellow-feeling. Rather, 'l'intérêt que nous prenons aux êtres de notre espèce multiplie notre bien-être propre, en exerçant notre sensibilité, et nous permet de prétendre à leur reconnaissance' (the interest we take in the beings of our species increases our own well-being several fold by exercising our sensibility, and allows us to make a claim on their gratitude).[24] Holbach

[22] *Lettre à d'Alembert* (*OC* v. 24; *CW* x. 269).

[23] Paul Henri Thiry, baron d'Holbach, *Système social* (Paris: Fayard, 1994; 1st pub. 1773), 130.

[24] Ibid. 221.

and Rousseau both start from the self's own expansiveness rather than from a reciprocal relationship, but the element of vulnerability is entirely missing from Holbach's text. On the contrary, in the light of Holbach's remark that 'l'homme est un morceau de cire, dont on fait ce qu'on veut' (man is a lump of wax that we fashion as we will),[25] the notion that our interest makes a claim on the other's gratitude not only returns us to the self-interested notion of compassion Rousseau was at pains to avoid in the *Discours*; it transforms the sociable commerce of favors into a one-way form of manipulation. It never occurs to Holbach to consider what it would be like to be the subordinate object of another's gaze. Far from identifying with that experience himself, as an author he speaks only from a position above and outside the system he describes, to readers who imagine themselves in the role of rulers, not of subjects.

It may be objected, however, that this is also the perspective Rousseau adopts in the *Contrat social*. In contrast with the tone of *Discours sur l'inégalité*, which is that of a man speaking to men (*OC* iii. 131; G 1, 131), the later work is cast in impersonal, even mathematical language. Moreover, Rousseau's invocation of the quasi-divine figure of the Legislator seems to suggest that manipulation and mystification are a necessity of political life. To answer these objections, we need to ask whether gratitude has a role to play in Rousseau's political theory.

DU CONTRAT SOCIAL

Rousseau's demystification of sociability in the *Discours* makes it understandable that the *Contrat social* should not appeal to the language of benefits and gratitude in laying the foundation of political right. Such language is also foreign to the republican tradition to which Rousseau appeals. Machiavelli's *Discourses*, several times cited by Rousseau, warn rulers against the 'vice of ingratitude' when it comes to rewarding military heroes, because these heroes may turn against the state,[26] but they ascribe no role to gratitude in the political order itself. More important are the energy of *virtù* and the controlled strife of contending parties. While Rousseau differed from his Florentine predecessor in

[25] Ibid. 100.

[26] Niccolò Machiavelli, *Discourses on Livy*, tr. Harvey J. Mansfield and Nathan Tarcov (Chicago: Chicago University Press, 1996), 64 (book I, ch. 29).

condemning factions, he, too, defined political virtue in terms of force of will rather than mutual dependence and reciprocity. Among French writers, he was not alone in this view, as we can see by comparing the *Contrat social* with another contemporary expression of the renewed vitality of the republican tradition in France, the abbé de Mably's influential *Entretiens de Phocion.* Although its subtitle is *sur le rapport de la morale avec la politique* (on the relationship between morality and politics), it makes almost no mention of the emotions, and says nothing about gratitude. Its emphasis is all on the austerity and vigilance of an undifferentiated *vertu.*[27]

Not all republicanism, however, repudiated the language of favor and gratitude. A Christian thinker like Calvin, who played a key role in the newly independent Republic of Geneva, made gratitude a foundational theme in his teaching.[28] The social contract could be cast in the covenant language of the Bible, with thanksgiving as the people's primary response to the ultimate sovereignty of God. There were a number of reasons, however, why despite his Genevan background Rousseau did not appeal to this tradition. In theology, the hardening of the doctrine of predestination in seventeenth-century Reformed orthodoxy, and then the movement of the Genevan clergy in the eighteenth century towards a more rationalistic form of theology verging on deism, had largely drained the notion of gratitude of its vitality and point. Neither the harsh nor the impersonally benevolent God of these writers was likely to inspire much gratitude.[29] On the political level, Rousseau was all too aware of Calvin's intolerance of dissent, and of the way Geneva's patrician families in his lifetime controlled the city behind a veil of republican rule. Thus, it is no surprise that the social contract as he presents it is a purely impersonal affair: the people contract with each other as equals without regard to their relative economic or other circumstances. It would seem that in a society founded on a will that is truly general, gratitude would have no place.

[27] Gabriel Bonnot de Mably, *Entretiens de Phocion, sur le rapport de la morale avec la politique, traduits du grec de Nicoclès, avec des remarques* (1764). The book was published anonymously.

[28] See B. A. Gerrish, *Grace and Gratitude: The Eucharistic Theology of John Calvin* (Minneapolis: Fortress, 1993).

[29] See Helena Rosenblatt, *Rousseau and Geneva: From the 'First Discourse' to the 'Social Contract'* (Cambridge: Cambridge University Press, 1997), and Maria-Cristina Pitassi, *De l'orthodoxie aux lumières: Genève 1670–1737* (Geneva: Labor et Fides, 1992).

Yet, the polity formed by the social contract cannot do without inner feelings of obligation altogether. Something is needed to motivate obedience to the laws even when no one is looking, and so Rousseau advocates the institution of a 'civil' religion. Rousseau speaks of religion in terms more like Machiavelli's than Calvin's, but he does not treat religious belief as merely a useful illusion to be controlled by secular authority. True, Rousseau's list of the civil religion's dogmas has a utilitarian ring: 'L'existence de la divinité puissante, intelligente, bienfaisante, prévoyante et pourvoyante, la vie à venir, le bonheur des justes, le châtiment des méchants, la sainteté du contrat social et des lois; voilà les dogmes positifs' (The existence of the powerful, intelligent, beneficent, prescient, and provident divinity, the life to come, the happiness of the just, the punishment of the wicked, the sanctity of the social contract and the laws; these are the positive dogmas) (IV.8, *OC* iii. 468; G 2, 142). But religion must do more than prevent actions contrary to law. It must generate what Rousseau in the preceding paragraph calls the *sentiments de sociabilité* that motivate good behavior even when legal enforcement is absent.

It is not clear how hope of reward and fear of punishment by themselves can serve this less immediate function. Calvin, who grounds obedience in a prior sense of gratitude, can show how the calculus of reward and punishment is to be subordinated to a wider appreciation of divine charity, based on the Christian idea of God.[30] But for Rousseau, Christianity is too narrowly dogmatic in its institutional forms, and too otherworldly in its primitive essence, to serve as the civil religion. In Hobbes, hope and fear are focused on sanctions in this world, but they also have a motivating context. His sentiments of sociability are grounded in a constant and pervasive awareness of the potential for violence in human life. Rousseau, on the other hand, believes men are not naturally disposed to aggression. Even more important, the institution of the social contract is predicated on each citizen's willingness to overlook the differences of money and power among them and to give everything over to the people as a whole. For Rousseau, the political equality and solidarity that results from this commitment is a sufficient guarantee against outbreaks of serious violence among fellow citizens.

It might be more accurate to say that the real guarantee is that the imaginative world of the society created by the contract leaves no room

[30] 'Obedience to the commandments of love *is* thanksgiving, which for Calvin is not only a liturgical but an ethical concept' (Gerrish, *Grace and Gratitude*, 126).

for the possibility of such conflict to be entertained. Here again, the contrast with Hobbes is instructive. The laws of nature which according to *Leviathan* generate sociability are also mediated through an exercise of reason that leads to clear and compelling conclusions. Rousseau's civil religion is also reasonable (in the sense that its dogmas do not offend reason), but it is not, indeed cannot be, the product of deliberation or debate. For Rousseau, arguments over religion lead either to sectarian conflict (if they stem from unreflective conviction) or to the disenchantment that follows from adopting a self-conscious, critical attitude toward belief—that is to say, the enlightened approach of the *philosophes*. Where there are solid guarantees against sectarian conflict, as in a society grounded in a truly general will (such as the Geneva Rousseau portrays in the *Discours* and the *Lettre à d'Alembert*), it is disenchantment which presents the greater danger.[31] In a context of peace and security, when most people unreflectively obey the law, the exercise of critical reason can only serve to alienate citizens from their community by encouraging them to give priority to their private interests and shrug off the burden of obligation. Thus, Rousseau presents the civil religion as something to be taken on faith. Sentiments of sociability can only emerge through a consciousness that is active but unreflective, in other words through the imagination.

Rousseau's discussion of the civil religion does not, however, tell us *how* that religion works, what it feels like from the inside. In one sense, this is to be expected, since the 'religion of the citizen' (as opposed to the individual 'religion of man' we will read about in *Émile*) is concerned only with external behavior, not with belief. The hearts of the people are not to be policed.[32] It should not matter to the government what

[31] Rousseau's reluctance to support open critique of Geneva's political system diminishes, however, after Geneva's condemnation of the *Contrat social* in 1762. The complexities of his thought in that later period are now being given renewed attention in their own right. See *La Religion, la liberté, la justice: un commentaire sur les 'Lettres écrites de la montagne'*, ed. Bruno Bernardi, Florent Guénard, and Gabriella Silvestrini (Paris: Vrin, 2005).

[32] In this respect Rousseau is closer to Spinoza, who declared that 'Scripture demands nothing from men but obedience.' See Baruch Spinoza, *Theological-Political Treatise*, tr. Samuel Shirley (2nd edn, Indianapolis: Hackett, 2001), 154. This was a radically revisionist reading of the Bible, but one which is consistent with Spinoza's view of God as the impersonal necessity of nature. In the absence of a reciprocal personal relationship, gratitude is meaningless. Cf. Hobbes: 'The right of nature whereby God reigneth over men, and punisheth those that break his laws, is to be derived, not from His creating them, as if He required obedience as of gratitude for His benefits, but from His irresistible power.' *Leviathan*, 235 (ch. 31).

emotion motivates obedience to the laws. However, once religious feelings start to be nurtured, it might not be possible to contain the results within the framework of the political order. Since by definition gratitude is not governed by legal obligation, its scope may exceed the limits defined by the social contract and thereby subvert them. Precisely because self-interested reason is absent, gratitude might blur the boundaries between citizens and outsiders (by appealing to the idea of universal Christian fraternity, for example). It might foster a desire for an intensity of emotional connection with others that competes with the requirements of orderly sociability by creating expectations of intimacy at odds with family and social hierarchies.[33] And yet, the God of the *Contrat social* is not merely an impersonal and all-seeing judge. Such a God could not inspire sentiments of sociability. It is noteworthy that Rousseau speaks, not of 'a' but 'the' Divinity, a unique agent who is 'beneficent, prescient, and provident'. These qualities evoke a more personal kind of relationship than one defined by self-interested hope and fear. One might say that Rousseau creates a space for gratitude in his civil religion—but leaves it vacant.

To understand the meaning of this gesture, we must attend to the way Rousseau presents his argument as well as to the content of what he says. For this space is located at the intersection of two different authorial perspectives. In much of the *Contrat social*, Rousseau, in the manner of Machiavelli or Holbach, speaks of religion from outside, looking at it in purely functional terms as something to be manipulated for the common good. When he writes matter-of-factly that the peoples of the past identified their kings with gods, each people having its own national deity (the ancient Israelites being no different in this respect from any other nation); and when he dismisses Christianity as undermining the citizens' whole-hearted allegiance to the state, Rousseau seems to be addressing a reader—a Machiavellian prince in waiting, perhaps—who will accept such a disenchanted point of view with equanimity.[34] But Rousseau does not always speak from outside the belief system he advocates, to readers who likewise see themselves as too enlightened to need the civil religion themselves. In the opening para-

[33] In the *Lettre à d'Alembert*, Rousseau does offer a vision of moral intimacy in his depiction of the Genevan festivals, but even there it must be tempered by the vigilance of the authorities—authorities (religious and secular) whose rule is not to be made the object of scrutiny. One can have social intimacy and clarity about its political foundations, but not both.

[34] Rousseau, *Contrat social* IV.8 (*OC* iii. 460–1; G 2, 43).

graph of the chapter on civil religion, Rousseau refers to an argument of Caligula's (IV.8, *OC* iii. 460; G 2, 142), already cited near the beginning of the *Contrat social* (I.2, *OC* iii. 353; G 2, 43), to the effect that, just as the shepherd is superior in nature to the sheep, the rulers of men are superior in nature to ordinary people. According to Caligula, either kings are gods, or subjects are beasts.[35] The tone of this earlier passage was one of indignation at the exploitation of religious feeling (directed, as in the *Discours sur l'inégalité*, at the natural law arguments of Grotius and Hobbes), not cynical acceptance. The chapter on civil religion echoes this protest with an ironic comment on those early peoples who took their kings for gods. 'Il faut une longue altération de sentiments et d'idées pour qu'on puisse se résoudre à prendre son semblable pour maître, et se flatter qu'on se trouve bien' (It takes a long degradation of sentiments and ideas before one can bring oneself to accept a being like oneself as master, and flatter oneself [into believing] that one will be well off as a result) (IV.8, *OC* iii. 460; G 2, 142).

In this comment Rousseau identifies with the subjects, not the prince, and the reader is clearly meant to share Rousseau's indignation that things should have come to such a pass. Consequently, the reader cannot wholly adopt the Machiavellian point of view on religion that dominates the rest of the chapter. Rousseau has reopened, from below as it were, a critical space between human and divine authority that national religions had collapsed. While the civil religion supports the social contract by giving it a sacred underpinning, it is crucial this space be preserved if the sentiments of sociability fostered by religion are not to accelerate what the *Discours sur l'inégalité* argues is society's inevitable decline into despotism, that is, into a society marked by the fusion of personal and legal authority in the hands of an absolute ruler. If not held in check, the dynamic of sociability, with its personalizing of relationships, including that between the citizens and God, will corrupt the generality and impersonality of law. This nightmare represents a modern, 'enlightened' version of the archaic theopolitical synthesis Rousseau denounces in his disenchanted history of religion.

It is precisely for this reason that Rousseau imagines the God of the civil religion in terms at once personal and general, as a purely potential

[35] For an interpretation of the curious frequency of references to Caligula in this work, see Felicity Baker, 'La Peine de mort dans le *Contrat Social*', in Marian Hobson, J. T. A. Leigh, and Robert Wokler, eds, *Rousseau and the Eighteenth Century: Essays in Memory of R. A. Leigh* (Oxford: Voltaire Foundation, 1992), 163–88.

object of gratitude. Religion thus provides a background matrix rather than a foundation for 'sentiments of sociability'. Not only does gratitude remain outside the realm of legal obligation (this is true in the discourse of sociability also), its object or content remains underdetermined. One might describe the dynamic of gratitude in the terms of Kantian esthetics and say it has 'purposiveness' without specific purpose. Gratitude supplements the general will, not by completing it through the addition of an affective element (which, once again, would be to corrupt its generality) but by forestalling the collapse of the political community into a system enclosed upon itself. Whether or not Rousseau's God exists (and the genuineness of Rousseau's declarations of religious belief remains a subject of scholarly debate), his most important function in the civil religion is to prevent citizens from taking any person—human or divine—as their political master. For this, they should be thankful—even though, in Rousseau's paradoxical logic, the thanksgiving cannot itself be made an object of understanding without spoiling the thanks. This may be one reason that, in contrast with many of his other writings, Rousseau does not make the anticipated reception (favorable or unfavorable) of the *Contrat social* a theme within the work.

A similar distancing can be found in the chapter of the *Contral social* (II.7) devoted to another figure who illustrates the movement between the 'inside' and 'outside' of Rousseau's political system: the Legislator. In the preceding chapter, Rousseau raises what he sees as a fundamental problem in the creation of any political community. The people's will is only truly general if it transcends their socio-economic, demographic, and other circumstances. Individuals, who can see clearly what their situation is, are liable to prefer self-interest to the general welfare. 'Les particuliers voient le bien qu'ils rejettent: le public veut le bien qu'il ne voit pas' (Individuals see the good they reject, the public wills the good it does not see) (II.6, *OC* iii. 380; G 2, 68). Someone from outside is needed in order to bridge the gap between understanding and will in devising the system of positive laws most appropriate to a specific political body. So difficult is the task that the chapter on the Legislator opens with Rousseau exclaiming that 'il faudrait des dieux pour donner des lois aux hommes' (it would require gods to give men laws) (II.7, *OC* iii. 381; G 2, 69). Absent any actual divine intervention, Legislators must make the gods speak through their mouths. Moses and Muhammad are thus not to be condemned as 'impostors' for presenting themselves as prophets of a divine lawgiver. They should be judged by their results. And Rousseau's criterion is a purely practical one. The survival over time of the peoples they shaped provides the only material proof that understanding and will have been harmoniously combined.[36]

Similarly, Rousseau claims that only if people believe they are submitting to the laws of nature (in the sense of rules independent of human desires) and not to the arbitrary will of any individual will they accept the 'yoke of public felicity' (II.7, *OC* iii. 383; G 2, 71). As with the civil religion, the perspective Rousseau adopts is that of the disenchanted and knowing observer, and his idealizing rhetoric about the superhuman qualities of the Legislator can be read as an endorsement of religious trickery. The problem with this interpretation is that Rousseau's artfulness is too transparent. His text highlights the gap between understanding and will it was the mission of Moses and Muhammad to bridge.

There are two possible inferences from this paradoxical feature of the text. Rousseau may want the ordinary reader to become as shrewd as the political philosopher, or he may want the philosophical reader to share some of the awe lesser mortals feel when they consider the Legislator's character and task. That both intentions may be at work here is suggested by the author's shifting position with respect to his argument. Rousseau tells us neutrally the Legislator must see all men's passions without experiencing any of them, but then he shifts to the first person: the Legislator must have no connection to 'our nature' while understanding it thoroughly; his happiness must be independent 'of us' and yet he must be willing to concern himself with 'our' happiness (II.7, *OC* iii. 381; G 2, 68).[37] Here Rousseau identifies with humanity's lowly condition rather than analyzing it from the outside.

Yet, having once again prepared the ground for a subjective response to the Legislator, Rousseau says nothing about what the response should be. The 'true politician' will admire the 'genius' of Moses and Muhammad (II.7, *OC* iii. 384; G 2, 72), but how are the citizens to react to their ('our') own Legislator? Are they ('we') to be grateful to the one who mediates understanding and will for us? One might expect so, but

[36] Rousseau does not mention Jesus as being one of these 'impostors', but not, I believe, for reasons of prudence only. Unlike Moses or Muhammad, Jesus did not found a people in the political sense. The epithet *imposteurs* comes from a widely circulated clandestine manuscript. See *'Le Traité des trois imposteurs' et 'L'Esprit de Spinosa': philosophie clandestine entre 1678 et 1768*, ed. Françoise Charles-Daubert (Oxford: Voltaire Foundation, 1999).

[37] One wonders to what extent this duality echoes the long debate about the two natures of Christ.

while Rousseau has brought us to the brink of gratitude, he leaves us there. For the Legislator's gift the citizens of the *Contrat social* give no thanks. Rousseau may not want to encourage the credulity that goes with idealizing a person rather than the laws themselves. On the other hand, the absence of any commemoration of the Legislator's initiative may suggest it is dangerous to be reminded of it too often. The prestige of the laws may be undermined by 'enlightened' understanding of their origin. Recalling the Legislator's initiative may encourage the citizens to become more politically assertive than is good for the stability of the state.[38]

Thus, 'we' cannot be like the credulous believers Rousseau talks about, but we cannot *not* be like them. We, too, must look outside ourselves for an agent possessing that combination of knowledge and will necessary to set our (or any) community on a firm foundation. Rousseau does not resolve the contradiction, and perhaps he simply has no answer. Another possibility is that his aim is not so much to propose a solution (he stresses he is not himself a legislator) as to prevent our imagination of politics from closing in upon itself even as he stresses the need for unity of will. He does not do this by fostering an explicit awareness of conflicting values; that would be too risky. Instead, he moves the reader from a self-congratulatory position of detachment to a place within the community of those looking for help, so that their neediness can be shared and appreciated. From there he directs our imagination beyond the boundaries of the political order, precisely by emphasizing that the possibility of its existence has been *given* by an agent outside it. He thus makes room for gratitude—but that is all. The premise of the book, after all, its promise to readers suffering under arbitrary regimes, was liberation from personal dependence on gifts and favors into the impersonal space of contractual law.

Rousseau conceptualizes the contract as a process through which the individual gives everything over to the whole and receives it all back as a citizen—that is, as a process in which nothing has changed materially but yet everything has changed in the mode of possession. Yet, despite the ingenuity with which he develops this conception, the genre of the political treatise does not accommodate the play between givenness as a reality to be acknowledged and givenness as a gift to be received with

[38] In the *Lettre à d'Alembert*, Rousseau warns that a play in Geneva commemorating the Escalade—the day in 1602 when Savoyard invaders were successfully repelled—would stir up too much warlike spirit in the people (*OC* v. 110 n.; *CW* x. 340 n.).

thanks. It is here that fiction, for all Rousseau's condemnation of the dangers of artifice and make-believe, can play an important epistemological as well as existential role. In his epistolary novel *Julie*, Rousseau's characters discuss gratitude in the letters they write, but they also dramatize it in their relationships with each other. Gratitude becomes at once an object of analysis and an occasion for feeling, one in which readers, too, are invited to participate.

JULIE, OU LA NOUVELLE HÉLOÏSE

Rousseau's novel offers a utopian vision of harmony on the estate of Clarens but never loses sight of the real world of power.[39] Gratitude for favors is proof of moral refinement in a *belle âme*, but we are also shown how the sense of obligation can be manipulated to advance the benefactor's self-interest. This is especially true where sexual desire is involved. At the very beginning of the story, St Preux tells his pupil Julie that he cannot accept payment for his lessons. If he were obliged to her family, acting on his passion for her would be a violation of trust. The 'editor' of the letters comments sententiously that being paid in gratitude makes the fault even greater. 'Malheureux jeune homme! qui ne voit pas qu'en se laissant payer en reconnaissance ce qu'il refuse de recevoir en argent, il viole des droits plus sacrés encore' (Unhappy youth! who does not see that in allowing himself to be paid with gratitude for what he refuses to accept in money, he violates even more sacred rights) (I.24, *OC* ii. 85 n.; *CW* vi. 70 n.). Later, Julie tells St Preux it would be wrong to use the peasant girl Fanchon as an intermediary for their secret letters. They have helped Fanchon in the past, but asking her to become complicit in their forbidden correspondence would be an abuse of her gratitude, forcing virtue to become the instrument of vice (II.18, *OC* ii. 258; *CW* vi. 211).

The imagined exploitation of gratitude for erotic ends takes increasingly lurid forms when the temporary stability of the Clarens *ménage* starts to break down. Julie, ostensibly happy in her marriage to M. de Wolmar, exhorts her former lover St Preux to marry her cousin Claire. If he remains single and celibate, she argues, he might take sexual

[39] Rousseau, 'Préface de la nouvelle Héloïse: ou entretien sur les romans entre l'éditeur et un homme de lettres' (Preface of the New Heloise or Conversation about novels between the editor and a man of letters) (*OC* ii. 23; *CW* vi. 5).

advantage of Fanchon's continuing gratitude to him as her benefactor. Of course, the reader understands that Julie is defending against her own love for St Preux, but the way she seizes once again on a possible abuse of gratitude is significant (VI.6, *OC* ii. 668; *CW* vi. 549). And in 'Les Amours de Milord Édouard Bomston', an episode Rousseau omitted from the published novel, we find this supposedly phlegmatic Englishman entangled with a worldly and married Roman marquise. She will not grant him her favors, but in order to keep him attached she procures for him a courtesan named Laura. Édouard's gratitude, we are told, was harder for him to contain than his love (*OC* ii. 751; *CW* vi. 614).

In other contexts, gratitude can prove equally corrosive of human dignity. Julie was engaged to Wolmar because he saved her father's life when they were serving together as officers in the Dutch army. M. d'Étange decided to repay his obligation by giving Wolmar his daughter for a wife. We are told it would be ungrateful of him to go back on his word simply because Julie was not consulted and has fallen in love with someone else. Rousseau clearly intends the reader to view the father's action as another perversion of gratitude (III.18, *OC* ii. 349; *CW* vi. 288). The dutiful Julie herself believes it would be a sin even to think that the gratitude she owes her parents might have limits. 'Depuis quand un cœur sensible marque-t-il avec tant de soin les bornes de la reconnaissance?' (Since when does a sensible heart so carefully mark the limits of gratitude?) (II.6, *OC* ii. 208; *CW* vi. 170). Rousseau avoids a direct confrontation of the issue by introducing a new factor into the story. Wolmar loses his fortune in the turmoil of Russian politics. Canceling the marriage now would suggest that money took precedence over loyalty. The implication is that even though the free ideal of gratitude may be distorted by custom or prejudice, the characters must conform to social expectation.

In his portrait of Wolmar, however, Rousseau puts gratitude in a different kind of context. He initially presents Wolmar to the reader as a man of rational and utilitarian outlook, a man who likes to observe humanity from above. In his detachment, Wolmar resembles the French philosophers Rousseau criticized in the *Discours* for their lack of sensibility. After rescuing Julie's father, however, Wolmar begins to change. He did not expect any gratitude for his good deed, but 'le cœur sensible et reconnaissant' (the sensible and grateful heart) of Julie's father gave him 'une meilleure opinion de l'humanité' (a better opinion of mankind) (IV.12, *OC* ii. 491; *CW* vi. 403). He draws closer to his fellow men, and although he claims he does so only to observe them more clearly, closer contact with people generates in this confirmed bachelor a desire to get married. The spectacle of another person's gratitude breaches his self-sufficiency just enough that he agrees to be Julie's husband and master of the Clarens estate.

Wolmar does not hesitate to exploit his servants' personal loyalty to Julie to ensure the good management of his household, yet there is one important exception to his patriarchal attitude that shows he has not changed entirely: he does not expect gratitude from his servants. He has trained them and given them work they enjoy, yet the very egotism by which he sets himself above them acts as a barrier to obligation. 'Il n'y a que l'intention qui oblige, et celui qui profite d'un bien que je ne veux faire qu'à moi ne me doit aucune reconnaissance' (Intention alone creates obligations, and a person who takes advantage of something I want only for myself owes me no gratitude) (IV.10, *OC* ii. 446; *CW* vi. 367). Of course, the servants do feel obliged, but the relationship retains an impersonal quality that prevents it from becoming oppressive. In this respect it is likened to the relationship between God and human beings. St Preux makes the reference explicit when he freely expresses his own gratitude to Wolmar for helping him return to virtue by sublimating his love for Julie. Since St Preux is not Wolmar's employee, gratitude is an appropriate response. The younger man's 'grateful soul' inspires him to say: 'je ne puis vous offrir, comme à Dieu même, que les dons que je tiens de vous' (I can offer you, as to God himself, only the gifts I have received from you) (V.8, *OC* ii. 611; *CW* vi. 500).[40] Knowing a return is not expected prevents St Preux's feeling of dependence from being experienced as a burden.

The other side of the coin is that although Wolmar appreciates the advantages he enjoys as Julie's husband and master of a vast estate, he does not himself express any gratitude for his good fortune. Like the Legislator of the *Contrat social*, his role is to be concerned with others' happiness while remaining independent. His role in the book may be God-like, but he himself is an atheist. Like Bayle before him, Rousseau wants to promote religious tolerance by showing that an atheist can be moral. Yet, if Wolmar's unbelief is not evidence of moral failure, it is the sign of a defective sensibility. The more vulnerable characters, Julie, St Preux, and Claire, need a strong mentor figure like Wolmar, but their

[40] Cf. 1 Chr. 29: 34, a verse made broadly familiar by its use in worship services.

dependence is offset by their delight in a capacity for sensibility that allows them to feel superior to the 'cold' Wolmar. At first, this distribution of qualities gives stability to the small circle of *belles âmes.* But Julie soon becomes dissatisfied. She secretly wishes for her husband's conversion, so that he, too, may discover the sweetness of grateful attachment. Whether her wish arises from concern about his salvation or from resentment at his lack of neediness, it suggests the emotional equilibrium of Clarens is deceptive. Julie is increasingly torn between her wifely loyalty and her never-extinguished passion for St Preux, and only the fatal illness that befalls her after saving her son from drowning allows her to give each of these ties its due in the frankness of a deathbed confession.

Milord Édouard's behavior illustrates the novel's ambivalent attitude toward gratitude in a different way. In the early part of the story this wealthy English peer offers Julie and St Preux one of his English estates as a refuge from the wrath of Julie's father. Deference to paternal authority prevents the lovers from accepting his proposal, but they are deeply grateful for it, especially since Édouard is not bound to them by blood or social obligation. Indeed, when Julie's parents discover her correspondence with St Preux and the latter is forced to leave with Édouard for Paris, only his obligation to his benefactor enables him to part from his mistress. Years later, after St Preux has been living at Clarens with Wolmar and Julie for some time, Édouard again asks his friend, this time as a favor to himself, to accompany him on a trip to Italy. Édouard has fallen in love with Laura, the courtesan procured for him by the marquise, and he is debating whether to marry her. He relies on St Preux to decide whether her character justifies this irregular match. Édouard writes: 'je me fais un plaisir de rendre tout commun entre nous: la reconnaissance aussi bien que l'attachement' (I take pleasure in making everything common between us, gratitude as well as attachment) (V.1, *OC* ii. 525–6; *CW* vi. 431). In a letter to Wolmar, however, Édouard belies this idea of reciprocal service. 'Vous savez que pour contenter sa reconnaissance et remplir son cœur de nouveaux objets, j'affectais de donner à ce voyage plus d'importance qu'il n'en avait réellement' (You know that in order to satisfy his gratitude and fill his heart with new objects, I affected to lend this journey more importance than it really had) (VI.3, *OC* ii. 649; *CW* vi. 534). Here is another form of that manipulation of gratitude about which the novel is so uneasy. Given Édouard's unease with the form his own gratitude has taken, it may be that what he is really affecting is detachment. Whatever the case, the incident underscores just how exceptional it is for gratitude not to be exploited as a tool of domination or as an escape from one's true responsibilities to oneself and others.

Can gratitude, then, ever expand the scope of the self's agency in a truly beneficial way? Two incidents suggest that it can, although, significantly, neither involves an obligation to other human beings. The first occurs during St Preux's stay in Paris, where he composes a lengthy critique of life in the French capital. In reply to Julie's suggestion that Parisian hospitality should make him more indulgent, he replies: 'L'estime et la reconnaissance que m'inspirent leurs bontés ne font qu'augmenter ma franchise' (The esteem and gratitude their kindnesses inspire in me only increase my candor) (II.19, *OC* ii. 262; *CW* vi. 215). The notion of an empowering gratitude is a striking one. Rousseau is clearly alluding to his own relationship with Parisian readers. Their positive response to his early writings had encouraged a career that he was confident would reach a pinnacle of acclaim with the publication of the novel he was now writing.[41] Yet, it is interesting that St Preux names no actual Parisians and indeed describes no personal acquaintances. The only exception is an ironic one, when he mistakes the enticements of brothel prostitutes for the hospitality of salon hostesses—another illustration of the dangers of confusing ethical attachments with erotic ones. Otherwise, the French politeness that empowers St Preux has an impersonal quality that prevents it from fostering dependence. Looking back at Wolmar, we may wonder whether his own privileged position, at once inside and outside the Clarens circle, is only tenable to the extent that he relates to the little society as a whole more than he does to any individual, even Julie. When she dies, he discovers in his grief feelings of fragility and dependence that lead him to the brink of religious conversion, but this triumph over insensibility also marks the end of his role as legislator for others. It is St Preux who will be entrusted with the education of Julie's children.

The empowering gratitude St Preux enjoys as a thinker and writer in Paris is not, however, available to ordinary people. The second kind of self-enhancing gratitude is one to which anyone may have access, since it

[41] We find the same kind of empowering gratitude in Rousseau's relationship with Madame de Warens—an elective relationship, determined neither by blood nor by legal ties. See Felicity Baker, 'The Object of Love in Rousseau's *Confessions*', in Patrick Coleman, Jayne Lewis, and Jill Kowalik, eds, *Representations of the Self from the Renaissance to Romanticism* (Cambridge: Cambridge University Press, 2000), 171–99.

involves the cultivation of a relationship with God. It begins negatively, with Julie worrying that her gratitude to God for the happy life she enjoys at Clarens is too self-regarding, merely 'a self-interested gratitude' (V.5, *OC* ii. 591; *CW* vi. 484). The assumption here, inherited from seventeenth-century Augustinian *moralistes*, is that self-interest robs sentiment of all moral worth. In one of his *maximes*, La Rochefoucauld had declared: 'Il est de la reconnaissance comme de la bonne foi des marchands: elle entretient le commerce; et nous ne payons pas parce qu'il est juste de nous acquitter, mais pour trouver plus facilement des gens qui nous prêtent' (Gratitude is like good faith in business. It keeps commerce going; and we do not pay up because it is right for us to discharge our debt, but so that we can more easily find people who will lend to us).[42] The difficulty of discerning genuine motivation led many eighteenth-century thinkers to define virtue in terms of practical results rather than of an unattainable (and unascertainable) purity of intention. Rousseau's insistence in the *Contrat social* that the citizen's motives should not be scrutinized is informed by this tradition.

The premise of *Julie* is that the heroine can become a virtuous wife and mother even though she had a sexual relationship before marriage and continues for the rest of her life to love someone other than her husband. Thus St Preux, who reports the discussion to us, seeks to calm Julie's scruples about her motives. Self-interest (in the legitimate primary sense of *amour de soi*), he claims, is what anchors us in the real world. Julie's gratitude to God, which arises from and nourishes her attachment to those around her, is right and good, precisely because it enhances her earthly life and prevents her from taking it for granted. She contrasts her gratitude with the misguided devotion of the 'mystics' whose lack of self-interest comes not from a full heart but from an empty brain (V.5, *OC* ii. 590; *CW* vi. 483).[43]

[42] La Rochefoucauld, *maxime* 223, in *Moralistes du XVIIe siècle*, ed. Jean Lafond (Paris: Laffont, 1992), 154; La Rochefoucauld, *Collected Maxims and Other Reflections*, tr. and ed. H. and A. M. Blackmore and Françoise Giguère (Oxford: Oxford University Press, 2007), 63.

[43] The lovers of *Julie*, like their creator, are also admirers of archbishop Fénelon, whose doctrine of *pur amour* radicalized the basic Christian idea that God should be loved for himself by claiming that any self-interest (ultimately, even interest in one's own salvation) tainted that love. In doing so, Fénelon transformed an idea that had long been invoked by Christian mystics as a kind of theological paradox into a principle of general application. The notion of *pur amour*, and the 'quietist', almost impersonal attitude toward salvation associated with it, left little room for gratitude at all.

What St Preux does not realize is that Julie's anxiety about the relation between this world and the next stems from her enduring passion for him. She longs to escape the conflict between this passion and her moral principles. St Preux feels some of the same stress, but the difference is that Julie cannot relate to anything—to domestic society, or to the wider world of Paris, or to God—in general terms. As a woman, her relationships are all particular and personal.[44] They have an admirably self-involving quality, but by the same token she cannot bridge the gap between dependence and autonomy through a self-enhancing, because impersonal, gratitude. Indeed, her reaction to life at Clarens is that she is 'too happy'. She cannot live both inside and outside her own world, and she feels most self-interested when she is most selfless. Her dilemma cannot be resolved, and so her death, and with it the end of the Clarens experiment, becomes inevitable. A political community depends for its cohesion on a Legislator whose work endures after his death. The Clarens community might survive the death of Wolmar, but it cannot handle the loss of the woman who was its presiding spirit. In the absence of Julie, the dream of reconciling reciprocity and authority, attachment and autonomy, is exposed as an illusion.

On the other hand, Julie's death does unite the novel's characters, and along with them Rousseau's readers, in a solidarity of grief. The fact that readers of both sexes and of various social conditions wept for Julie suggests that they, too, felt oppressed by social structures unable to accommodate their emotions.[45] As author, Rousseau plays the role of a different kind of Legislator. Instead of establishing a constitution within which the general will can find political expression, he provides through his novel a capacious imaginative framework in which his readers find, and then give, articulate form to feelings that hitherto had remained inchoate. The outpouring of appreciative letters Rousseau received shows how grateful readers were for the gift.[46]

[44] For details of Rousseau's views of gender differences in this regard, see the discussion of Sophie's education in the fifth book of *Émile*.

[45] For a discussion of the social accommodation of emotion in the period, see the second half of William M. Reddy, *The Navigation of Feeling: A Framework for the History of Emotions* (Cambridge: Cambridge University Press, 2001).

[46] See Robert Darnton, 'Readers Respond to Rousseau: The Fabrication of Romantic Sensitivity', in *The Great Cat Massacre and Other Episodes in French Cultural History* (New York: Basic Books, 1984), ch. 6; Claude Labrosse, *Lire au XVIIIe siècle: La Nouvelle Héloïse et ses lecteurs* (Lyon: Presses universitaires de Lyon, 1985).

ÉMILE, THE TUTOR, AND THE VICAIRE SAVOYARD

Is it possible to say something more encouraging on a practical level about the way individuals can live successfully in society, connected to others by gratitude yet autonomous and self-possessed? This is one of the tasks Rousseau sets for himself in *Émile*. Whereas the *Discours sur l'inégalité* emphasized the independence and self-sufficiency of man in the state of nature, *Émile* acknowledges that man is by nature weak and therefore destined to be sociable. The contradiction between the two texts may be explained by the difference in their purpose. The *Discours*, even in its evocation of pity, was intended to provide a critical perspective on social life, while *Émile* moves toward a more constructive vision, in which positive emotional attachment plays a major role. In the state of nature, there is no room for love; human couplings are random, instinctual, and short-lived.[47] In the first part of *Émile*, which focuses on the negative education of nature, there is no question of love either, but in book four, the tutor starts preparing Émile for the life-long partnership of marriage. It is still true that 'tout attachement est un signe d'insuffisance: si chacun de nous n'avait nul besoin des autres il ne songerait guère à s'unir à eux' (every attachment is a sign of insufficiency. If each of us had no need of others, he would hardly think of uniting himself with them). But now Rousseau adds: 'Ainsi de notre infirmité même naît notre frêle bonheur' (from our very infirmity is born our frail happiness) (*OC* iv. 503; *E*, 221). Only God, by virtue of his omnipotence, is truly self-sufficient and therefore happy in solitude. Because human beings are weak, they can only love if they need someone else, and a person who does not love cannot enjoy such happiness as is available on earth.[48]

It is at the age when Émile's sexual desires begin to stir, and his need for a partner becomes acute, that Rousseau introduces the idea of attachment to other people and the notion of gratitude in particular. This does not mean the ideal of self-sufficiency is abandoned altogether,

[47] For a provocative treatment of this issue, see Susan Meld Shell, '*Émile*: Nature and the Education of Sophie', in Patrick Riley, ed., *The Cambridge Companion to Rousseau* (Cambridge: Cambridge University Press, 2001), 272–301.

[48] Recall that for Rousseau what distinguishes God (or the Legislator) is that he loves in the absence of any need of his own.

but because erotic desire is so powerful Émile needs both human and divine support to help defend his autonomy even as he opens himself to the vulnerability of love. Before he meets the woman of his dreams, therefore, Émile must be initiated into social relationships in a manner that recognizes his need for support without undermining his feeling of self-possession. Émile's education in sociability will cultivate in him sentiments of friendship and gratitude that his tutor can call upon in order to bind Émile to himself (as Édouard did with St Preux), but not for the tutor's benefit. The latter's only goal is to help Émile contain the wayward force of his desires.

Rousseau's concern here is not primarily with morality in the conventional sense. If sexual love is dangerous, it is because it can result in excessive attachment to a particular person at the expense of commitment to a general ideal or principle. In this respect, the problem is analogous to that of loyalty to a national leader, a national god, or even to the national community itself, considered as an empirical entity and not as a contractual structure.[49] Thus, before meeting and marrying Sophie, Émile will be encouraged by the tutor to picture an ideal woman who can provide a standard by which the merits of real women can be judged. As always with Rousseau, an element of distance and impersonality in emotion is necessary to give the self some room for maneuver.

Realistically, however, Émile cannot become emotionally attached without investing in the particularity of another person. The function of gratitude, as Rousseau conceives it, is to help deal with this problem. Rousseau begins by postulating a basic reciprocity in the development of attachment. 'En devenant capable d'attachement, il [Émile] devient sensible à celui des autres . . . On aime ce qui nous fait du bien; c'est un sentiment si naturel!' (In becoming capable of attachment, [Émile] becomes sensitive to that of others . . . We like what does us good. It is so natural a sentiment!) (*OC* iv. 520–1; *E*, 233–4). The feeling is natural because it responds to a 'what' (*ce*) rather than a 'who'. That is to say, it is not burdened by reflection on what the other's intentions might really be. Because the evidence is necessarily uncertain, such an examination

[49] For Rousseau's wariness about the identification with the national community, see Patrick Coleman, '"Aimer les lois": l'objet de l'éducation républicaine chez Rousseau', in Michael Böhler, Etienne Hofmann, Peter H. Reill, and Simone Zurbuchen, eds, *Republikanische Tugend: Ausbildung eines Schweizer Nationalbewusstseins und Erziehung eines neuen Bürgers. Contribution à une nouvelle approche des Lumières helvétiques* (Geneva: Slatkine, 2000), 459–70.

may well generate anxiety and thus uncomfortable feelings of dependence on the object. Rather, the natural response is to the effect itself, and it is immediate and unreflective. A side benefit is that Émile's gratitude gives the tutor a potential 'empire' over him, provided the tutor not demand Émile be grateful but instead allow him to arrive at gratitude on his own.

The tutor's relationship with Émile includes an element of control because attachment, and the sociability that derives from it, is the source of other feelings in addition to love. In seeking out 'what does us good', men may look on other people as instruments of their own well-being. As in the *Discours sur l'inégalité*, awareness of other people leads to reflection and comparison, activities which inevitably pervert legitimate self-interest into vanity. As soon as Émile begins to compare himself to other people, he wants to be in the 'first position' (*OC* iv. 23; *E*, 235). He makes himself the center of his world. Rousseau warns his readers that Émile's education into sociability should not begin with courts and salons. The brilliance of these assemblies can only provoke vanity or envy, while social success will give Émile a taste for power.

Instead, education in sociability should focus on the suffering that is the common lot of humanity. Picking up another theme of the *Discours*, Rousseau shows how the emotion of pity allows Émile to exercise his imagination and sensibility in a way that allows him to feel his own power, but only through identification with, and appreciation for, the weakness of others. By putting himself imaginatively in their place, he no longer makes himself the center of his own world, yet without actually giving up anything of his own. Of course, Émile must learn about more positive forms of power, but he will not do so through direct contact with men who rule others and whose place he would then want to occupy. Instead, he will read Thucydides and Plutarch, who will inspire him to be brave and bold, but who will also inoculate him against delusions of invincibility.

Similarly, when Rousseau wants to show gratitude in action, he surprises us by adopting the same indirect approach, as if gratitude were as dangerous to handle as power. And indeed, we have just seen how the tutor's control over Émile is based on his pupil's sense of obligation.[50] Yet, the tutor does not make gratitude an object of esthetic contemplation,

[50] If the tutor is not likely to abuse his power, it is because he is an exceptional individual, of course, but also because he is not Émile's father. His position is socially marginal and also limited in time.

as in the spectacle of the angry man. Émile himself will not witness actual displays of gratitude. He might be tempted to bestow favors himself just for the pleasure of putting people in his debt (an experience memorably dramatized in *Les Liaisons dangereuses* when the rake Valmont makes a show of giving alms to some poor folk who then fall to their knees and give him the new experience of being worshipped like a god). Worse, Émile might feel resentment at his inability, for lack of resources, to become a benefactor. There will be no dramatic initiation into gratitude comparable to the episode of Robert's garden. At most, the tutor will allow Émile a little agency by letting him give small alms when he thinks the tutor is not looking. Nor is Émile made to reflect on his own gratitude to the tutor until he is able to see him as a fellow sufferer. The tutor, he comes to realize, has sacrificed his own career and social life (including the possibility of marriage) to devote himself to his pupil's upbringing. In principle, though, the tutor's role in the pupil's life is an instrumental one. At some point Émile will leave his tutor behind and strike out on his own, and so the bond of gratitude is limited in scope. The tutor is not supposed to be a fully developed character with whose past or future Émile is called upon to engage, even in imagination. As a contemporary analogy to one of Plutarch's *Lives*, therefore, Rousseau tells the story of the Vicaire savoyard and the boy he rescued from degradation.

Although the Vicaire's 'Profession de foi' is not directly tied to the narrative of Émile's development, it is the culmination of Rousseau's exploration of gratitude's role in human flourishing. The Vicaire does not speak in Rousseau's name, and the boy of the story, who listens to the Vicaire's speech, is not supposed to be the future author of *Émile* either, only a fellow citizen who passes the speech on to him. Yet, this does not mean that Rousseau disagrees with the Vicaire or that his ideas bear only a contingent relation to the rest of the text. Rather, in addition to serving as a defense against the French censor, this relay of voices is designed to prevent the exploitation of the gratitude expressed in the 'Profession de foi' by any power, political, ecclesiastical, or even authorial. It is just because what the Vicaire says is vitally important and an integral part of the book that Rousseau does his best to present it as a 'sentiment... for examination', not as a rule to follow (*OC* iv. 558; *E*, 260).

As we saw in the last chapter, the discursive context of the Vicaire's 'Profession de foi' blends dramatic fiction with autobiographical testimony, personal voice, and discursive generality. The confident authorial first person of the main text of *Émile* gives way to the more vulnerable figure of someone who as a boy had been made angry and bitter by mistreatment. He would have fallen into vice had he not met a kindly priest who helped him escape from the hospice where he was confined. The boy forgets his benefactor and is soon punished for his 'ingratitude' by falling again into distress. The prodigal returns, however, and is welcomed back. Like Émile's tutor, the priest does not boast of the help he gives the boy. Instead, like Milord Édouard he pretends to need the boy's help in his research, thus instilling in him 'le noble sentiment de la reconnaissance' (the noble sentiment of gratitude) (*OC* iv. 562; *E*, 264). What attaches the boy even more to the priest is that the benefactor deserves compassion himself: a youthful love affair with a parishioner has spoiled his chances for advancement in the church. But while conforming outwardly to the dogmas and rituals of the Catholic church, the Vicaire holds to his own unorthodox theological system. This system he imparts to his protégé with a mixture of humility and pride designed to foster in the boy a similar mixture of gratitude to a higher power and confidence in his own.

Against the materialist *philosophes*, the Vicaire argues that the universe must have been created by an intelligent will external to it. Man, who shares the ability to act by free will and not by determined motion alone, is the king of creation. Not only does he have power to master the animals, his capacity for wonder proves his superiority over the whole world of matter. It takes little reflection to realize, however, that man did not earn this position through any merit of his own. Thus gratitude is a natural response to the Creator. 'De mon premier retour sur moi naît dans mon cœur un sentiment de reconnaissance et de bénédiction pour l'Auteur de mon espèce, et de ce sentiment mon premier hommage à la divinité bienfaisante' (From my first return to myself there is born in my heart a sentiment of gratitude and benediction for the Author of my species; and from this sentiment my first homage to the beneficent divinity) (*OC* iv. 583; *E*, 278).

When the Vicaire then turns to the human world around him, he sees a different picture. Disorder reigns; people do not occupy the social position they deserve. God himself is not to blame, because an omnipotent God can only will the good.[51] Man creates his own misery by taking the human tendency to think of oneself first as evidence that he really is the center of the universe. He should instead look to God, who

[51] For Rousseau, it is lack of power that generates ill will.

as creator is the true center of a cosmic order obscured by humanity's errors and perverted by its wayward will.

Overcoming one's attachment to the things of this world and contemplating the majestic order of the universe leads to a second, higher response of gratitude. The divine favor involved here is not the power to rule the earth, but the prospect of eventual liberation from the burden of earthly existence, including all relationships of dependence and power. It follows from this that the Vicaire will not ask anything specific of God: petitionary prayer would betray a misunderstanding of what divine providence is all about. The Vicaire's confidence in his ultimate release is not, however, the empty, escapist mysticism Rousseau condemned in *Julie*. On the contrary, the Vicaire never stops focusing on the needs of the self here below for reassurance and emotional stability. And yet, the Vicaire's faith is not for Rousseau merely a projection onto the cosmos of the self's desire for order. The voice of conscience, which expresses an innate love of order and leads us to look beyond ourselves, is for Rousseau independent of all self-interest.[52] As in the *Contrat social*, Rousseau wants to define a place for the self at once within and outside the system of mutual obligations, which allows the self to flourish only by destroying its independence. Because the Vicaire's gratitude is not tied to any concrete earthly benefit or to a benefactor who needs any favor in return, it allows him, albeit by anticipation, to be more wholly who he is: '*moi* sans contradiction, sans partage' (*me* without contradiction or division) (*OC* iv. 604–5; *E*, 293). In the end, the Vicaire will feel grateful, not for having his needs met, but for no longer having needs at all. Here at last is the gratitude vital to human happiness without the dependence that spoils it.

If we ask how the gratitude fostered by faith can protect the Vicaire's protégé from delinquency, the answer does not lie in any religious prohibition. The Vicaire ends his speech with a general warning against bad habits, but he says nothing about specific rules of behavior. This is because the 'vice' against which he warns the boy is psychological rather than moral in origin. Social oppression had made the boy feel depressed and unworthy, and so the primary function of gratitude is to restore him

[52] For discussion about where conscience as a normative voice fits within Rousseau's conception of human nature, see Henri Gouhier, *Les Méditations métaphysiques de Jean-Jacques Rousseau* (2nd edn, Paris: Vrin, 1984). For a different interpretation of Rousseau's religious views, see Victor Gourevitch's challenging essay 'The Religious Thought', in Riley, *The Cambridge Companion to Rousseau*, 193–246.

to himself. As an attachment based on the contemplation of an attractive and order-creating Other, it involves no self-alienating desire and seeks no reward other than a heightened sense of integration.

Whether the lessons of the 'Profession de foi' will be of any use to Émile is another question. In his political education, Émile's role was that of a spectator who contemplated the great men of history from a distance, the better to appreciate their courage without losing sight of their vulnerability. He is not being educated to be a ruler himself. The 'Profession de foi' is also focused on the value for the anonymous boy of sympathetic contemplation. The Vicaire himself gives his speech against the backdrop of a beautiful landscape—but one in which no people can be seen (*OC* iv. 565; *E*, 266). He tells us that he now fulfills his priestly duties conscientiously and without anxiety, but he accepts that these duties exclude intimate involvement with individuals. Nor is his protégé's gratitude said to spill over into other relationships. Despite the warmth of its theistic overtones, the Vicaire's faith has no interpersonal concreteness. This did not matter to the readers of Rousseau's day. If the charms of 'natural religion' are now hard to see, the enthusiastic response of Rousseau's readers reminds us that for Rousseau's contemporaries the attraction of religion that seemed to combine personal validation with a saving sense of distance and impersonality should not be underestimated.

But while in politics and religion Émile can preserve a measure of detachment, it is difficult to see how this could be true in love. Émile is raised so as to be able to live productively in any country and to adopt any reasonable expression of faith, but his marriage implies a lasting bond with a specific woman. Thus the prospect for success in love is not encouraging. While *Émile* does end with the hero happily united with his bride, the treatise's abortive novelistic sequel, *Émile et Sophie, ou les solitaires*, shows the marriage breaking down very quickly once the lovers have to deal with each other as real people. Even the original *Émile* ends in a kind of palinode. Instead of Émile bidding his tutor farewell as he sets off with Sophie, Rousseau has the young man beg the tutor to stay on, complaining that he cannot do without his guidance (*OC* iv. 868; *E*, 480). The gift of self-possession cannot, it seems, be received, enjoyed, and passed on to others without something going wrong.

Perhaps in the end the only exception to this rule is to be found in the relationship between the author and his readers, but even there the process is a risky one. If *Julie* provided an imaginative context in which dreams of psychological and social integration could be contained, *Émile* underscores what is problematic in trying to apply imaginative paradigms to particular real-life contexts. It is also ironic that the book Rousseau considered to be his most constructive and helpful work should be the one condemned most severely, and that the part of the book for which the author expected the most gratitude, the 'Profession de foi', should be the target of the attack. While many readers, including many within the church, responded enthusiastically to the Vicaire's preaching,[53] *Émile* was condemned by religious authorities in both Paris and Geneva. In his reply to the archbishop of Paris, Christophe de Beaumont, Rousseau would write: 'Je connaissais trop les hommes pour attendre d'eux de la reconnaissance' (I knew men too well to expect gratitude from them) (*OC* iv. 1003; *CW* ix. 80), but it was clear that he had expected it, and that his bitter experience of unexpected persecution lies behind his later ambivalence about doing and receiving favors in the *Rêveries.*

UNFINISHED BUSINESS

And yet, in the unfinished tenth *promenade* that concludes the *Rêveries* as we have them, Rousseau returned to the subject of gratitude in the form of a tribute to Madame de Warens, whose *bienveillance* inspired in him 'avec la reconnaissance des sentiments plus tendres que je n'en distinguais pas' (along with gratitude, more tender feelings which I did not distinguish from it). This encounter, he writes 'décida de toute ma vie' (determined my fate) (*OC* i. 1098; *CW* viii. 89, tr. modified). In terms that recall the 'Profession de foi', Rousseau celebrates the fact that, far from creating a relationship of dependence, Madame de Warens's generosity allowed him to experience 'cet unique et court temps de ma vie où je fus moi pleinement sans mélange et sans obstacle et où je puis véritablement dire avoir vécu' (this unique and brief time in my life when I was myself, fully, without admixture and without obstacle, and when I can genuinely say that I lived). He goes on to develop the paradoxical nature of the relationship: 'Je ne pouvais souffrir l'assujettissement, j'étais parfaitement libre, et mieux que libre, car assujetti par mes seuls attachements, je ne faisais que ce que je voulais faire' (I could

[53] See, among others, Philippe Lefebvre, *Les Pouvoirs de la parole: l'Église et Rousseau, 1762–1848* (Paris: Éditions du Cerf, 1992).

not bear subjection; I was perfectly free and better than free, for bound only by my affections, I did only what I wanted to do) (*OC* i. 1098–9; *CW* viii. 89–90).[54] There is no doubt that this experience was crucial to the development of Rousseau's creative talent. The grateful responses of many ordinary readers show that they, too, felt their sense of self quickened and enhanced by their acquaintance with Rousseau through his works.

What explains, then, the difficulty in mediating gratitude and independence that emerges into the open within *Émile* and then is acted out in the relationship between author and public? One may only speculate, but setting to one side the depth of the religious, political, and cultural problems he tries to address, Rousseau seems to be haunted by a double bind of anxiety. Only a reader who has become independent, whose judgment has been emancipated from obligation to society, can recognize Rousseau's fundamental goodness, that is, his moral innocence. If Rousseau knows himself to be innocent, it is only because a unique set of circumstances have freed him from the blinders of social conditioning, circumstances that others have not known but which they can access in their imaginations by reading his works. And yet that same independence also leaves readers free to judge Rousseau as they will, that is to say, in ways Rousseau cannot control. If they feel grateful to Rousseau, they should judge him favorably. Whether that gratitude becomes in itself a resented experience of dependence, of reader on author, or vice versa—as often happened in his own life—is a real risk, one which, again, Rousseau cannot control. Nor does he have the confidence in social progress that allows him to place any hope in eventual vindication of the inherent value of his works irrespective of their author's faults. To have to rely on the gratitude of posterity is a prospect that holds little appeal for Rousseau.

In this respect, he differs greatly from his erstwhile friend Diderot. As we shall see in the next chapter, however, the dynamic of gratitude, and of anger, in *Le Neveu de Rameau* also reflects anxieties about authorship.

[54] See note 41.

6

Resentment and Reflection in *Le Neveu de Rameau*

Le Neveu de Rameau is the frankest and freest of all Diderot's works, but also the one most shrouded in secrecy. Not only was the satire not published during the author's lifetime, even in clandestine form, it is never so much as mentioned in Diderot's other writings or in the correspondence with his friends. Even Diderot's executor Naigeon, who oversaw the posthumous publication of other controversial works when the Revolution made that possible, seems to have been unaware of the *Neveu*'s existence. Although the text originated, at least in part, from a very public quarrel over Palissot's play *Les Philosophes*, which portrayed Diderot as a duplicitous character bent on subverting the moral order, none of the author's contemporaries heard the bitter anger of 'Moi's' complaints against the enemies of Enlightenment.[1] Nor were they confronted by the provocative character of 'Lui', based on the composer Jean-Philippe Rameau's real-life nephew, whose resentful and sometimes obscene tirades against social hypocrisy might well have sparked the reader's ire as well. On the other hand, since Diderot kept the work a secret, he incurred no debt of gratitude to friends for endorsing or publishing it. Absent from the *Neveu*, for example, are the appreciative references to Grimm we find in Diderot's *Salons*, *La Religieuse*, or *Jacques le fataliste*, in whose confidential newsletter these daring works first saw the light of day. Absent, too, is the resentment at Grimm's interference that surfaces here and there in those same works, and which might explain why he did not entrust him with *Le Neveu de*

[1] The scholarly consensus that Diderot first drafted his satire in 1761 or 1762 and revised it over a period of years into the 1770s has recently been challenged by Henri Coulet. He argues it was written only in the early 1770s and that allusions to earlier events are deliberate anachronisms. For a judicious discussion, see Nicholas Cronk's introduction to *Rameau's Nephew and First Satire*, tr. Margaret Mauldon (Oxford: Oxford University Press, 2006).

Rameau. Absent also, finally, is any mention in the text of Rousseau, the former friend who had become in Diderot's eyes a monster of ingratitude as well as an enemy of Enlightenment, and who is arguably silently present in the background of the work.[2] *Le Neveu de Rameau* appears to be the most extroverted of Diderot's works, yet at the same time it seems to be the most self-contained. The most deeply dialogic of Diderot's dialogs was never brought by its author into actual conversation with others. One might say that in the *Neveu* the author dialogs with himself. This is surely true, but the secrecy surrounding the work makes us wonder about the social stakes of this inner exchange.

It is hard to imagine a writer as self-reflexive as Diderot not turning the conditions of the work's composition into one of the themes of the work itself, and so a possible starting-point for exploring the paradox of a non-dialogic dialog may be found in a moment of the dialog where Diderot remarks that even silence can be expressed in sound. Lui is in the midst of one of his musical impressions by which he imitates in rapid succession the sounds of an entire orchestra of instruments. His voice also evokes a wide variety of scenes and moods: 'un orage, une tempête, la plainte de ceux qui vont périr, mêlée au sifflement des vents, au fracas du tonnerre; c'était la nuit avec ses ténèbres, c'était l'ombre et le silence, car le silence même se peint avec des sons' (a storm, a tempest, the moans of the dying mingling with the whistling of the wind and the crashing of the thunder; night, with its darkness; shadows and silence—for sound can portray silence itself).[3] In its immediate context, this passage explores what it means to say that music imitates nature. Diderot is reaching beyond conventional notions of imitation as a clear correspondence of art to its object toward an esthetic of the sublime, in which music allows us to hear even what in nature has no sound. This passage suggests that Diderot's silence about the work, and its relationship to what the speakers of the dialog say, might be discerned within the text itself. I will argue that the place to look is where the dialog between the

[2] The case for Rousseau as an inspiration for the satire has been forcefully made in Donal O'Gorman, *Diderot the Satirist* (Toronto: University of Toronto Press, 1971). He points to Diderot's bitter remarks about Rousseau's ingratitude in his manuscript 'Tablettes', 143–4 and 216–17. See John Pappas and Georges Roth, 'Les "Tablettes" de Diderot', *Diderot Studies* 3 (1961), 309–20.

[3] Diderot, *Le Neveu de Rameau*, in *Œuvres*, ed. Laurent Versini (Paris: Laffont, 1994–7), ii. 678. Unless otherwise indicated, all quotations from Diderot are from this edition, abbreviated as V. References to the *Neveu* in volume ii of this edition will be given in the text by page number only, followed by page references to Mauldon's fine translation, which I have occasionally ventured to modify in order to highlight a specific linguistic point.

characters is at its sharpest and yet most elusive: when it addresses anger and resentment at personal dependence, and the gratitude (or ingratitude) that may also result from acknowledging such dependence.

In one or another of its forms, anger appears at every stage of the dialog. The nephew himself, or 'Lui', is angry at having been banished from the household of the financier Bertin, where he was employed as court jester and general factotum. He had lived there in comfort, despite the humiliation of having to constantly find new ways to praise Bertin's intelligence and new roles for Bertin's mistress, the mediocre actress Mlle Hus. The philosopher, 'Moi', expresses righteous indignation at Lui's servility, but he also berates him, somewhat ironically, for failing to show gratitude toward his benefactor, even though it is precisely this fault that proves Lui still clings to his moral dignity. Matching irony for irony, Lui laments the lack of moral fiber that prevents him from becoming as single-minded in corruption as the courtier Bouret and other virtuosos of flattery. Lui also exposes the hidden resentment in Moi, who has not forgotten the social humiliations he had to endure in his impoverished youth, even though the now-established man of letters would prefer not to dwell on them. This old resentment emerges in new form as Lui challenges Moi's hard-won sense of philosophical equanimity. In an even more serious blow to his self-image as a *philosophe*, Moi finds to his dismay that as the dialog progresses he cannot untangle admiration for Lui's skill as a performer from contempt for his immorality.

The thematic salience of anger is underscored by the generic framing of the text as a satire in the Roman tradition.[4] A quotation from one of Horace's satires (II.7) appears as an epigraph, while echoes of Juvenal and Persius may also be found throughout the work.[5] The characteristic

[4] The dialog's actual title, according to the manuscript, is *Satyre seconde* (623). For a discussion of this title, see Stephen Werner, *Socratic Satire: An Essay on Diderot and Le Neveu de Rameau* (Birmingham, Ala: Summa, 1987).

[5] The scholarship on Diderot's relationship to Horace is well known enough not to be rehearsed here. For Persius, see the *Neveu* (658), the 'Satyre première' (V ii. 591), and the 'Satire contre le luxe à la manière de Perse' in the *Salon de 1767* (V iv. 586–90); G. Charlier and L. Hermann, 'Diderot annotateur de Perse', *RHLF* 35 (1928), 39–63; and Roland Desné, 'Diderot correcteur d'une traduction des "Satires" de Perse', in *Éditer Diderot, Studies on Voltaire and the Eighteenth Century* 254 (1988), 233–42. A number of critics have sought to place *Le Neveu de Rameau* in the Menippean tradition, and certainly such factors as the mix of tones and themes make the connection a plausible one. Arguing against it, however, is the fact that when Diderot takes inspiration from Lucian or Rabelais, as he does in *Jacques le fataliste*, he puts it to comic rather than satirical use. On the Menippean tradition, see Howard D. Weinbrot, *Menippean Satire Reconsidered: From Antiquity to the Eighteenth Century* (Baltimore: Johns Hopkins University Press, 2005).

form of Roman satire is a multi-layered mini-drama of anger. Slaves, parasites, or reprobates complain of their ill-treatment and expose the corruption of the good citizens around them, and yet their angry outbursts are also an occasion for the reader's scorn, since these characters have neither the social nor the moral standing required for their resentment to be taken seriously. On the other hand, the righteous indignation of the satirist who laughs at his unworthy characters may itself be undermined by his own unthinking conventionality or his inability to control his own passions.[6] For all its ironies, however, Roman satire never seriously questions the distinction between those whose anger in defense of personal reputation or public good may be socially legitimate, and those who by virtue of their low status do not deserve to have their anger taken seriously. The Horatian satire quoted at the beginning of the *Neveu* is set in the topsy-turvy world of the Saturnalia, but although status hierarchy is temporarily suspended, it remains a given. In Diderot's text, by contrast, Lui justifies his resentment with a claim to moral dignity which may be ridiculous but which is also given a pathetic dimension more reminiscent of Rousseau than of ancient Rome.[7]

Nor does ancient satire entertain the possibility that philosophy as such may be rife with internal contradictions. Would-be wise men betray their principles, but in classical satire the philosophical way of life is never at odds with itself.[8] In *Le Neveu de Rameau*, on the other hand, Lui's challenge to Moi goes beyond exposing the *philosophe*'s complacency or making him acknowledge the corruption of respectable and even of enlightened society. That kind of pressure Moi will ultimately welcome as an occasion to expand the scope of his thinking, to become more truly a philosopher. If Lui is truly disturbing, it is because, as we shall see, he raises the discomforting issue of the *philosophe*'s dependence on an agency outside himself, not for approval or respect, but for the very material with which he thinks. The eccentric Lui may be a phenomenon of nature, but he is not simply an object readily available for analysis. As Lui points out, Moi is driven by his desire for stimulation

[6] A relevant text here is Juvenal's ninth satire, too obscene, perhaps, to be mentioned even in as uninhibited a work as *Le Neveu*.

[7] In his *Essai sur les règnes de Claude et de Néron*, Diderot praises Seneca's Stoic virtue, yet he concludes his discussion of the philosopher's *De ira* by declaring: 'La raison, sans les passions, serait presque un roi sans sujets' (Reason without the passions is almost like a king without subjects) (V i. 1173).

[8] Lucian may be a partial exception to this rule, but it is significant that Diderot never invokes him on this topic.

to seek out men such as Lui; he also needs Lui to open up to him. This gives their relationship an interpersonal dimension even though Moi likes to think he is merely and impersonally observing the behavior of a curious natural specimen. To acknowledge an epistemological debt to Lui would be to undermine the sense of detached autonomy so important to the Enlightenment thinker.

This is not to say that Diderot believed that philosophers escape all external determinations. On the contrary, Diderot's materialist views made him emphasize the thinker's location within an already constituted dynamic of matter and speech in motion.[9] Generally speaking, however, the implications of epistemological dependence for the philosopher *as a person* are not addressed. Diderot prefers to think of human beings as complex but imperfectly organized nodes of relations within a larger system rather than as persons in the humanistic sense. When he makes an exception to this rule, he does so not as an end in itself but to make a broader epistemological point. The *Lettre sur les aveugles*, for example, focuses on the ways the blind English mathematician Saunderson makes rational sense of the world around him despite his infirmity. There is pathos in Saunderson's description of himself as a 'monster' or freak of nature, deprived of the benefits of sight. Yet, Diderot's real aim is to discredit arguments for the existence of God on the basis of the world's design. Saunderson's plight is exploited chiefly for its polemical value, with much of the *Lettre* being devoted to the ingenuity with which Saunderson has compensated for his infirmity. From an epistemological point of view, his dependence is not greater than our own, only different, and the reader's attention is directed primarily outwards, to the complexity of the natural circumstances which condition any knowledge.[10]

A more complicated dramatization of dependence occurs in *Le Rêve de d'Alembert*. Diderot's former partner in the direction of the *Encyclopédie* is stripped of his dignity by being portrayed in his sleep. We are shown how the free associations of his dream speech generate erotic fantasies and culminate in a nocturnal emission. Here the philosopher's

[9] See Jean Starobinski's classic discussion of Diderot's tendency to use other people's words as a springboard for thought and his predilection for the dialog form in 'Diderot et la parole des autres', *Critique* 296 (1972), 3–22.

[10] By contrast, in the *Additions à la Lettre sur les aveugles*, composed in 1782 and thus possibly Diderot's last text, Diderot paints a more sentimental portrait of a blind woman, Mélanie de Salignac, who expresses her gratitude for all the kindness she has received from others (V i. 190).

lack of self-possession, the dependence of his thought on physical processes beyond his control, is vividly dramatized, but the sleeping d'Alembert of the dialog does not realize what is going on. He does not, therefore, experience any humiliation, and so there is no occasion for anger at having his nocturnal fantasies revealed to a stranger, or at being turned into an object of scientific scrutiny in the dialog between his companion Julie de Lespinasse and Doctor Bordeu.[11] Any resentment he might later express, or that the reader might be tempted to attribute to him, would in any case be undercut by the nature of his predicament: his indignities make him a figure of comedy.[12]

In any case, it is Bordeu who is the real philosopher in the *Rêve*, and the doctor's impersonal medical gaze remains untroubled by emotion. Dependence on his patient as a source of medical knowledge does not undermine the status or integrity of a physician, whose clinical mission is more practically oriented than the philosopher's. The clear separation between one body and another in the medical situation stands also in marked contrast to the disturbing fluidity of organic boundaries in d'Alembert's vision of swarming bees. D'Alembert is not suffering from a contagious disease, after all, but only dreaming. Mlle de Lespinasse's emotional autonomy is not in doubt either, even though she is a woman. Her relationship to d'Alembert was purely platonic, and so she is easily able to overcome her own momentary discomfort with the experiment and discuss sexual matters with a detachment that matches the doctor's. As in the *Lettre sur les aveugles*, then, the philosopher's dependence on the objects of his thought is not thematized as an occasion for an emotional response of appreciation or resentment.

Even Diderot's dialog on the esthetics of acting, the *Paradoxe sur le comédien*, tends toward the impersonal. Its main thesis, that actors are better able to communicate emotions consistently and convincingly when they do not feel them, is persuasively argued, but it is developed solely in terms of the mastery of technique. It does not explore how the

[11] On the contrary, gratitude to the doctor for bringing to light and demystifying the secrets of the body might be a more appropriate response, did not Julie's modesty, on the one hand, and d'Alembert's celibate state, on the other, preclude any dwelling on this gratitude.

[12] Thus the anger expressed by the characters in Diderot's *Jacques le fataliste* is a matter for laughter. That of Mme de la Pommeraye would be only a partial exception. Her single-minded vindication of what she feels is owed to her is impressive, but, as in Diderot's other tales of infidelity, it is disproportionate to its occasion, and so evidence of error rather than of philosophical judgment.

achievement of such mastery might affect the actor's own self or the spectator who admires its display. One can understand perhaps why Diderot would want to avoid this issue, since those who criticize the theater on moral grounds, including Rousseau in his *Lettre à d'Alembert*, liked to argue that the actor's habit of pretense leads to duplicity in real life. However, the whole dialog is governed by another kind of absolute imperative. Diderot's own test for good acting—whether he can understand the play even when he blocks his ears so as not to hear the dialog—suggests that what is most important is that the feelings expressed on stage be clearly and unmistakably discernible to anyone and everyone. The emotional complexities in the achievement and comprehension of dramatic communication can be safely ignored as long as the demand for epistemological certainty is satisfied.

The blending of reflective philosophical dialog and vehement Roman satire in *Le Neveu de Rameau* suggests that in this work Diderot is now ready to risk the philosopher's self-image in a more open exploration of his personal relationship to the provocations of the world around him. These provocations are embodied in the figure of Rameau's nephew, a man whose opinions, social behavior, and displays of esthetic virtuosity range from the pathetically contemptible to the intellectually bracing to the disturbingly sublime. Moi describes Lui as 'un grain de levain qui fermente et qui restitue à chacun une portion de son individualité naturelle' (a grain of yeast that ferments, and restores to each of us a bit of his natural individuality) (624/4, tr. modified). To respond to him dispassionately is therefore to miss the opportunity he provides for regaining that individuality. The nephew does more than offer material for observation: he presents Moi with an occasion for experience. The fact that Moi needs to seek out the nephew suggests such opportunities are rare and precious, and so it can be said that by making himself available Lui is doing Moi a favor. Acknowledging such a benefit, however, stands at odds with the *philosophe*'s sense of autonomous agency. As we shall see, the paradox of the *Neveu* is that this tension arises even though, indeed in part because, interaction with the nephew enhances Moi's sense of his ability to deal with the world on his own. Moi's encounter with Lui dramatizes an experience of epistemological dependence which produces complex results. It generates denial and angry resentment, but a more positive appreciation as well. This latter response will be intellectually and temperamentally 'philosophical' in a way that is difficult to define, since, unlike Bordeu's reaction to d'Alembert or Saunderson's response to the cosmic order, it seeks to transcend rather than merely dismiss the dependence that generates satiric anger and dialogic gratitude.

ANGER AND SATIRIC DIGNITY

Lui's anger at his banishment from the household of the opulent financier Bertin provides Diderot with a convenient way to denounce the foolishness and corruption of the rich while exposing the angry parasite's own contradictions. In adopting this kind of satirical structure, Diderot's classical model is less that of Horace II.7 than of Juvenal's ninth satire, the only one that author composed in dialog form. Juvenal's satirical persona asks the gigolo Naevolus why he looks so thin and why his good humor has changed to gloom. Naevolus launches into a long complaint about his ungrateful patron, who has not properly rewarded him for all his services. Not only has Naevolus prostituted himself to the patron's vanity and sexual desires, he has also ensured the future of the patron's family by fathering children with his wife—something the patron himself, who prefers to take the passive role in homosexual intercourse, was loath to do. Yet, despite the bitterness of his critique, Naevolus nurtures an equally vulgar fantasy of wealth and power, and his righteous indignation is further undermined by his fear that the poem's speaker will repeat what he has said. His cowardice makes him unworthy of his anger.[13]

Diderot's Lui can be just as servile as Naevolus, but he is no coward. Or rather, he is no more a coward than anyone else in eighteenth-century French society, where philosophic prudence, in Diderot's view, is not a betrayal of bold speech but its necessary complement. The contrast found in Juvenal between the satirist's willingness to accept the consequences of *parrhesia* (bold speech) and the parasite's fear is not to be found in Diderot.[14] Indeed, he was irked when Rousseau adopted his motto (also from Juvenal),[15] since he viewed Rousseau's willingness 'to

[13] See *Juvenal and Persius*, ed. and tr. Susanna Morton Braund (Cambridge, Mass.: Harvard University Press, 2004). For commentary, see S. H. Braund, *Beyond Anger: A Study of Juvenal's Third Book of Satires* (Cambridge: Cambridge University Press, 1988).

[14] For an important recent study of *parrhesia* in the ancient world and beyond, see Michel Foucault, *Le Gouvernement de soi et des autres: cours au Collège de France, 1982–1983* (Paris: Hautes Études, Gallimard Seuil, 2008).

[15] Juvenal, *Sat.* IV.91. Diderot responded to Rousseau's motto in his 'Tablettes' by citing another line from Juvenal, 'Qui Curios simulant, et Bacchanalia vivunt' (roughly

risk his life for the truth' as a theatrical gesture devoid of any real sacrifice, whereas at that moment Diderot himself, as editor of the controversial *Encyclopédie*, faced a genuine political threat. Diderot could not afford grand gestures if he was going to complete his task. Lui's pragmatism is thus not in itself something to be scorned.

Yet, neither is the claim to moral dignity that grounds Lui's anger. Here we see another difference between Diderot and his Roman sources. When Moi advises Lui to beg Mlle Hus, Bertin's mistress, to intercede for his pardon, Lui agrees at first, but then he rebels. 'Il faut qu'il y ait une certaine dignité attachée à la nature de l'homme, que rien ne peut étouffer' (it must be that man's nature comprises a certain dignity, which nothing can stifle) (635/17, tr. modified), not even the long habit of mercenary servility. Lui is willing to abase himself, but only on his own terms: 'je veux bien être abject, mais je veux que ce soit sans contrainte' (I'm quite willing to be abject, but I want to be abject without constraint) (652/38). Moi's initial reaction is contemptuous: 'votre dignité me fait rire' (your dignity makes me laugh) (652/38). He advises Lui to have 'le courage d'être gueux' (the courage to be a pauper) (635/17) if he doesn't like the way his patrons treat him. Yet, as a man who himself suffered his share of humiliation in his rise to a comfortable position in society, Moi cannot take his talk of courage too far.[16]

More important, Moi's critique is undermined by his readiness to identify with Lui's way of looking at things. It is Moi who salaciously details the attractions of Mlle Hus's backside, which Lui is called upon to kiss, perhaps not just metaphorically, as part of his apology. Of course, in Diderot's eighteenth century, prurient fantasies are not necessarily incompatible with *philosophie*; indeed freedom from puritanical prejudice is a mark of the philosophic spirit. But Moi also finds himself laughing at Lui's dramatic demonstration of how to procure a young bourgeois girl for a rich seducer (636/18). This is taking libertine

translatable as: 'who present themselves as virtuous men yet live disorderly lives) (*Sat.* II.3). See Pappas and Roth, 'Les "Tablettes" de Diderot', 318. Diderot had used the same quotation in his discussion of satire in his article 'Encyclopédie' (V i. 405).

[16] We should beware of identifying the Moi of the dialog so closely with Diderot himself that we fill in what is not said about Moi with what we know of Diderot's biography. Moi is not presented in this text as someone who has been imprisoned for his beliefs or taken great risks in order to complete the *Encyclopédie.* While Diderot's silence on these issues may reflect his modesty, the result is that the Moi of the text is a more superficial character, and, as critics have remarked, more *bien-pensant* than the author himself.

freedom too far. Moi is aware of the contradiction, which affects his own righteous indignation, and the dignity that grounds it. 'Vingt fois un éclat de rire empêcha ma colère d'éclater; vingt fois la colère qui s'élevait au fond de mon cœur se termina par un éclat de rire. J'étais confondu de tant de sagacité et de tant de bassesse' (Again and again a roar of laughter prevented my rage from bursting forth; again and again the rage rising in my heart became a roar of laughter. I was dumbfounded by such shrewdness and such depravity) (637/19–20).

It is true that satire often includes some questioning of the satirist's own standing, and a reversal of the positions initially held by the dialog partners had long been part of the genre's poetic complexity. The theme is more prominent in Horace than in Juvenal, and indeed Moi's reaction at this point of the *Neveu* echoes that of the master in the satire from which Diderot draws his epigraph. In Horace's poem, the slave Davus, taking advantage of the freedom of the Saturnalia, exposes the master's complicity in social corruption. Davus' rant may be a second-hand pastiche of philosophical diatribe,[17] but it makes the master so uncomfortable that in a fit of pique he puts an end to the conversation. Abandoning reason for passion, he threatens Davus with punishment, but in so doing puts himself on the same level as his slave. Similarly, Moi's ambivalence mirrors the lack of single-mindedness in Lui. Since it was precisely Lui's lack of constancy that most disqualified his claim to dignity, Moi finds his own authority undermined as well.

The two situations, however, are contextualized very differently. In the Roman poem, the ironic reversal of positions illustrates a principle of traditional wisdom: no one is truly wise, and even fools may sometimes speak the truth. In Diderot's dialog, human foolishness is not simply a failure to see the truth because passion prevents us from thinking rationally. It is the product of an internal division within the reflecting mind whose rationality is always embodied, and therefore affected by a more general tension between natural and perverted feeling. A truly philosophical response to foolishness must therefore go beyond satirical scorn. It must include a more self-reflective and self-involving inquiry, one in which feeling as well as thought is seen as a potential path to insight, and thought as well as feeling is viewed as a possible source of error. This shift of viewpoint corresponds to a change

[17] Davus admits he learned his philosophical lessons from 'Crispinus' porter' (*quae Crispini docuit me janitor*), Crispinus being himself a pompous moralist (Horace, *Sat.* II.7, 45; I.4).

in the principle governing the exchange of authority and other qualities between people of 'superior' and 'inferior' status, in the dialog and in society at large. Instead of showing that all share in the weakness (or occasional insight) of their common humanity, contrasted with the higher wisdom attained only by a true philosopher or enjoyed by a god, these exchanges illustrate the workings of an internally differentiated system operating within the one realm of ordinary nature.[18]

The existence of such a system is first suggested rhetorically, in Diderot's repeated use of chiasmus in the dialog. As Jean Starobinski has shown in one of his illuminating essays on the *Neveu*, Diderot uses this rhetorical figure to illustrate the reversibility of roles and the generally topsy-turvy nature of the world Moi and Lui inhabit.[19] He also points to a peculiar feature of Diderot's use of chiasmic structures. While the symmetry of the figure suggests that the dynamic of reversal and exchange of properties is self-enclosed, turned in upon itself, in the *Neveu* the words that compose the figure do not all belong to the same semantic level. This opens up the chiasmus so that it becomes part of a more exploratory understanding of the complexities of social exchange. The most extended example of this kind of chiasmus is particularly relevant for our purposes, since it involves the exchange of favors and the emotions or dispositions associated with such an exchange.

The passage begins with Lui chuckling about the jokes people are making about Mlle Hus's increasing weight. Moi recoils:

Moi.—Vous n'êtes pas de ces gens-là?
Lui.—Pourquoi non?
Moi.—C'est qu'il est au moins indécent de donner des ridicules à ses bienfaiteurs.
Lui.—Mais n'est-ce pas pis encore de s'autoriser de ses bienfaits pour avilir son protégé?
Moi.—Mais si le protégé n'était pas vil par lui-même, rien ne donnerait au protecteur cette autorité.
Lui.—Mais si les personnages n'étaient pas ridicules par eux-mêmes, on n'en ferait pas de bons contes. (666)

[18] For a more extended and critically sophisticated account of Diderot's understanding of system and systematicity in relation to dialog, see Julie Candler Hayes, *Reading the French Enlightenment: System and Subversion* (Cambridge: Cambridge University Press, 1999), 142–83.

[19] Jean Starobinski, 'Sur l'emploi du chiasme dans *Le Neveu de Rameau*', *Revue de métaphysique et de morale* 89 (1984), 182–96.

Me: But surely you're not one of those people.
Him: Why not?
Me: Because at the very least it's bad manners to tell tales that ridicule your benefactors.
Him: But isn't it even worse to use one's own position as benefactor to vilify one's protégé?
Me: But if the protégé were not vile already, nothing would give the benefactor the power to do that.
Him: But if the individuals concerned were not themselves ridiculous, people wouldn't tell those great stories. (55)

Starobinski points to the peculiar juxtaposition of esthetic terms such as 'ridicule' and 'great stories' with moral ones such as 'vile' and 'vilify'.[20] Their use in the chiasmus suggests their equivalence even as we remain aware of the distinction between them. Is the *bons* of *bons contes* a purely esthetic goodness covering or compensating for the moral turpitude of the tales? The importance of the question goes beyond the immediate context, since the scandalous *Neveu de Rameau* as a whole surely counts as one of these problematic *bons contes.*

The relationship between moral and esthetic judgment is of course a recurring theme in Diderot's text, and Starobinski's analysis helpfully focuses on the slipperiness in Diderot's treatment of the problem. Yet, the ease with which the text passes from one kind of goodness to another suggests this chiasmic exchange should be read against a different background. If we consider the pleasurable goodness of the tales in terms of social appropriateness, and if such appropriateness involves not just the sharing of laughter but an ongoing negotiation of one's status in the eyes of others, then the sharpness of the distinction between the esthetic and the moral is somewhat blunted. The chiasmic jousting of Moi and Lui occurs in the midst of an ongoing argument about the right to be angry. Since assessing the legitimacy of anger involves considerations of cultural as well as moral status, one cannot define the disparity between 'ridicule' and 'vilify' as one of simple opposition between moral and esthetic judgment. Both actions are forms of insult, and as such are at one in giving rise to anger in the offended person.

[20] Jean Starobinski, 'Sur l'emploi du chiasme dans *Le Neveu de Rameau*', *Revue de métaphysique et de morale* 89 (1984), 184.

How that anger may be expressed or transcended is of course subject to various kinds of judgment, but the underlying point in question here is the 'dignity' of the subject. As we have seen, dignity in the *Neveu* involves both inner moral character and exterior qualities related to social status and personal appearance. Diderot's use of chiasmic structures may be viewed as an attempt to organize these factors into some kind of systematic relationship. In what sense that *system* can be subjected to judgment is the concern of the passage that follows the exchange between Moi and Lui cited above. In Lui's depiction of what he calls the *pacte tacite* (tacit agreement) the dynamic of the text shifts from a tight chiasmic exchange to a more differentiated exposition and evaluation of insult and anger.

THE *PACTE TACITE*

Lui's presentation of the *pacte tacite* is intended to untangle the personal and the impersonal aspects of the relationship between 'benefactors' like Bertin, and 'protégés' such as himself. Lui has just described how he was driven out of Bertin's household for taking his role as jester too far and exposing his patron to ridicule. He paints a scathing portrait of Bertin and his mistress, Mlle Hus. To Moi's objection that insulting one's benefactor is an 'indecent' thing to do, Lui replies angrily:

> Est-ce ma faute, lorsqu'ils se sont encanaillés, si on les trahit, si on les bafoue? Quand on se résout à vivre avec des gens comme nous et qu'on a le sens commun, il y a je ne sais combien de noirceurs auxquelles il faut s'attendre . . . Il y a un pacte tacite qu'on nous fera du bien, et que tôt ou tard nous rendrons le mal pour le bien qu'on nous aura fait. Ce pacte ne subsiste-t-il pas entre l'homme et son singe ou son perroquet? (666–7)
>
> Is it my fault, if, when they're in that company, they're betrayed and ridiculed? When people choose to live with people like us, if they've any sense, they must be prepared for all manner of low-down tricks . . . There's a tacit agreement that they'll treat us well, and that sooner or later we'll return evil for the good they've done us. Isn't there such a pact between a man and his monkey or his parrot? (55)

On one level, Lui's 'tacit agreement' is a parody of the unwritten code of civility.[21] Ingratitude is here the expected response to a favor. It follows

[21] The pact also reverses the biblical injunction to return good for evil (Rom. 12: 21; Matt. 5: 39), but while Diderot evokes this ethic in telling the story of M. Pelletier in *Jacques le fataliste*, he does not do so in the *Neveu*.

that the benefactor has no right to be angry when he is disrespected. Instead of affirming the dignity of the person offended, anger deprives him of the prestige of being a benefactor, turning him into an object of ridicule, the butt of what Lui calls 'great stories'. On the other hand, the recipient's ingratitude is also given another meaning. For someone like Rousseau, it marks an attempt to reject the inferior status that went with the acknowledgment of obligation. It was the subordinate's way of proclaiming his dignity as an independent human being. Lui will have none of this. He compares the recipient of a favor to a partially domesticated animal. Monkeys and parrots mimic the gestures or speech of a human being, but they are driven by sheer instinct, a force beyond human control. Indeed, as Lui describes it, the system of favors, instead of fostering the mutual recognition of both parties, giving them the opportunity to acknowledge their need for each other, is entirely depersonalizing. If recipients are animals, then all will be well as long as the benefactor realizes this (666/55). If he doesn't, he will be reduced to the animal level himself, uttering inarticulate and impotent screeches (*hauts cris*) when they bite the hand that feeds them. Of course, the philosophers who wrote about favors always warned their readers to take into account the character and position of the person on whom they were considering bestowing a benefit.[22] But prudence could never be a matter of mechanically applying a rule, for to approach the matter in this way would go against the ethos of liberality. In contrast to this tradition, the prudence of a benefactor operating in the context of the *pacte tacite* is of a kind that admits of no exceptions. It is the prudence of the zoo visitor who knows not to put a hand through the bars of a predator's cage (667).

The *pacte tacite*, then, is really the law of the jungle. The pact is not left unstated because it reflects the discretion and consideration of a refined culture, but because it describes an instinctive awareness of how nature operates in the raw. The interaction between a human being and a monkey or a parrot is based on a 'tacit' understanding only in the sense that the monkey cannot speak at all and the parrot's speech is only a series of squawks. On the other side, it should go without saying that the benefactor is a fool if he doesn't put self-preservation first. The whole passage can be seen as an ironic inversion of the Enlightenment cliché about the 'cry of nature', that voice of instinctive goodness which erupts

[22] Cicero, *De officiis*, I.42; Seneca, *De beneficiis*, II.15–16.

to attack social violence and corruption in the name of a more profound reality.[23] Here Lui cries out only to remind us of the even more fundamental reality of the unspoken rules of animal behavior.

This is not, however, the end of the story. The word *pacte* stands in tension with the word *tacite*, since it evokes a very different basis for human interaction: that of a compact by which agents bind themselves voluntarily to a foundational agreement. Rousseau, for example, uses the word to designate the foundational social contract.[24] Whereas the rules of animal behavior belong to the sub-legal realm of natural regularity, the laws of a compact transcend both natural instinct and that basic human self-interest which generates primitive forms of law. As such, the compact has a quasi-religious dimension. Diderot may have differed with Rousseau on social contract theory and the role of inspired lawgivers, but he, like other materialist *philosophes*, did not hesitate to speak of 'the laws' as 'sacred', since they form the linchpin of ordered freedom, the highest expression of human community. In the course of his speech, Lui echoes this language, and in so doing adopts a different viewpoint on the actions he depicts. Speaking of the man who lost his hand to the zoo animal, he says:

> Tout cela est écrit dans le pacte tacite. Tant pis pour celui qui l'ignore ou qui l'oublie. Combien je justifierais par ce pacte universel et sacré, de gens qu'on accuse de méchanceté, tandis que c'est soi qu'on devrait accuser de sottise! (667)
>
> It's all spelled out in the tacit agreement. Hard luck for anyone unaware of that agreement, or who has forgotten it. How often would I not invoke this universal, sacred compact to justify those we accuse of malice, when it is we ourselves and our own stupidity that we should accuse? (56)

In other words, it is the foolish victim who failed to respect the terms of the compact. Of course, Lui is being ironic. There is nothing sacred about bites or betrayals. But why use such exalted language at all if the aim is to dissolve the reciprocity of favors into the law of the jungle?[25]

The real purpose is to justify Lui's indignation. That benefactors are foolish enough to get angry at their ungrateful protégés does not in itself give Lui a *reason* to be angry in turn. Only if their foolishness is culpable can they be 'accused', to use Lui's term, of a fault. According to Lui, benefactors should know better. But how might they acquire

[23] Diderot discusses 'le cri de la nature' in his 'Satyre première' (V ii. 582).

[24] Jean-Jacques Rousseau, *Du contrat social* I.6 (*OC* iii. 360).

[25] One of the little-noticed silences of the dialog is that while it discusses all kinds of moral and esthetic rules it never discusses political law.

that knowledge? The laws of a political compact are normally spelled out explicitly, and preserved in written form. Knowledge of a *pacte tacite*, by contrast, is gained through experience of the world. But if the failure to learn from experience is culpable, that experience must differ from the natural life of the jungle, where normative expectations about what people should or shouldn't know have no place.

Animals, of course, never fail to learn from their experience. This is true not only in nature: smarter animals, such as dogs, can be trained by humans to learn perverted lessons. The story of Bouret's dog, who was trained by his own master to fear him and to respond positively instead to the image of the Garde des Sceaux, the minister of justice Bouret wanted to flatter (655–7/41–3), provides an interesting transition between the impersonal experience of nature and the more personalized learning provided by what we call the world. Bouret's dog loved his master, and so he was naturally puzzled and pained when Bouret started to beat him. Bouret then put on a costume and mask that made him look like the official he was trying to please. After an initial moment of cognitive dissonance, the dog begins to respond to his 'new' master instead of Bouret. When the minister arrives for a visit, the apparently spontaneous welcome the dog gives him secures the powerful man's goodwill.

The benefactors Lui criticizes should have learned similar lessons. Their sophisticated minds should have helped them understand what happens to other people in their world, and what is likely to happen to them. They have no excuse for getting angry when one of their entourage repays their generosity with ingratitude. The self-deception of vanity—the illusion that there will be exceptions to the universal rule—plays a part, no doubt, in their failure to learn, but given the larger argument of the text, the decisive factor would seem to be their grossness of sensibility. This is certainly the case with Bertin. The sycophants around Bertin's table may also be deluded about their merits, but they have enough finesse to appreciate the jokes made at their expense. Bertin, on the other hand, is mired in his stupidity. Despite Lui's best efforts, he remains immune to irony and refuses to acknowledge the laws of social rapacity illustrated by his dinner guests. His failure is not only culpable; it also constitutes an offense against Lui, who has done him the favor of trying to educate him. From this point of view, Lui's ingratitude is eclipsed by that of his supposed benefactor, for which is the greater favor: the gift of money or the gift of enlightenment?

This is true even if enlightenment, following the rules of the *pacte tacite*, comes, as it must, at the recipient's expense. Lui's exploitation of Bertin may reflect the law of the jungle, but his teaching puts Bertin under an obligation which can be called 'sacred' inasmuch the favor consists less of a particular benefit within the system of worldly exchange than of insight into the nature of that world. An insight of this magnitude should elicit in the recipient an especially profound response of gratitude, however debased in other respects the source of that insight might be. This is a key point, since, as we shall see in a moment, the dialog as a whole raises the question of whether Moi, too, owes Lui a debt of gratitude for the insight he gains from Lui's performances. Here, at least, the text seems to endorse Lui's claim that since he did his ironic best to educate Bertin, his anger at his former patron is justified.

THE RIGHTS OF GENIUS

While Lui's claim to legitimate anger is in itself not absurd, it is undermined by the instability of his character. He cannot sustain his role, and the passions associated with it, over time. As Diderot emphasizes from the beginning of the dialog, everything about Lui is in constant flux: his temperament, his social location, even his physical appearance.

> Aujourd'hui, en linge sale, en culotte déchirée, couvert de lambeaux, presque sans souliers, il va la tête basse, il se dérobe, on serait tenté de l'appeler pour lui donner l'aumône. Demain, poudré, chaussé, frisé, bien vêtu, il marche la tête haute, il se montre, et vous le prendriez au peu près pour un honnête homme. (624)
>
> One day, in grubby linen, torn breeches, and rags, virtually barefoot, he goes about with his head down, avoiding people, and you'd be tempted to call him over and slip him a coin or two. The next, powdered, shod, curled, well dressed, he goes about with head high, he wants to be noticed, and you'd be likely to take him for a gentleman, or near enough. (4)

If anger is defined as the appropriate response to a slight to one's dignity, Lui's self is too changeable, his dignity too evanescent, for it to be slighted more than momentarily. The day he explains the laws of the *pacte tacite*, he has only recently been expelled from Bertin's, and so he is still in good moral shape. But he is on the way down into abjection and self-hatred, and at the beginning of the dialog he endures Moi's sarcasm without protest. 'Ce n'est rien, ce sont des moments qui passent' (It's nothing. These moments quickly pass) (631/12).

In the course of the dialog, however, Moi's sustained attention provides Lui with enough temporal continuity for the latter to change his attitude. When Moi first runs into him, Lui speaks briefly about his expulsion from Bertin's house, but he does not give a detailed explanation for what seems at first to be the understandable but hardly dignified resentment of an unsuccessful beggar. Moi's appreciation of Lui's talents as a mimic gives the nephew a feeling of confidence which enables him to claim the righteous indignation he expresses in his speech about the *pacte tacite.* In his play-acting, Lui turns his protean character from a liability into an asset. Moi feels compelled to take him seriously as a source of insight into reality. Artistic genius may be a way to compensate for personal shortcomings and give Lui the dignity that until now had been merely one of those momentary moods.

There are two problems with this strategy. The first is that to be successful, the art Lui creates must itself endure over time. Diderot explores this issue early in the dialog by having Moi cite Racine as an exemplar of the literary genius whose deplorable character is forgotten while the glory of his works lives on. Moral judgments of Racine the man have lost their pertinence; the work endures, endowed with its own authority. Later on, however, the value of this example is diminished when the discussion turns to Lui's uncle, the composer Jean-Philippe Rameau, another artist whose unpleasant character might be redeemed by his musical talent. Unfortunately, Rameau's glory is fading as the French public begins to recognize the superiority of Italian music. Posterity cannot be counted on to vindicate esthetic judgments indefinitely, with the consequence that the artist's personal faults may once again come to the fore. How much more uncertain, then, is Lui's attempt to recover his dignity through artistic creation. His talent is for live performance, not for composing works of art that might last as long as his uncle's. When Moi asks Lui how it is that 'avec la facilité de sentir, de retenir et de rendre les plus beaux endroits des grands maîtres, avec l'enthousiasme qu'ils vous inspirent et que vous transmettez aux autres, vous n'ayez rien fait qui vaille' (with your gift of experiencing, remembering, and reproducing the most beautiful passages from the great masters, with the passion they inspire in you and you convey to others, you yourself have not created anything worthwhile) (686/78), Lui can only hang his head and blame the stars. They failed to give him the genius to create the kind of art that silences moral reproach by endowing the artist with a second form of dignity grounded in art's victory over time.

It appears that Moi has scored a decisive point against Lui, and indeed this passage marks the transition to the concluding section of the text.[26] In the concluding section of the *Neveu*, Lui continues to challenge Moi's preconceptions, but he is no longer able to undermine his partner's basic self-confidence. Yet, the process by which Moi is empowered to reassert himself has not been given proper attention, because at first sight it stands at odds with the rest of the text. After all, Moi no more than Lui can take comfort from the notion that personal dignity can be won from the victory of genius over time. For if Lui is not such a genius neither is Moi.[27] In the dialog, when Lui challenges Moi's still-precarious status as a philosophical writer, Moi falls back on his personal commitment to virtue for reassurance. In one of his longer speeches, Moi boasts that he takes more pleasure in writing 'a satisfying page' than in pursuing the pleasures of the flesh. But he does not pursue this artistic claim very far. On the contrary, he cites Voltaire in order to assert the priority of activism over art. 'C'est un sublime ouvrage que *Mahomet*; j'aimerais mieux avoir réhabilité la mémoire de Calas' (*Mahomet* is a sublime work; but I would rather have rehabilitated the memory of Calas) (649–50/34).[28] Voltaire's campaign on behalf of Calas, a Protestant from Toulouse unjustly tortured and executed for the alleged murder of his son, was one of the highlights of Enlightenment activism, and Diderot was correct in predicting that posterity would remember Voltaire for this accomplishment as much as for his (now largely unread) tragedies. No doubt Diderot hoped that his own work on the monumental *Encyclopédie* would earn him similar fame as an agent of Enlightenment. On the other hand, *Le Neveu de Rameau* ends with some skepticism about expectations for the future. Lui's famous parting line, 'rira bien qui rira le dernier' (he that laughs last, laughs best) (695/89), not only implies that Moi's hopes (or Diderot's) may be misplaced; it also undercuts the meaning of survival over time. Lui does not in fact argue that his creative or philosophical superiority

[26] See Henri Coulet's introduction to *Le Neveu de Rameau* in Diderot, *Œuvres complètes*, ed. Herbert Dieckmann, Jacques Proust, and Jean Varloot, 24 vols to date (Paris: Hermann, 1975–), xii. 39.

[27] Diderot himself was far from confident that his life would be validated by the posthumous success of his works.

[28] A close parallel to these remarks may be found in the chapter on anger in Diderot's *Essai sur les règnes de Claude et de Néron* (V i. 1170).

will be vindicated by posterity, only that he might outlive his opponent. The persistence of identity is reduced to physical survival. We are back to the world of animal nature. No wonder, then, that in the same speech in which he praises Voltaire, Moi's celebration of virtuous living and writing focuses on the immediate pleasure it gives rather than on such traditional philosophical arguments about the difference between short- and long-term interests, or anything else that sacrifices the present to the future. Moi's recovery of nerve must therefore have another basis.

ADMIRATION, OBLIGATION, AND ENVY

Up to now, we have been assuming that the right to anger, and the dignity associated with it, rested on the stability over time of the self's identity. Yet, if we look at the overall rhythm of *Le Neveu de Rameau*, this connection may not be a necessary or exclusive one. Diderot's satire is a series of provocations and responses which value reflective complexity and witty profundity in the moment over extended and integrated achievement. When Lui mimics a wealthy libertine's seduction of a shop-girl or the things he would do if he himself were rich, what win Moi's applause are his rapid shifts from one role to another such that time is condensed into a series of almost simultaneous actions. Anger, too, may legitimately be taken, as Pope's *Dunciad* had shown, at the offensive durability of dullness, which fails to recognize the merits, not just of enlightened philosophy, but of intensity and complexity of sensibility. It was precisely Bertin's lack of sensibility that gave rise to Lui's most pointed resentment. Bertin's identity is all-too stable; the financier's foolish anger is a function of his dullness. The righteousness of Lui's indignation can thus be validated by the brilliance of his performances, even though they leave no permanent legacy. Their merit lies in their evocative power, a power all the more impressive in that Lui's sole instrument is his own body. Not only does he transcend the spatial limitations of that body by conveying the sounds produced by a whole orchestra of players, he seems to transcend the temporal basis of music itself. In his *Essai sur l'origine des langues*, Rousseau had argued that all musical effects were predicated on measured intervals of time. Silence is a structured interval between sounds. The silence conveyed by Lui is something more; the embodied presence of Lui and his seamless outpouring of sound points, in fact opens out, to an absence beyond it.

This momentary transcendence of the body in the body is what elicits Moi's admiration.

For just the same reason, however, Moi also sees where Lui falls short. 'Admirais-je? Oui, j'admirais! Étais-je touché de pitié? J'étais touché de pitié; mais une teinte de ridicule était fondue dans ces sentiments, et les dénaturaient' (Was I filled with admiration? Yes, I was. Was I moved to pity? Yes, I was; but a tinge of ridicule blended with these feelings, and denatured them) (677/68). The formulation of Moi's reaction here is significant. He does not counter an esthetic judgment with a 'higher' moral one; on the contrary, the moral sentiment of pity is trumped by the ostensibly more trivial criterion of ridiculous appearance. Moreover, the verb 'denature', which elsewhere in Diderot and other Enlightenment discourse is strongly pejorative, suggestive of moral perversion, is taken in a different sense, as signifying a necessary separation from instinctive feeling in the critical consciousness of the observing subject. We are reminded here of Rousseau's paradoxes in the *Discours sur l'inégalité* about humanity's progress involving a separation from nature one should deplore, but which one should also applaud for giving us the self-consciousness that allows us make judgments of value. What makes Lui ridiculous is the same thing that makes his performances an object of Moi's admiring wonder: his triumph over the body's limitations happens at the expense of his sense of self. While in simple *saynètes* like the seduction scene Lui is able to suggest ironic awareness in his performance, when he turns to music that awareness disappears. Just after underscoring Lui's ability to paint silence in sound, Moi goes on to describe Lui's condition as the scene winds down.

Sa tête était tout à fait perdue. Épuisé de fatigue, tel qu'un homme qui sort d'un profond sommeil ou d'une longue distraction, il resta immobile, stupide, étonné. Il tournait ses yeux autour de lui, comme un homme égaré qui cherche à reconnaître le lieu où il se trouve. Il attendait le retour de ses forces et de ses esprits; il essuyait machinalement son visage. (678)

He had completely lost touch with reality. Utterly spent, like someone emerging from a deep sleep or a long trance, he stood there motionless, stupefied, astounded. He gazed all around, as would a man who had mistaken his way and was trying to discover where he was. As he waited for his strength and his wits to return, he kept automatically wiping his face. (69)

This depiction of Lui stands in sharp contrast to Diderot's portrait of the self-conscious actor in the *Paradoxe sur le comédien.* For our purposes, what is interesting is that at this moment the Lui described by

Moi resembles the Bertin portrayed by Lui at other moments of the dialog. We see the same rigid and mechanical behavior that made Bertin a legitimate target of ridicule and resentment. Here Moi's mockery robs Lui of his dignity, and in so doing undermines Lui's right to take angry offense. In this passage, Diderot returns to the norms of Roman satire.

Yet, as we saw in the discussion of the *pacte tacite*, there was another dimension to Lui's claim to anger. This had less to do with his personal dignity than with the value of the lessons he imparted to Bertin, lessons that should have moved Bertin to gratitude. The financier's failure to acknowledge his obligation violated an implicit rule of the compact. In the dialog as a whole, Lui also serves as Moi's teacher. As Moi says in the prologue, he is happy to encounter the disreputable Nephew because talking with him stimulates his thinking and reveals things he would not otherwise have occasion to see for himself. Does Moi's relationship to Lui fall under the conventions of the *pacte tacite*? Has Lui done Moi a favor? If so, then Moi's focus on Lui's ridiculous appearance could be taken as an attempt to deny any corresponding obligation. Indeed, the ostensibly self-sufficient Moi, ironically echoing Bertin, may well resent his dependence for insight on a man he does not esteem.

It might be objected that the opportunity to observe Lui's antics does not involve a favor, any more than would the observation of any natural process. Moi speaks of Lui as a kind of natural phenomenon, that 'grain of yeast' that restores a bit of our natural individuality (624/4). Dependence on yeast for one's philosophical bread is not for Diderot a matter for either gratitude or resentment. This is also true of other kinds of learning: the Diderot of the *Lettre sur les aveugles* does not feel personally indebted to Saunderson for his edifying example, nor does the Diderot of the *Paradoxe sur le comédien* owe anything to the great stage actress Clairon for her performance. In the *Rêve de d'Alembert*, Bordeu is under no obligation to the sleeping philosopher for having witnessed his dream, although it might be argued that here, as in the other instances, the observer enjoys a privilege that is not available to all, and that what he observes is something special, having to do with the exceptionally expressive capacities of certain individuals. In *Le Neveu de Rameau*, however, Diderot evinces, at least implicitly, some awareness of this interpersonal dimension of the observational experience in the language he uses to describe Lui's function. While the fermentation image suggests a material process, the word 'restitution' anticipates what Lui says later on about the social value of parasites like himself. By taking money from the rich for music lessons he did not know how to give, Lui says, 'I helped them to make restitution' for what they themselves had unjustly acquired. Speaking of all social classes, he adds: 'Nous faisons justice les uns des autres sans que la loi s'en mêle' (We mete out justice to one another without benefit of law) (646/31). The comment is ironic, but the key point is that 'restitution' refers to human agency, driven in part by the emotion of anger, and not to an impersonal natural process. What Lui is saying is also not so different from what Diderot writes in a contribution to the *Histoire des deux Indes* about early human societies, in which anger provided the crucial motor of justice before the institution of a legal system.[29] Restitution belongs to the tacit agreement, which as we have seen is at once an instinctive process through which natural equilibrium is recovered and a sacred compact worthy of respect.

Furthermore, what Lui is restituting here is each person's 'natural individuality', and this, too, involves more than clarifying their place in the natural order of the species. As a general statement, the claim also suggests that the philosopher is among those whose individuality becomes more apparent to the observer, who in this case is himself. Certainly, in the course of the dialogue, Moi is led to experience a range of feelings with new intensity and to reflect with unaccustomed sharpness on the interplay between feelings, moral convictions, and esthetic sensibility. This experience comes from engagement with Lui as much as it does from observation. The dialog between them is much more personal in quality that of the *Lettre* or the *Rêve*. It thus seems appropriate to ask whether the recovery of one's individuality is not a benefit for which the recipient should feel grateful.

Diderot does not address the issue explicitly, and indeed the genre of *Le Neveu de Rameau* seems to rule the question out of bounds. In Roman satire, the poet or his persona cannot owe anything to the slave, gigolo, or fool who provides him with entertaining or even enlightening material. Such people simply do not have the standing required for their actions to constitute a favor. Seneca argues against this position, saying that just as one gets angry when slaves do less than their duty demands, it is proper to feel gratitude when they do more, but the strain in the text suggests the weight of the prejudice.[30] More broadly,

[29] See Diderot's contributions to Raynal's *Histoire des deux Indes* (V i. 599). See also the *Essai sur les règnes de Claude et de Néron* (V i. 1167–8).

[30] Seneca, *De beneficiis*, III.18–19.

the lowly of whatever sort, not to mention those who abase themselves by pursuing dishonorable professions, are generally disqualified as benefactors. Despite the influence of Christianity and humanistic thinking, this assumption persisted into the eighteenth century. *Le Neveu de Rameau* opens with Moi sitting on a bench in the Palais-Royal, at that time a dubious neighborhood frequented by prostitutes and their clients. The place is not chosen by accident. On one level, it allows Moi to introduce a striking analogy: 'mes pensées, ce sont mes catins' (my thoughts are my little flirts) (623/3).[31] The place where he sits illustrates the *libertinage* of his thought-process: he is happy to entertain, at least for a moment, any seductive idea without regard for its propriety or philosophical gravitas. But it also guarantees that Moi will not owe anything to the people inhabiting the scene for providing him with the stimulation he needs. Those who hire prostitutes owe them money but not gratitude. The figure of the nephew emerges out of this background. He, too, is 'kept' by his patrons. His witty and eccentric character amuses but earns him no respect. Moi's own attitude is clear enough. 'Je n'estime pas ces originaux-là', he says (I hold such eccentrics in low esteem) (624/4). Lui may well have 'great stories' to tell, but the education he provides about life in the street instills no sense of obligation.[32] In this respect, as in many others, he stands in sharp contrast with such revered pedagogical figures as Rousseau's Vicaire savoyard or the Mentor of Fénelon's *Télémaque.*

Yet, in a reversal of roles that also belongs to satiric tradition, Lui insinuates that Moi's deprecation of Lui is a desperate attempt to hide his own weakness. In a passage describing what he would do if he were rich, Lui says that he and his friends would cut all the famous *philosophes* down to size, including, he says to Moi, 'tous ces petits Catons comme vous, qui nous méprisent par envie, dont la modestie est le manteau de l'orgueil, et dont la sobriété est la loi du besoin' (all those petty stoics like you, who despise us out of envy, cloak their pride in modesty, and live soberly out of necessity) (647/32). What gives the barb a special sting is the way Moi is distinguished from the other writers on Lui's list. Earlier in Lui's speech, Voltaire, Buffon, Montesquieu, and d'Alembert are accused of inflating their merits, but only Moi is accused of puffing himself up at the expense of other people, and of looking down on them

[31] 'Flirt' is perhaps too mild, but 'whore' would be too crude in this context.

[32] Compare the very different kind of 'contract' between servant and master in *Jacques le fataliste.*

out of resentment of their talent or success. The envious Moi is thus linked to the Palissots and other resentful second-rate writers Lui lampoons throughout the dialog—with Moi's complicity. The only difference is that Moi is better at disguising his envy. Instead of openly competing for prestige, he has donned the mantle of austerity and made a show of virtuous scorn for worldly success. The charge is all the more insidious, since it echoes Diderot's bitter critique of Rousseau.[33] If Lui has hit the mark, then little wonder if Moi is not grateful for the lesson.

Of course, Lui is equally deluded about his abilities, or rather, he can face reality only intermittently, and one aspect of that reality is that he himself is unwilling to embrace virtuous poverty. When Moi suggests 'il vaudrait mieux se refermer dans son grenier, boire de l'eau, manger du pain sec, et se chercher soi-même' (it would be better to sequester yourself in a garret, live on dry bread and water, and attempt to know yourself), Lui replies, 'je n'ai pas le courage' (I haven't the courage) (687/80). The suffering and sacrifice are such that he cannot believe anyone is capable of adopting that life (692/86). One can infer from this that when Lui attacks Moi he is revealing his own envy of Moi's relative self-sufficiency. The dialog also makes it clear that Lui's inability to produce a work of art marks him as a failure in his own eyes.

Yet, Moi does envy one thing about Lui: his frankness. He says things openly that the respectable Moi cannot—and that Diderot, the creator of both Moi and Lui, can only explore in a dialog he does not discuss with anyone. As Eric Walter has pointed out, an underlying motive for composing *Le Neveu de Rameau* was Diderot's uncomfortable realization that despite his best efforts, he had not attained the independence he desired. The status boundary separating him from the Grub Street writers of his day was not as secure as he would have liked. Moi's scornful envy of Lui arises, not from a resentful recognition of his talents, but from a reluctant identification with his social condition, a condition to which Lui can at least give eloquent expression, whereas Moi is forced by his philosophical persona to sweep it under the rug.[34] It is Lui, not Moi, who enjoys the *parrhesia* of Diogenes, the philosopher 'qui n'a rien et qui ne demande rien' (who has nothing and asks for nothing) (692/86), and so can speak his mind.

[33] See n. 15.

[34] Eric Walter, 'Les "Intellectuels du ruisseau" et *Le Neveu de Rameau*', in Georges Benrekassa, Marc Buffat, and Pierre Chartier, eds, *Études sur le 'Neveu de Rameau' et le 'Paradoxe sur le comédien' de Denis Diderot* (Paris: Cahiers Textuel, 1992), 43–59.

As the author of the work, Diderot is of course the source of Lui's eloquence just as much as he is of Moi's evasions. One could therefore argue that the dialog's energy constitutes in itself a response to Lui's challenge. The relation of resentful envy between the two characters is internalized and transcended on the level of literary creation. Diderot the author would achieve the self-sufficient comprehensiveness that eludes both Moi and Lui. Yet, the general tendency of *Le Neveu de Rameau* is to be skeptical of any claims of this sort. Earlier we saw how the specious genius of Lui's one-man band performances does not, in the end, represent a triumphant display of self-sufficiency, but rather a comically reductive form of reflective mastery which hardly serves to support his right to anger. The transcendence of Moi's obligation of gratitude through the character's link to a comprehensive authorial consciousness is equally problematic, if less explicitly so. The opening scene in which Moi describes himself indulging in the controlled libertinage of thought is a dramatization of the consciousness, not only of Moi, the character in the story, but also of the reflective consciousness looking at the character from the outside. 'C'est moi qu'on voit, toujours seul, rêvant sur le banc d'Argenson' (It's me you see there, invariably alone, sitting on the d'Argenson bench) (623/3). Here, Moi is a spectacle for others. The fact that this external voice does not make itself heard in the subsequent dialog does not mean that the perspective it represents has disappeared from the scene. Rather, it accompanies Moi in his reflective consideration of Lui's performances. As a consequence, the issue of Moi's obligation to Lui cannot be settled by weighing the relative personal status of the dialog partners. If Lui is not just a character in the world of the dialog but a voice of otherness within the author, then the issue is also a challenge to the integrity of the higher consciousness of the artist. To put the question in somewhat paradoxical terms, what might it mean for the author to be obliged, and then grateful—or resentful—in relation to himself?

BEYOND ANGER AND GRATITUDE: THE SUBLIME

In *Le Neveu de Rameau*, a possible answer to this question may be found in Diderot's exploration of the dynamic of the sublime. Like other eighteenth-century writers, Diderot is fascinated by those objects or occasions the comprehension of which challenges the self's ability to go beyond the limits of our ordinary understanding, and of our ordinary tolerance for perceptual pleasure or pain. The violence of a storm at sea, for example, is not a pleasant sight, but contemplating it (from a safe place on land) gives pleasure to the extent that our mind can rise above sensation to a higher comprehension of the dynamism of nature.[35] An action or a work of art expressing that dynamism could also be appreciated for its sublime qualities, even though it did not conform to our usual criteria of moral goodness or esthetic beauty. As has been often remarked, widespread interest in the sublime marked a shift in attention and in valuation from the orderly character of the object to the ordering powers of the human subject, and in this respect reflected a general tendency of modern thought.

But we can also see in Diderot a second reason for interest in the sublime. As Anthony Kenny has pointed out, Enlightenment empiricism, in supposing that the mind knows nothing but its own ideas, makes the self a 'solitary inner perceiver' and so runs the risk of solipsism.[36] How can we be certain our perceptions really do convey knowledge of external reality? Descartes had solved the problem by proving the trustworthiness of God to his own satisfaction, but such a priori arguments were rejected by his Enlightenment successors. The question was made the more acute by the widening acceptance, and not just by traditional skeptics, of the notion that much of what passed for 'knowledge' of the world was a projection of human hopes or fears. From this perspective, the opening image of *Le Neveu de Rameau* takes on a different meaning from the one usually given to it. While it may seem to symbolize Diderot's openness to unconventional thinking, stimulated by the erotic activity around the Palais-Royal, the description of his thoughts as 'flirts' (623/3) points to a drama played out wholly within the philosopher's mind. Indeed, the text emphasizes the thinker's isolation, as he sits alone on the d'Argenson bench. While Moi goes on to say that he likes to observe the chess-players in the Café de la Régence, the only person whom he engages in conversation is Lui. This

[35] For recent discussion of the sublime in France, see Baldine Saint Girons, *Fiat Lux: une philosophie du sublime* (Paris: Quai Voltaire, 1993), and Dominique Peyrache-Laborgne, *La Poétique du sublime de la fin des Lumières au romantisme* (Paris: Champion, 1997).

[36] Anthony Kenny, *The Rise of Modern Philosophy: A New History of Western Philosophy*, vol. iii (Oxford: Clarendon Press, 2004), 239. See also Jessica Riskin, *Science in the Age of Sensibility: The Sentimental Empiricists of the French Enlightenment* (Chicago: University of Chicago Press, 2002), 50. Diderot had acknowledged the problem in his discussion of Berkeley and Condillac in his *Lettre sur les aveugles* (V i. 164).

is because only Lui restores to him, as he does to others, a share of his 'natural individuality' (624/4). As we have seen, Moi sidesteps the issue of whether this 'restitution' might impose some obligation on the recipient, and now we can see why. Such a favor might be too great to be repaid. For it can be argued that the restitution of Moi's individuality, or sense of self, is predicated on the power of Lui's performances to put him in touch with the reality that exists outside himself. This power and this experience are complementary illustrations of the sublime.

In discussions of the sublime its role in resolving epistemological anxieties has been much less prominent than its function as a catalyst for the expression and celebration of the power of human intellect and will. To acknowledge the role of the sublime in overcoming philosophical solipsism would be to undermine the very autonomy the sublime is invoked to demonstrate. To invoke the sublime as a weapon in the fight against imaginative timidity and conventionality was all well and good. It was part of the Enlightenment's campaign for social and esthetic emancipation. The problem of solipsism, however, is not one that can be solved simply by greater effort. The answer has to come from a source beyond the self, beyond even the 'nature' available to and addressed by the self in the ordinary course of events, and which seems so nicely to fit the capacities of human understanding. The question arises of whether we owe any gratitude to the agency assuring us of our connection to this wider reality. This would be the case if the power experienced in the sublime is ultimately that of a personal agent. As a number of thinkers have recently argued, an unexamined insistence, not just that this was not, but that it could not be, the case, is what made the sublime a key category in the development of modern secular thought.[37]

From the time of Longinus up until the eighteenth century, examples of the sublime included the mighty acts of God, and the dynamism of nature could also be attributed to a divine source. As the idea of a personal God, in the eyes of the *philosophes*, came to be seen as itself a mythical projection, the sublime could only provide a link with a reality truly independent of human wishes if it stood in contrast with anything suggesting a personal or providential divinity. Thus, we see the sublime linked to ideas of the terrible and even the criminal. The sublime could also be experienced in works of art that upset conventional notions of beauty, so that indeed the esthetic sublime was no

[37] See John Milbank, *Theology and Social Theory* (2nd edn, Malden, Mass.: Blackwell, 2006), 101–44.

longer the highest form of cosmic beauty but something defined over against the beautiful.[38] Here, too, the genius that enabled the work to be transparent to deeper reality was distinct from the personality the artist shared with ordinary men. Whereas the latter were bundles of contradictions resulting from the play of clashing internal and external influences, the sublime man, whether artist or criminal, is all of a piece. The strength of his passion makes his actions immune to the 'inconsistencies' that characterize most human behavior, or, in the case of someone like Racine, makes his human faults irrelevant to the judgment of his works.[39] This higher unity of intention and expression evokes wonder and even admiration in the subject who considers it. 'On crache sur un petit filou, mais on ne peut refuser une sorte de considération à un grand criminel: son courage vous étonne, son atrocité vous fait frémir. On prise en tout l'unité de caractère' (People spit on a petty thief, but cannot refuse a kind of respect to a great criminal. His courage astounds, his cruelty terrifies. People value unity of character in everything) (669/58). It takes the spectator outside of himself into a new realm of esthetic experience, in which moral judgments prove to be inadequate.

But whereas the transcendence of ordinary moral categories in religious experience led to awe and submission before divine power and grace, the result in the secular experience of the sublime is very different. It still begins with a move beyond moral judgment. As Moi remarks to Lui near the beginning of the dialogue, 'vous ne faites grâce qu'aux hommes sublimes' (your judgment only spares men who are sublime) (625/6, tr. modified). Sublimity is immune to satire, and in particular to the anger or resentment that animates its critique. But it does not follow that the contemplating subject is summoned to acknowledge any positive personal connection to the sublime otherness he experiences. We may, for example, marvel at Racine's ability to transcend his defects and produce works of genius, but his plays are not a gift for which we should be grateful. This is because Racine the man did not 'give' them to anyone. Not only was Racine not a generous man personally—this indeed was one of his chief faults—but the artist's human agency was

[38] This concern has reappeared again in some postmodern re-appropriations of the sublime and the religious. For an overview, see Philip Shaw, *The Sublime* (London: Routledge, 2006), and especially David Bentley Hart, *The Beauty of the Infinite* (Grand Rapids, Mich.: Eerdmans, 2003), 43–93.

[39] Diderot, letter to Sophie Volland, 31 July 1762 (V v. 397).

really only a mediator through which the impersonal dynamic of nature found expression.

Not that the artist's role is purely a passive one. On the contrary, the *Paradoxe sur le comédien* and the *Salons* show Diderot's admiration for those artists who can exert the discipline required to get their emotional selves out of the way so that the cries and gestures of nature can be communicated without distortion. This self-mastery depends on the artist's internal 'organization', to use Diderot's expression. It results from an exceptionally well-regulated interaction of the material relationships that in increasingly complex layers make up the individual human being. To the extent that the regulatory capacity of the artist's mind and sensibility is enhanced by—or enhances—relationships with other people, it does so, to use the musical metaphor suggested in the *Rêve de d'Alembert*, by means of a harmonic 'resonance' analogous to an acoustic echo, rather than through the giving or receiving of gifts or favors. Thus, early in *Le Neveu de Rameau*, before he comes to a more critical view of Lui's talent, Moi responds to one of the nephew's musical pantomimes by assuring us that 'les accords résonnaient dans ses oreilles et dans les miennes' (the harmonies were resounding in my ears as well as in his own) (639/22). This resonance is a matter for aesthetic appreciation, even sympathetic participation, but not a springboard for interpersonal intimacy. Thus at this most fundamental level of experience Moi need not feel any gratitude to Lui. Furthermore, whatever obligation he might have for insights Lui gives him about social interaction can be dismissed if those insights can be recast as deriving from this more basic and impersonal experience.

As we have seen, Moi's general strategy has been to downplay the value of Lui's artistic and argumentative performances. This deprecation extends to Lui's exemplification of sublimity. 'Quelque sublime que vous soyez, un autre peut vous remplacer' (However sublime you might be, someone else could replace you) (634/16, tr. modified). Lui had responded, 'difficilement' (with difficulty), but as he himself shows in his description of the Bertin household and the parasitic pact, even the most talented jesters are replaceable. Thus Lui, in an ultimate attempt to salvage his dignity by distinguishing himself from the crowd, invokes the more difficult and rare sublime of evil. 'S'il importe d'être sublime en quelque genre, c'est surtout en mal' (If there's any area in which it really matters to be sublime it is, above all else, in wickedness) (669/58). In reading this passage, most critics have underscored the tension between the esthetic valuation of a concentrated expression of character which provokes strong sensations, and the immoral nature of the actions. To focus on this feature of the sublime, however, is to miss what is new in this passage. The tension between art and morality has already been fully explored in the dialog. As O'Gorman has argued, the figure of the 'great criminal' is invoked, not as a phenomenon to be addressed in its own right, with all its attendant challenges to moral philosophy, but rather simply to show that Lui falls short of even this ideal.[40] We also already know that Lui does not possess unity of character, and never will. He can only point to the sublime of evil, not embody it.

Thus, when Diderot has Lui go on to tell the story of the Avignon renegade, it is with a different purpose. In this story, told with a gleeful *sang-froid* designed to shock the reader, a con man on the run betrays his Jewish benefactor twice over, first by tricking him out of his fortune, and then by denouncing him to the Inquisition. He is a monster of ingratitude. But Diderot is not interested in the psychology of such a 'sublime' criminal, whose character (in contrast to that of Lui) is not developed at all. The important thing is how Moi handles the story he hears. The interest of the sublime of 'wickedness' is that it provides a rare test of the self's capacity to deal with a reality that, precisely because it is recognized as evil (and not just amoral), must surely be independent of the self. Diderot is still enough of a believer in natural goodness that he assumes moral evil cannot be a projection of the self's own desires.

The renegade story also differs from Lui's other tales in that it does not lead the teller to disappear into the tale. On the contrary, Lui takes some distance from the horror of the events themselves by analyzing the nature of the renegade's sublimity. He remarks that 'la grandeur de caractère résulte de la balance naturelle de plusieurs qualités opposées' (greatness of character comes from a natural balance between several antithetical qualities) (670/60). Elsewhere in the dialog, Moi would have picked up the formula, one of many in which Lui echoes what Moi (or Diderot himself) might say, and continued the debate. But here Moi expresses some discomfort with the idea of Lui playing the philosopher's role. 'Et laissez là vos réflexions, et continuez votre histoire' (Enough of your ruminations; get on with your story), he says. And yet Moi needs Lui's mediation to come to his own judgment. Soon afterwards, Lui interrupts his account of how the renegade manipulated his host's fears

[40] O'Gorman, *Diderot the Satirist*, 105.

of persecution because he notices Moi is absorbed in his thoughts. 'Mais vous ne m'écoutez point, à quoi rêvez-vous?/Moi.—Je rêve à l'inégalité de votre ton tantôt haut, tantôt bas' (But you're not paying attention. What are you thinking about?/Me: I'm thinking about the way your tone varies; sometimes it's high-flown, sometimes familiar and low) (670/60). Moi has trouble believing that Lui is faithfully reproducing the renegade's language, which seems to him inconsistent, at odds with the unity and balance of the sublime. Lui retorts that his account is a faithful one, and the dialog partners agree that the renegade was overacting. In this first part of the passage, Moi and Lui are at one in abstracting from the content of the drama, the better to display their ability to handle it with equanimity.

This solidarity, however, only serves to accentuate the contrast between the two characters' reactions at the end of the story. When Moi learns that the Avignon Jew was burned at the stake while his former guest calmly took possession of his fortune, he is shocked by Lui's tone, which is now far too *égal*. 'Je ne sais lequel des deux me fait le plus d'horreur, ou de la scélératesse de votre renégat, ou du ton dont vous en parlez' (I don't know which of the two horrifies me more: the villainy of your renegade, or the tone in which you speak of it) (671–2/62). Lui's detachment—and by implication, the detachment he himself had just displayed—now becomes an object of distaste. Lui goes on to perform 'an extraordinary fugue-like song' which absorbs the earlier high and low tones into a complex musical whole. This dynamic integration of opposing musical (and, implicitly, moral) values at first generates in Moi an intense inner conflict. 'Je ne savais, moi, si je devais rester ou fuir, rire ou m'indigner. Je restai . . . Je devins sombre malgré moi (For my part, I couldn't decide whether to stay or leave, laugh or be angry. I stayed . . . In spite of myself, I was overcome with depression) (672/62). The repeated *moi* ('for my part', 'myself') emphasizes the struggle to maintain control of the self in the face of serious challenge. Once again, Lui notices Moi's distraction, and asks if he is feeling ill. Moi replies: 'un peu; mais cela passera' (a little, but it will pass), echoing Lui's reference to the 'moments that quickly pass' near the beginning of the dialog (631/12), to which reference was made above. Lui probes the wound: 'Vous avez l'air soucieux d'un homme tracassé par quelque idée fâcheuse' (You look anxious, as if you're worrying about some disturbing idea). Moi agrees, but does not explain further. Instead, after 'un moment de silence de sa part et de la mienne' (a moment's silence on his part and mine), he changes the subject by asking Lui, 'Que faites-vous à présent?' (What are you doing now?) (672/63).

This moment of silence, I would argue, is the pivotal moment of the dialog, the moment that makes possible that recovery of nerve that launches the last section of the *Neveu.* It reproduces on the level of Moi's interaction with Lui that ultimate stage in Lui's musical transports when he showed that even silence could be depicted in sound. Indeed, the two scenes are linked by the added detail that Lui's 'silence' takes the form of walking up and down whistling and humming (672/63). The triviality of his whistling stands in ironic contrast with the sublimity of his earlier performance. Its function is to point to Moi's very different silence, which is no longer that of the bourgeois philosopher, dazzled into speechlessness by Lui's virtuosity. Rather, in this silence Moi takes in and processes the 'disturbing idea' that upset him. The fact that to do so Moi abandons dialog, Diderot's favored mode for dealing with challenging ideas, suggests that Moi must, and can, undertake this task himself, independently of others.

But why should the processing of a disturbing idea take place in silence? 'Je commençais à supporter avec peine', Moi says, 'la présence d'un homme qui discutait une action horrible, un exécrable forfait, comme un connaisseur en peinture ou en poésie examine les beautés d'un ouvrage de goût' (I was beginning to find it hard to tolerate the presence of a man who could discuss a horrible deed, an abominable, heinous crime, the way a connoisseur of painting or poetry discusses the beauty of a fine work of art) (672/62). Lui's attitude toward social corruption has always been one of detached appreciation for the cleverness involved, but the renegade's reprehensible action, which resulted in another man's persecution and death, turns wit into obscenity. Yet, Moi does not pronounce judgment on Lui. He does not chase him away, as Bertin did when he could no longer bear the sight of Lui in his house. Nor does he turn away himself and leave the scene. The disturbing idea to which Lui refers a few lines later, and which Moi acknowledges with a laconic 'that's so' before lapsing into his silence, can only be Moi's realization that he can remain in Lui's presence, and, moreover, that he wants to do so.

What Moi discovers, but what he cannot admit out loud, is that listening to Lui's horrible story, made even more horrible by Lui's detached attitude and then by its transposition into a musical fugue, has tested and confirmed his capacity to deal with a difficult reality. Even more, given the renewed energy with which he takes on Lui's challenge in the rest of the dialog, the experience has enhanced Moi's sense of his powers of apprehension. For Moi, the disturbing idea is thus ultimately a welcome one because it confirms his connection with a reality beyond his own fancies. The philosopher who began with a desire to be teased out of his solipsistic ruminations has here achieved his goal, which could only happen when faced with a spectacle devoid of the easy seductiveness of the Palais-Royal prostitutes or even the more complex charm of Lui's eccentricities.

Moi's experience of the sublime signifies that, in the end, his relationship to Lui is not an interpersonal one. The sublime moves us beyond the realm of satirical anger or envy. Moi can experience the sublime only through the presence of Lui, just as in music silence can be heard only within the texture of sound. But Lui is too alienated to serve as a personal mediator or messenger of what comes to expression in him. Indeed, his expressive powers are at their fullest when in a sense he is not present, to himself or to Moi. To whom, then, could Moi be said to owe a debt of gratitude?

When the dialog resumes, Lui again displays his virtuosity as critic and as performer, but Moi no longer feels threatened or undermined by Rameau's challenge to his values or by any sense that he owes Lui any debt. On the contrary, he punctures the nephew's pretensions by drawing attention to his lack of achievement. When Moi asks Rameau why he has not accomplished anything worthwhile (686/78), he can do so because he has gained a more secure confidence in his own achievement. This has finally little to do with Moi's successful completion of an enduring work of art or philosophy. That is a matter for posterity to decide, and, as Lui says in the line that concludes the dialog (Moi and the author behind him being content to leave him the last word), 'Rira bien qui rira le dernier' (He that laughs last, laughs best) (695/89). Rather, the crucial issue is Moi's capacity here and now to contain an experience of a reality that, in a way at once disturbing and reassuring, retains the key quality of being external to him, and thus continues to guarantee in return the reality of that self as separate from the outside world.

Moi's enhanced sense of autonomy is shown by his playful identification with the figure of Diogenes in the last part of the dialog. Here, Moi shows that he can dispense with the protective image of the respectable bourgeois philosopher. Diogenes was known for his proud self-sufficiency, and the mention late in the dialog of his occasional lover, the courtesan Laïs (693/87), recalls the famous line: 'I possess her, she does not possess me', well known to Diderot.[41] This allusion brings us back to Moi's references to prostitution at the beginning of the dialog. The easy self-satisfaction of the earlier passage gives way to a more tough-minded confidence that the seductions and snares of the outside world will not jeopardize the integrity or the individuality of his self.

Moi's silence in the renegade episode may also represent Diderot's own silence about *Le Neveu de Rameau* itself. The refusal to allow anyone to share or participate in the development of his most dialogic work may not be as puzzling as it appears. It may be that Diderot felt that his circle of friends did not provide him with points of view that were external enough, that he was too closely entangled with them, and the familiar intellectual and social networks to which they belonged as much as he, to generate real dialog on the issues of dignity and dependence, of anger and gratitude, that lie at the heart of the *Neveu de Rameau*. It would not be the least of Diderot's many paradoxes that the work most attuned to the social and cultural networks he had to negotiate as a writer should also be the most self-contained. How such artistic self-containment could itself be construed as a vital mode of social engagement, despite or even because of its ironic character, is a question Diderot also left to posterity, that is to say, to his Romantic and post-Romantic heirs.

[41] Diderot, *Pensées sur l'interprétation de la nature*, no. 27 (V i. 1569–70).

Conclusion

Deciding when and whether social interactions are best regulated by a code of law or by informal rules of civility is not an issue that concerned Enlightenment writers alone. It may be true, as Rémi Brague has recently argued, that some pre-modern worldviews do not draw any sharp distinction between different kinds of norm, and we should certainly beware of imposing a simplistic interpretive grid on complex and shifting patterns of ideas.[1] Yet, it seems fair to say that thinkers in all modern societies reflect in some way on the philosophical basis for preferring one of these alternatives over the other, and on the practical implications of doing so. The tension between these ways of imagining social order may appear more or less explicitly in the self-understanding of any particular culture, and more or less saliently in its practices. At any given historical moment, individual persons may be helped to flourish more fully by reforming (or reinforcing) the rule of law or the habits of mutual consideration. Ideally, these efforts should go hand in hand, but the relation between them may take very different forms. In some contexts, for example, law may be identified with tradition and *mœurs* or civil society may be viewed as the realm more open to innovation and more accommodating of difference. In others, it is custom that is seen as more resistant to change and legislation that appears more amenable to revisionary initiative. As in recent debates over the civil rights of racial, sexual, or religious minorities, it is not always easy, either as a matter of principle or of strategy, to decide where to focus one's energies.

I have argued in this study that the tension between these two ways of conceptualizing the basis of social relationships took on particular

[1] 'In the word *nomos,* the notion of law is not disentangled from that of manners [*mœurs*].' He cites as evidence Plato's remark (*Laws* VII.793a) that unwritten customs should not be called laws, contrary to common practice. Rémi Brague, *La Loi de Dieu* (2005; corrected repr. Paris: Gallimard 'Folio', 2008), 41.

urgency for writers of the French Enlightenment. Part of the explanation lies in the cultural situation they confronted. In early modern France, the coexistence of an absolutist definition of political sovereignty with an idealized notion of the civilizing power of *politesse* aggravated the imaginative tension between the formal and informal rules, sometimes to the point of radical opposition. Another contributing factor was the challenge for the writers themselves of gaining secure and respected status within that society, caught as they were between dependence on networks of favor and patronage in *la cour et la ville*, and the uncertain validation of their print persona in the public sphere of print. By asserting their entitlement to anger, or, alternatively, their claims to have transcended the disturbance of vehement emotion, Enlightenment authors could defend and illustrate the dignity of their calling and at the same time offer philosophical warrant for their interventions. Equally significant, I have argued, was the rhetoric of emotion adopted by writers to foster or forestall experiences of gratitude in their readers, or to negotiate the gratitude patrons or public expect of authors they applaud. Understanding how these emotional dispositions were defined and deployed helps us to appreciate what is at stake in claiming literary or intellectual authority.

The reconfiguration of the cultural roles played by discussions and displays of emotional dispositions after the upheaval of the French Revolution is another fascinating story that is only beginning to be told. Certainly, the ways anger and gratitude were analyzed, appropriated, or repudiated were significantly affected by events. The very distinction between 'good' and 'bad' anger, for example, had to be rethought after the trauma of the Terror. In a recent study of the changing place of anger in British Romanticism, Andrew Stauffer writes: 'For Romantic-period writers, anger was a locus of rational justice and irrational savagery, and determining its place in society and in their own work as a tool or weapon confronted them with an urgent task.'[2] One might add that the notion of transcending or otherwise freeing oneself from anger required equally urgent rethinking in the light of the disturbing spectacles of impassive rationality offered by Terrorists like Saint-Just. Judith Miller has also recently cast new light on the problematic appeals made during the Directory to Stoic

[2] Andrew Stauffer, *Anger, Revolution, and Romanticism* (Cambridge: Cambridge University Press, 2005), 2.

firmness in confronting and controlling revolutionary and counter-revolutionary violence.[3]

As for gratitude, its political importance was given new acknowledgment by the institution of the Panthéon, with its famous inscription *Aux grands hommes la patrie reconnaissante.* By suggesting that great writers such as Voltaire and Rousseau were, like statesmen, owed a common public debt rather than a sum of personal obligations, the Revolution marked a shift in the dynamic of favor and gratitude away from the early modern model of civility toward a less personal kind of relationship, although one that remained distinct from the domain of law. In nineteenth-century France, some writers would certainly enjoy an unprecedented form of cultural prestige, one which cannot be captured by the vocabulary of benefactor and grateful recipient. It is not clear, however, that in the age of what Paul Bénichou called *les mages romantiques*, which was also the age of what Sainte-Beuve called *la littérature industrielle*, the relationship between author and reader should be defined in terms of leader and follower, or of producer and consumer.[4] Rejecting both of these models, later writers like Baudelaire would argue, by a further dialectical twist, that rejection by the uncomprehending crowd ('Mène-t-on la foule dans les ateliers . . . ?' (Does one bring the crowd into the studios))[5] is the artist's real badge of distinction. Such an attitude would, of course, entail a corresponding shift in the kind of value assigned or denied to anger in the writer's response to the world.[6]

[3] See Judith A. Miller, 'After Sentiment: The Stoic "Real" of the Directory', paper presented at the conference of the Western Society for French History, Albuquerque, November 2007. Miller's forthcoming publications offer insightful perspectives on attitudes toward emotion in the revolutionary period.

[4] Paul Bénichou, *Les Mages romantiques* (Paris: Gallimard, 1988), his examples being Lamartine, Vigny, and Hugo; Charles-Augustin Sainte-Beuve, 'La Littérature industrielle', *Revue des deux mondes*, 1 September 1839.

[5] Charles Baudelaire, 'Projet de préface pour Les *Fleurs du mal*', in *Œuvres complètes*, ed. Claude Pichois (Paris: Gallimard, 1975), i. 185.

[6] These values were of course subject to ironic reversal. For one suggestive example, see Baudelaire's prose poem 'Portraits de maîtresses', in which a man resembling the poet complains about his too-perfect mistress who prevents him from enjoying 'les bénéfices que j'aurais pu tirer de ma folie personnelle . . . Pour comble d'horreur, elle n'exigeait pas de reconnaissance, le danger passé. Combien de fois ne me suis-je pas retenu de lui sauter à la gorge, en lui criant: "Sois donc imparfaite, misérable! afin que je puisse t'aimer sans malaise et sans colère!"' (all the benefits I could have drawn from my personal madness . . . The final horror was that she never asked for thanks once the danger had passed. How many times did I stop myself from screaming at her: 'You wretch, be imperfect for a change! so that I can love you without feeling uneasy and angry!' Baudelaire, *Œuvres complètes*, i. 348; *The Prose Poems and La Fanfarlo*, tr. Rosemary Lloyd (Oxford: Oxford University Press, 1991), 95.

Among nineteenth-century writers, however, the one who provides the most appropriate coda to the story told in this book is Alexis de Tocqueville. He took up what was most fruitful in the legacy of Montesquieu but which had been more admired than assimilated by other Enlightenment writers, that is to say, a nuanced sociological and historical contextualization of an *esprit des lois* that encompassed both legislation and *mœurs*, and which could be extended to emotional dispositions. Moral considerations are not irrelevant to this enterprise, but they are tempered by an acute awareness of the interrelationship of all the circumstances in which individual actions and judgments are embedded. A striking example of this approach, which illustrates both continuities and discontinuities with eighteenth-century portrayals of anger, is the contrast between the character of white Americans in slave and free states Tocqueville develops in *De la démocratie en Amérique*:

L'Américain du Sud, dès sa naissance, se trouve investi d'une sorte de dictature domestique; les premières notions qu'il reçoit de la vie lui font connaître qu'il est né pour commander, et la première habitude qu'il contracte est celle de dominer sans peine. L'éducation tend donc puissamment à faire de l'Américain du Sud un homme altier, irascible, violent, ardent dans ses désirs, impatient des obstacles; mais facile à décourager s'il ne peut triompher du premier coup.

The southerner is born into a sort of domestic dictatorship. From the beginning, life teaches him that he is born to command, and the first habit he acquires is that of effortless domination. The southerner's upbringing all but ensures that he will be arrogant, quick-tempered, irascible, violent, ardent in his desires, and impatient of obstacles, but easily discouraged if triumph is not immediate.

The Northerner, on the other hand,

ne voit pas d'esclaves accourir à son berceau . . . A peine est-il au monde que l'idée de la nécessité vient de toutes parts se présenter à son esprit; il apprend donc de bonne heure à connaître exactement par lui-même la limite naturelle de son pouvoir . . . Il est donc patient, réfléchi, tolérant, lent à agir, et persévérant dans ses desseins.

has no slaves to wait on him in his cradle . . . From the moment he comes into the world, the idea of necessity is borne in on him; hence he learns early on to gauge precisely, on his own, the natural limit of his power . . . He is therefore patient, reflective, tolerant, slow to act, and persevering in his designs.[7]

[7] Alexis de Tocqueville, *De la démocratie en Amérique*, in *Œuvres*, ed. André Jardin et al. (Paris: Gallimard, 1991–2004), ii. 436; *Democracy in America*, tr. Arthur Goldhammer (New York: Literary Classics of the United States, 2004), 433.

There are clear echoes of *Émile* here, as well as of Montesquieu. Tocqueville's fundamental moral judgment is equally clear, but there is no suggestion, as there is in Rousseau, that the tension between North and South is amenable to any simple moral pedagogy. This is because, considered from the perspective of political history, the Southerner has the defects, but also the qualities, of aristocracies, while the Northerner has the qualities, but also the faults, of the middle class.[8] One of Tocqueville's major themes is that the overall health, moral and social, as well as the survival over time, of the political community, requires elements of both outlooks, and so the eighteenth-century style division of Americans into two types is only the first step in a complex argument. Neither righteous indignation nor philosophical equanimity can any longer productively be discussed in the language of ancient virtue or evaluated simply in terms of individual moral dignity. Any resolution will involve a complex set of considerations governed by an overarching concern for human freedom and dignity but tempered by an appreciation for the gains and losses in any 'progress' from one social ethic to another.

The same outlook characterizes Tocqueville's remarks on gratitude, which form part of his attempt to capture aspects of the shifting relationship between 'liens sociaux' and 'liens naturels' that cannot be captured by a priori moral or political categories. In a key passage in the second volume of his great work, he begins by observing that what had seemed to be the natural deference of the vassal toward the lord has vanished with the abolition of the feudal system. 'Maintenant, ces deux hommes ne se connaissent plus. La crainte, la reconnaissance et l'amour qui les liaient ont disparu. On n'en trouve point la trace' (Now the two men no longer recognize each other. The fear, gratitude, and love that bound them together have vanished. Not a trace remains). But while the legal equality established by democracy destroys the power of old conventions—and their civilizing along with their oppressive power—it does not leave a moral vacuum. While democracy 'fait disparaître entièrement la plupart des sentiments qui naissent de ces conventions . . . elle ne fait que modifier les autres, et souvent elle leur donne une énergie et une douceur qu'ils n'avaient pas' (completely eliminates most of the sentiments born of those conventions . . . it merely modifies the others and often imparts to them an energy and gentleness they did not previously

[8] Tocqueville, *Démocratie*, 437; *Democracy*, 434.

possess).[9] That is to say, it allows feelings that arise from natural relationships, as opposed to particular social ones, not only to come to the fore, but to do so in a more refined form. Emotions such as gratitude do not in fact disappear; rather, they can be expected to re-emerge in other places and other ways, if we allow ourselves to perceive them. The contrast is not between 'society' and 'nature' as such, or between free and rule-bound behavior, but between different ways of mediating the relationship between feelings and rules, that is to say, between what William Reddy calls different emotional regimes.[10]

Tocqueville's approach to the social dynamic of emotions is thus significantly different from that of the writers examined in this book. At the same time, it grew out of an appreciation of the tensions in the work of his Enlightenment predecessors that extends far beyond his explicit reflections in *L'Ancien Régime et la Révolution.* The example of Tocqueville, who in his writing was also reflecting on his own situation as the son of an enlightened but proudly aristocratic family, also suggests how productive renewed attention to the emotional as well as the intellectual tensions in Enlightenment writing might be in reflecting on the social and cultural tensions of our own day. Demands for recognition and sensitivity to slight have taken new forms in postmodern debates over 'identity politics'. New attention to the dynamics and appropriateness of gratitude may be found across a range of contemporary writings from self-help books to reflections on gift-giving and other forms of openness to the other as fundamental to a non-reductive ethics that, if not explicitly religious, may be termed 'post-secular'.[11] How writers define their own cultural role in the light of these considerations, and what kind of authority they may claim in articulating them, remains an open question.

[9] Tocqueville, *Démocratie*, 711; *Democracy*, 691.

[10] William M. Reddy, *The Navigation of Feeling: A Framework for the History of Emotions* (Cambridge: Cambridge University Press, 2001), 55.

[11] The later work of Derrida, along with that of Lévinas, has been particularly influential here. For a sample of other recent perspectives, see Robert A. Emmons and Michael E. McCulloch, eds, *The Psychology of Gratitude* (New York: Oxford University Press, 2004).

Bibliography

PRIMARY SOURCES

Aristotle, *On Rhetoric: A Theory of Civic Discourse*, tr. George A. Kennedy (New York: Oxford University Press, 1991).

Baudelaire, Charles, *Œuvres complètes*, ed. Claude Pichois, 2 vols (Paris: Gallimard, 1975).

—— *The Prose Poems and La Fanfarlo*, tr. Rosemary Lloyd (Oxford: Oxford University Press, 1991).

Challe, Robert, *Difficultés sur la religion proposées au père Malebranche*, ed. Frédéric Deloffre and François Moureau (Geneva: Droz, 2000).

—— *Journal d'un voyage fait aux Indes orientales (du 16 février 1690 au 10 août 1691)*, ed. Frédéric Deloffre and Jacques Popin, 2 vols (new edn, Paris: Mercure de France, 2002).

—— *Les Illustres Françaises*, ed. Jacques Cormier and Frédéric Deloffre (Paris: Livre de poche, 1996).

—— *Mémoires, Correspondance complète, Rapports sur l'Acadie et autres pièces*, ed. Frédéric Deloffre with Jacques Popin (Geneva: Droz, 1996).

Cicero, Marcus Tullius, *Cicero on the Emotions: Tusculan Disputations 3 and 4*, tr. and with commentary by Margaret Graver (Chicago: Chicago University Press, 2002).

—— *De officiis*, tr. Walter Miller, Loeb Classical Library (London: Heinemann, 1913; repr. 1975).

—— *On Duties*, ed. M. T. Griffin and E. M. Atkins (Cambridge: Cambridge University Press, 1991).

—— *On Obligations*, tr. P. G. Walsh (Oxford: Oxford University Press, 2000).

Descartes, René, *Les Passions de l'âme*, ed. Pascale d'Arcy (Paris: GF-Flammarion, 1996).

—— *Meditations métaphysiques* (édition bilingue), ed. Jean-Marie Beyssade and Michelle Beyssade (Paris: GF-Flammarion, 1992).

—— *Meditations on First Philosophy, with Selections from the Objections and Replies*, ed. Michael Moriarty (Oxford: Oxford University Press, 2008).

Diderot, Denis, *Œuvres*, ed. Laurent Versini, 5 vols (Paris: Laffont, 1994–7).

—— *Œuvres complètes*, ed. Herbert Dieckmann, Jacques Proust, and Jean Varloot, 24 vols to date (Paris: Hermann, 1975–).

—— *Rameau's Nephew and First Satire*, tr. Margaret Mauldon (Oxford: Oxford University Press, 2006).

Du Marsais, César Chesneau, *Examen de la religion, ou doutes sur la religion dont on cherche l'éclaircissement de bonne foi*, ed. Gianluca Mori (Oxford: Voltaire Foundation, 1998).

Hobbes, Thomas, *Le Citoyen ou les fondements de la politique*, ed. Simone Goyard-Fabre (Paris: GF-Flammarion, 1982).

—— *Leviathan: With Selected Variants from the Latin Edition of 1668* (Indianapolis: Hackett, 1994).

—— *On the Citizen*, ed. and tr. Richard Tuck and Michel Silverthorne (Cambridge: Cambridge University Press, 1998).

Holbach, baron d', *Système social* (Paris, 1773: repr. Paris: Fayard, 1994).

Horace, *Satires, Epistles, and Ars Poetica*, ed. H. R. Fairclough (London: Heinemann, 1929).

Inwood, Brad, and Gerson, L. P., tr., *Hellenistic Philosophy: Introductory Readings* (2nd edn, Indianapolis: Hackett, 1998).

Juvenal and Persius, *Satires*, ed. and tr. Susanna Morton Braund (Cambridge, Mass.: Harvard University Press, 2004).

Lafond, Jean, ed., *Moralistes du XVIIe siècle: de Pibrac à Dufresny* (Paris: Laffont, 1992).

La Rochefoucauld, François de, *Collected Maxims and Other Reflections*, tr. and ed. H. and A. M. Blackmore and Françoise Giguère (Oxford: Oxford University Press, 2007).

Mably, Gabriel Bonnot de, *Entretiens de Phocion sur le rapport de la morale avec la politique: traduits du grec de Nicoclès, avec des remarques* (The Hague, 1764).

Machiavelli, Niccolò, *Discourses on Livy*, tr. Harvey A. Mansfield and Nathan Tarcov (Chicago: University of Chicago Press, 1996).

Malebranche, Nicolas, *Œuvres*, ed. Geneviève Rodis-Lewis and Germain Malbreil, 2 vols (Paris: Gallimard, 1979–92).

—— *Traité de morale*, ed. Jean-Pierre Osier (Paris: GF-Flammarion, 1996).

Marivaux, Pierre Carlet de Chamblain de, *Théâtre complet*, ed. Henri Coulet and Michel Gilot, 2 vols. (Paris: Gallimard, 1993–4).

—— *Up from the Country*, tr. Leonard Tancock, and *Infidelities* and *The Game of Love and Chance*, tr. David Cohen (Harmondsworth: Penguin, 1980).

—— *La Vie de Marianne*, ed. Frédéric Deloffre (Paris: Garnier, 1963).

—— *Œuvres de jeunesse*, ed. Frédéric Deloffre and Claude Rigault (Paris: Gallimard, 1972).

Nicole, Pierre, *Essais de morale*, vol. i (Geneva: Slatkine, 1971).

Pascal, Blaise, *Les Provinciales, Pensées, et opuscules divers*, ed. Gérard Ferreyrolles and Philippe Sellier (Paris: La Pochothèque, 2004).

Pinot-Duclos, Charles, *Considérations sur les mœurs*, ed. F. C. Green (Cambridge: Cambridge University Press, 1939).

Plato, *The Republic*, tr. G. Grube, rev. C. D. C. Reeve (Indianapolis: Hackett, 1992).

Plutarch, *Essays*, tr. Robin Waterfield, ed. Ian Kidd (New York: Penguin, 1992).

Preston, A. W., *Life, Love, and Laughter in the Reign of Louis XIV: A New Translation of Robert Challe's Novel 'Les Illustres Françaises'* (Brighton: Book Guild, 2008).

Prévost, Abbé, *Histoire du Chevalier Des Grieux et de Manon Lescaut*, ed. Jean Sgard (Paris: GF-Flammarion, 1995).

Pufendorf, Samuel, *On the Duty of Man and Citizen according to Natural Law*, ed. James Tully, tr. Michael Silverthorne (Cambridge: Cambridge University Press, 1991).

Rousseau, Jean-Jacques, *The Collected Writings of Rousseau*, ed. Roger D. Masters and Christopher Kelly, 12 vols to date (Hanover, NH: University Press of New England, 1990–).

—— *Confessions*, tr. Angela Scholar, ed. Patrick Coleman (Oxford: Oxford University Press, 2000).

—— *The Discourses and Other Early Political Writings*, ed. and tr. Victor Gourevitch (Cambridge: Cambridge University Press, 1997).

—— *Emile*, tr. Allan Bloom (New York: Basic Books, 1979).

—— *Œuvres complètes*, ed. Bernard Gagnebin and Marcel Raymond, 5 vols (Paris: Gallimard, 1969–95).

—— *The Social Contract and Other Later Political Writings*, ed. and tr. Victor Gourevitch (Cambridge: Cambridge University Press, 1997).

Sade, Marquis de, *Œuvres*, ed. Michel Delon, 3 vols (Paris: Gallimard, 1990–8).

Sainte-Beuve, Charles-Augustin, 'La Littérature industrielle', *Revue des deux mondes*, 1 September 1839.

Sales, François de, *Œuvres*, ed. André Ravier (Paris: Gallimard, 1969).

Scudéry, Madeleine de, *Clélie: histoire romaine*, ed. Chantal Morlet, 5 vols (Paris: Champion, 2001–5).

Seneca, Lucius Annaeus, *Moral and Political Essays*, ed. John M. Cooper and J. F. Procopé (Cambridge: Cambridge University Press, 1995).

—— *Entretiens, Lettres à Lucilius*, ed. Paul Veyne (Paris: Laffont, 1993).

Smith, Adam, *The Theory of Moral Sentiments*, ed. D. D. Raphael and A. L. Macfie, in *The Glasgow Edition of the Works and Correspondence of Adam Smith* (Oxford: Clarendon Press, 1976–83), vol. i.

Sorel, Charles, *Histoire comique de Francion*, 1633 edn, ed. Fausta Garavini, Anne Schoysman, and Anna Lia Franchetti (Paris: Gallimard, 1996).

Spinoza, Benedict, *Theological-Political Treatise*, tr. Samuel Shirley, introduction and annotation by Seymour Feldman (2nd edn, Indianapolis: Hackett, 2001).

Tocqueville, Alexis de, *De la démocratie en Amérique*, in *Œuvres*, ed. André Jardin et al., 3 vols (Paris: Gallimard, 1991–2004).

—— *Democracy in America*, tr. Arthur Goldhammer, Library of America (New York: Literary Classics of the United States, 2004).

SECONDARY SOURCES

Abecassis, Jack, 'The Fragility of Philosophy: Passions, Ancient and Modern', *MLN* 110 (1995), 918–42.

Alberg, Jeremiah, *A Reinterpretation of Rousseau: A Religious System* (New York: Palgrave Macmillan, 2007).

Albertan-Coppola, Silviane, 'L'Anti-épicurianisme: l'épicurianisme des Lumières', *Dix-huitième siècle* 35 (2003), 309–18.

Anderson, W. S., 'Anger in Juvenal and Seneca', *University of California Publications in Classical Philology* 19.3 (1964), 127–96.

Andrew, Edward, *Patrons of Enlightenment* (Toronto: University of Toronto Press, 2006).

Apostolidès, Jean-Marie, *Le Prince sacrifié: théâtre et politique au temps de Louis XIV* (Paris: Éditions de Minuit, 1985).

Aronson, Ronald, *Living without God: New Directions for Atheists, Agnostics, Secularists, and the Undecided* (Berkeley: Counterpoint, 2008).

Artigas-Menant, Geneviève, *Du secret des clandestins à la propagande voltairienne* (Paris: Champion, 2001).

—— and Popin, Jacques, eds, *Leçons sur 'Les Illustres Françaises' de Robert Challe: actes de la table ronde de Créteil, 9 janvier 1993* (Paris: Université de Paris XII, 1993).

Attridge, Derek, *The Singularity of Literature* (London: Routledge, 2004).

Baczko, Bronisław, *Job, mon ami: promesses du bonheur et fatalité du mal* (Paris: Gallimard, 1997).

Baker, Eric, 'Lucretius in the European Enlightenment', in Stuart Gillespie and Philip Hardie, eds, *The Cambridge Companion to Lucretius* (Cambridge: Cambridge University Press, 2007), 274–85.

Baker, Felicity, 'La Peine de mort dans le *Contrat social*', in Marian Hobson, J. T. A. Leigh, and Robert Wokler, eds, *Rousseau and the Eighteenth Century: Essays in Memory of R. A. Leigh* (Oxford: Voltaire Foundation, 1992), 163–88.

—— 'The Object of Love in Rousseau's *Confessions*', in Patrick Coleman, Jayne Lewis, and Jill Kowalik, eds, *Representations of the Self from the Renaissance to Romanticism* (Cambridge: Cambridge University Press, 2000), 171–99.

Basset, Lytta, *Le Pardon originel: de l'abîme du mal au pouvoir de pardonner* (Geneva: Labor et Fides, 1994).

—— *Sainte Colère: Jacob, Job, Jésus* (Paris: Bayard, 2004).

Bell, Michael, *Open Secrets: Literature, Education, and Authority from J.-J. Rousseau to J. M. Coetzee* (Oxford: Oxford University Press, 2007).

Bénichou, Paul, *Le Sacre de l'écrivain 1750–1830: sur l'avènement d'un pouvoir spirituel laïque en France* (Paris: Corti, 1973).

—— *Les Mages romantiques* (Paris: Gallimard, 1988).

Benrekassa, Georges, Buffat, Marc, and Chartier, Pierre, eds, *Études sur le 'Neveu de Rameau' et le 'Paradoxe sur le comédien' de Denis Diderot* (Paris: Cahiers Textuel, 1992).

Berchthold, Jacques, '*Vitam impendere vero*', *Europe* 84.390(October 2006), 141–60.

Bernardi, Bruno, Guénard, Florent, and Silvestrini, Gabriella, eds, *La Religion, la liberté, la justice: un commentaire des 'Lettres écrites de la montagne' de Jean-Jacques Rousseau* (Paris: Vrin, 2005).

Biet, Christian, *Droit et littérature sous l'ancien régime: le jeu de la valeur et de la loi* (Paris: Champion, 2002).

Böhler, Michael, Hofmann, Étienne, Reill, Peter H., and Zurbuchen, Simone, eds, *Republikanische Tugend: Aussbildung eines Schweizer Nationalbewusstseins und Erziehung eines neuen Bürgers. Contributions à une nouvelle approche des Lumières helvétiques* (Geneva: Slatkine, 2000).

Bost, Hubert, *Pierre Bayle* (Paris: Fayard, 2006).

Brague, Rémi, *La Loi de Dieu* (2005; con. edn, Paris: Gallimard, 2008).

Braund, S. H., *Beyond Anger: A Study of Juvenal's Third Book of Satires* (Cambridge: Cambridge University Press, 1988).

——and Most, Glenn W., eds, *Ancient Anger: Perspectives from Aristotle to Galen* (Cambridge: Cambridge University Press, 2003).

Brewer, John and Staves, Susan, eds, *Early Modern Conceptions of Property* (London: Routledge, 1995).

Bury, Emmanuel, *Littérature et politesse: l'invention de l'honnête homme (1580–1750)* (Paris: Presses universitaires de France, 1996).

Cave, Terence, *Recognitions: A Study in Poetics* (Oxford: Oxford University Press, 1988).

Charles-Daubert, Françoise, ed., *Le 'Traité des trois imposteurs' et 'L'Esprit de Spinosa': philosophie clandestine entre 1678 et 1768* (Oxford: Voltaire Foundation, 1999).

Charlier, G., and Hermann, L., 'Diderot annotateur de Perse', *RHLF* 35 (1928), 39–63.

Charvet, John, *The Social Problem in the Philosophy of Rousseau* (Cambridge: Cambridge University Press, 1974).

Coleman, Patrick, 'Constant and the *Froissement* of Form', *Historical Reflections/Réflexions historiques* 28.3 (2002), 385–96.

——*Reparative Realism: Mourning and Modernity in the French Novel, 1730–1830* (Geneva: Droz, 1998).

——*Rousseau's Political Imagination: Rule and Representation in the 'Lettre à d'Alembert'* (Geneva: Droz, 1984).

——Lewis, Jayne, and Kowalik, Jill, eds, *Representations of the Self from the Renaissance to Romanticism* (Cambridge: Cambridge University Press, 2000).

Cooper, Laurence, *Rousseau, Nature, and the Problem of the Good Life* (University Park, Pa: Pennsylvania State University Press, 1999).

Coulet, Henri, *Marivaux romancier: essai sur l'esprit et le cœur dans les romans de Marivaux* (Paris: Armand Colin, 1975).

Darnton, Robert, *The Great Cat Massacre and Other Episodes in French Cultural History* (New York: Basic Books, 1984).

Daumas, Maurice, *La Tendresse amoureuse: XVIe–XVIIIe siècles* (Paris: Hachette, 1997).

Davis, Natalie Zemon, *The Gift in Sixteenth-Century France* (Madison: University of Wisconsin Press, 2000).

DeJean, Joan, *Ancients against Moderns: Culture Wars and the Making of a Fin de Siècle* (Chicago: University of Chicago Press, 1997).

Delumeau, Jean, *Le Péché et la peur: la culpabilisation en Occident, XIIIe–XVIIIe siècles* (Paris: Fayard, 1983).

Denis, Delphine, and Spica, Anne-Elisabeth, eds, *Madeleine de Scudéry: une femme de lettres au XVIIe siècle: actes du colloque international de Paris, 28–30 juin 2001* (Arras: Artois presses université, 2002).

Derrida, Jacques, *Donner la mort* (Paris: Galilée, 1999).

—— *Donner le temps* (Paris: Galilée, 1989).

DeSilva, David A., *Honor, Patronage, Kinship and Purity: Unlocking New Testament Culture* (Downers Grove, Ill.: Intervarsity Press, 2000).

Desné, Roland, 'Diderot correcteur d'une traduction des "Satires" de Perse', Éditer *Diderot, Studies on Voltaire and the Eighteenth Century* 254 (1988), 233–42.

Didier, Béatrice, *La Voix de Marianne: essai sur Marivaux* (Paris: Corti, 1987).

Dixon, Thomas, *From Passions to Emotions: The Creation of a Secular Psychological Category* (Cambridge: Cambridge University Press, 2003).

Duchêne, Roger, *Les Précieuses ou comment l'esprit vint aux femmes* (Paris: Fayard, 2001).

Elliott, Matthew A., *Faithful Feelings: Rethinking Emotion in the New Testament* (Grand Rapids, Mich.: Kregel, 2006).

Emmons, Robert A., and McCulloch, Michael E., eds, *The Psychology of Gratitude* (New York: Oxford University Press, 2004).

Farrell, John, *Paranoia and Modernity: Cervantes to Rousseau* (Ithaca, NY: Cornell University Press, 2006).

Fisher, Philip, *The Vehement Passions* (Princeton: Princeton University Press, 2002).

Force, Pierre, *Self-Interest before Adam Smith: A Genealogy of Economic Science* (Cambridge: Cambridge University Press, 2003).

Foucault, Michel, *Histoire de la sexualité 3: le souci de soi* (Paris: Gallimard, 1984).

—— *Le Gouvernement de soi et des autres: cours au Collège de France, 1982–1983* (Paris: Hautes Études: Gallimard Seuil, 2008).

Fried, Michael, *Absorption and Theatricality: Painting and Beholder in the Age of Diderot* (Berkeley and Los Angeles: University of California Press, 1980).

Fumaroli, Marc, *La Diplomatie de l'esprit: de Montaigne à La Fontaine* (Paris: Hermann, 1994).

Gans, Eric, 'The Victim as Subject: The Esthetico-Ethical System of Rousseau's Rêveries', *Studies in Romanticism* 21.1 (Spring 1982), 3–32.

Gerrish, B. A., *Grace and Gratitude: The Eucharistic Theology of John Calvin* (Minneapolis: Fortress Press, 1993).

Gevrey, Françoise, ed., *Marivaux et l'imagination* (Toulouse: Éditions universitaires du sud, 2002).

—— *L'Illusion et ses procédés: de 'La Princesse de Clèves' aux 'Illustres Françaises'* (Paris: Librairie J. Corti, 1988).

Gillespie, Michael, *Nihilism before Nietzsche* (Chicago: University of Chicago Press, 1995).

Godelier, Maurice, *L'Énigme du don* (Paris: Fayard, 1996).

Goldingay, John, 'Anger', in *New Interpreter's Dictionary of the Bible* (Nashville: Abingdon Press, 2006–9), i. 156–8.

Goldzink, Jean, 'Des *Difficultés sur la religion* aux *Illustres Françaises*: écarts et interprétations', *RHLF* 101 (2001), 313–24.

Gordon, Daniel, *Citizens without Sovereignty: Equality and Sociability in French Thought, 1670–1789* (Princeton: Princeton University Press, 1994).

Gouhier, Henri, *Les Méditations métaphysiques de Jean-Jacques Rousseau* (2nd edn, Paris: Vrin, 1984).

Graver, Margaret, *Stoicism and Emotion* (Chicago: Chicago University Press, 2007).

Groethuysen, Bernhard, *Origines de l'esprit bourgeois en France* (Paris: Gallimard, 1927).

Hadot, Pierre, *Qu'est-ce que la philosophie antique?* (Paris: Gallimard, 1995).

—— *What is Ancient Philosophy?*, tr. Michael Chase (Cambridge, Mass.: Harvard University Press, 2002).

—— *Philosophy as a Way of Life: Spiritual Exercises from Socrates to Foucault*, ed. Arnold I. Davidson, tr. Michael Chase (Oxford: Blackwell, 1995).

Harris, William V., *Restraining Rage: The Ideology of Anger Control in Classical Antiquity* (Cambridge, Mass.: Harvard University Press, 2001).

Hart, David Bentley, *The Beauty of the Infinite* (Grand Rapids, Mich.: Eerdmans, 2003).

Hayes, Julie Candler, *Reading the French Enlightenment: System and Subversion* (Cambridge: Cambridge University Press, 1999).

Herdt, Jennifer A., *Putting on Virtue: The Legacy of the Splendid Vices* (Chicago: University of Chicago Press, 2008).

Hirschman, Albert O., *Exit, Voice, and Loyalty: Responses to Decline in Firms, Organizations, and States* (Cambridge, Mass.: Harvard University Press, 1970).

Hobson, Marian, Leigh, J. T. A., and Wokler, Robert, eds, *Rousseau and the Eighteenth Century: Essays in Memory of R. A. Leigh* (Oxford: Voltaire Foundation, 1992).

Jacob, Margaret C., 'The Enlightenment Critique of Christianity', in *The Cambridge History of Christianity*, vii: *Enlightenment, Reawakening and Revolution 1660–1815* (Cambridge: Cambridge University Press, 2006), 265–82.

James, Susan, 'The Passions and the Good Life', in Donald Rutherford, ed., *The Cambridge Companion to Early Modern Philosophy* (Cambridge: Cambridge University Press, 2006), 198–220.

Jasinski, René, *Molière et Le Misanthrope* (Paris: Armand Colin, 1951).

Kahn, Victoria, Saccamano, Neil, and Coli, Daniela, eds, *Politics and the Passions 1500–1850* (Princeton: Princeton University Press, 2006).

Kelly, Christopher, *Rousseau's Exemplary Life: The Confessions as Political Philosophy* (Ithaca, NY: Cornell University Press, 1987).

Kenny, Anthony, *The Rise of Modern Philosophy: A New History of Western Philosophy*, vol. iii (Oxford: Clarendon Press, 2004).

Klein, Melanie, *Envy and Gratitude, and Other Works 1946–1963:The Writings of Melanie Klein*, vol. iii (London: Hogarth Press, 1975).

Kołakowski, Leszek, *God Owes Us Nothing: A Brief Remark on Pascal's Religion and on the Spirit of Jansenism* (Chicago: University of Chicago Press, 1995).

Komter, Aafke E., *Social Solidarity and the Gift* (Cambridge: Cambridge University Press, 2005).

Konstan, David, *The Emotions of the Ancient Greeks: Studies in Aristotle and Classical Literature* (Toronto: University of Toronto Press, 2006).

Kozul, Mladen, 'Péril extrême du discours d'autrui, ou le destinataire piégé: *Difficultés sur la religion* entre Descartes et Malebranche', in Jacques Cormier, Jan Herman, and Paul Pelckmans, eds, *Robert Challe: sources et héritages* (Louvain: Peeters, 2003), 263–78.

Labrosse, Claude, *Lire au XVIIIe siècle: 'La Nouvelle Héloïse' et ses lecteurs* (Lyon: Presses universitaires de Lyon, 1985).

Lafond, Jean, *La Rochefoucauld: augustinisme et literature* (Paris: Klincksieck, 1977).

Lefebvre, Philippe, *Les Pouvoirs de la parole: l'Église et Rousseau, 1762–1848* (Paris: Éditions du Cerf, 1992).

Lejeune, Philippe, 'Le Peigne cassé', *Poétique* 25 (1976), 1–29.

Levi, Anthony, *French Moralists: The Theory of the Passions 1585 to 1649* (Oxford: Clarendon Press, 1964).

Lilti, Antoine, *Le Monde des salons: sociabilité et mondanité à Paris au XVIIIe siècle* (Paris: Fayard, 2005).

McConnell, Terrance C., *Gratitude* (Philadelphia: Temple University Press, 1993).

McIntosh, Mark A., *Mystical Theology: The Integrity of Spirituality and Theology* (Malden, Mass.: Blackwell, 1998).

MacIntyre, Alisdair, *Dependent Rational Animals: Why Human Beings Need the Virtues* (Chicago: Open Court, 1999).

Magendie, Maurice, *La Politesse mondaine et les théories de l'honnêteté en France au XVIIe siècle, de 1600 à 1660* (Paris: Alcan, 1925).

Mall, Laurence, *Émile, ou, les figures de la fiction* (Oxford: Voltaire Foundation, 2002).

Marion, Jean-Luc, *Étant donné: essai d'une phénoménologie de la donation* (Paris: Presses universitaires de France, 1997).

Masters, Roger D., *The Political Philosophy of Rousseau* (Princeton: Princeton University Press, 1968).

Menemencioglu, Melâhat, 'Gallouin-Don Juan, une clé pour Robert Challe', *RHLF* 79 (1979), 981–93.

Mercier, Roger, *La Réhabilitation de la nature humaine 1700–1750* (Villemonble: La Balance, 1960).

Meyer, Michel, *Le Philosophe et les passions: esquisse d'une histoire de la nature humaine* (Paris: Librairie générale française, 1991).

Milbank, John, 'Can a Gift Be Given? Prolegomena to a Future Trinitarian Metaphysic', *Modern Theology* 11 (1995), 119–61.

—— *Theology and Social Theory: Beyond Secular Reason* (2nd edn, Malden, Mass.: Blackwell, 2006).

Mori, Gianluca, and Mothu, Alain, eds, *Philosophes sans Dieu: textes athées clandestins du XVIIIe siècle* (Paris: Champion, 2005).

Moriarty, Michael, *Fallen Nature, Fallen Selves: Early Modern French Thought II* (Oxford: Oxford University Press, 2006).

Muellner, Leonard Charles, *The Anger of Achilles: Mēnis in Greek Epic* (Ithaca, NY: Cornell University Press, 1996).

Murphy, Nancey, and Brown, Warren S., *Did my Neurons Make Me Do it? Philosophical and Neurobiological Perspectives on Moral Responsibility and Free Will* (Oxford: Oxford University Press, 2007).

Nadler, Stephen, ed., *The Cambridge Companion to Malebranche* (Cambridge: Cambridge University Press, 2000).

Naudin, Pierre, *L'Expérience et le sentiment de la solitude dans la littérature française de l'aube des Lumières à la Révolution: un modèle de vie à l'épreuve de l'histoire* (Paris: Klincksieck, 1995).

Newsom, Carol A., *The Book of Job: A Contest of Moral Imaginations* (New York: Oxford University Press, 2003).

Nussbaum, Martha, *The Therapy of Desire: Theory and Practice in Hellenistic Ethics* (Princeton: Princeton University Press, 1994).

—— *Upheavals of Thought: The Intelligence of Emotions* (Cambridge: Cambridge University Press, 2001).

O'Gorman, Donal, *Diderot the Satirist: 'Le Neveu de Rameau' and Related Works: An Analysis* (Toronto: University of Toronto Press, 1971).

Pappas, John, and Roth, Georges, 'Les "Tablettes" de Diderot', *Diderot Studies* 3 (1961), 309–20.

Peyrache-Leborgne, Dominique, *La Poétique du sublime de la fin des Lumières au romantisme: Diderot, Schiller, Wordsworth, Shelley, Hugo, Michelet* (Paris: Champion, 1997).

Pitassi, Maria-Cristina, *De l'orthodoxie aux lumières: Genève, 1670–1737* (Geneva: Labor et Fides, 1992).

Placher, William, *The Domestication of Transcendence: How Modern Thinking about God Went Wrong* (Louisville, Ky: Westminster John Knox Press, 1996).

Porter, Jean, *Nature as Reason* (Grand Rapids, Mich.: Eerdmans, 2005).

Postan, Gail Kern, Rowe, Katherine, and Floyd-Wilson, Mary, eds, *Reading the Early Modern Passions: Essays in the Cultural History of Emotion* (Philadelphia: University of Pennsylvania Press, 2004).

Poulet, Georges, 'Marivaux', in *Études sur le temps humain II: la distance intérieure* (Paris: Plon, 1952), 1–34.

Ray, William, *Story and History: Narrative Authority and Social Identity in the Eighteenth-Century French and English Novel* (Cambridge, Mass.: Blackwell, 1990).

Raynaud, Philippe, and Rials, Stéphane, eds, *Dictionnaire de philosophie politique* (Paris: Presses universitaires de France, 1996).

Reddy, William M., *The Navigation of Feeling: A Framework for the History of Emotions* (Cambridge: Cambridge University Press, 2001).

Ribard, Dinah, *Raconter, vivre, penser: histoire(s) de philosophes, 1650–1766* (Paris: Vrin, 2003).

Ricœur, Paul, *Parcours de la reconnaissance: trois études* (Paris: Stock, 2004).

Riley, Patrick, ed., *The Cambridge Companion to Rousseau* (Cambridge: Cambridge University Press, 2001).

Riskin, Jessica, *Science in the Age of Sensibility: The Sentimental Empiricists of the French Enlightenment* (Chicago: University of Chicago Press, 2002).

Rosenblatt, Helena, *Rousseau and Geneva: From the 'First Discourse' to the 'Social Contract', 1749–1762* (Cambridge: Cambridge University Press, 1997).

Rosenwein, Barbara, ed., *Anger's Past: The Social Use of an Emotion in the Middle Ages* (Ithaca, NY: Cornell University Press, 1998).

—— 'To be the Neighbor of Saint Peter', in *The Social Meaning of Cluny's Property, 909–1049* (Ithaca, NY: Cornell University Press, 1989).

Saarinen, Risto, *God and the Gift: An Ecumenical Theology of Giving* (Collegeville, Minn.: Liturgical Press, 2005).

Saint Girons, Baldine, *Fiat Lux: une philosophie du sublime* (Paris: Quai Voltaire, 1993).

Salaün, Franck, ed., *Pensée de Marivaux* (Amsterdam: Rodopi, 2002).

Saller, Richard P., *Personal Patronage under the Early Empire* (Cambridge: Cambridge University Press, 1982).

Seigel, Jerrold, *The Idea of the Self: Thought and Experience in Western Europe since the Seventeenth Century* (Cambridge: Cambridge University Press, 2005).

Shaw, Philip, *The Sublime* (London: Routledge, 2006).

Shklar, Judith, *Men and Citizens: A Study of Rousseau's Social Theory* (Cambridge: Cambridge University Press, 1969).

Solomon, Robert C., *True to our Feelings: What our Emotions Are Really Telling Us* (New York: Oxford University Press, 2007).

Spitzer, Leo, 'A propos de *La Vie de Marianne* (Lettre à M. Georges Poulet)', *Romantic Review* 44 (1953), 102–26.

Starobinski, Jean, 'Diderot et la parole des autres', *Critique* 296 (1972), 3–22.

—— 'La Prosopopée de Fabricius', *Revue des sciences humaines* 41 (1976), 83–96.

—— 'Sur l'emploi du chiasme dans *Le Neveu de Rameau*', *Revue de métaphysique et de morale* 89 (1984), 182–96.

Stauffer, Andrew, *Anger, Revolution, and Romanticism* (Cambridge: Cambridge University Press, 2005).

Stephen, Leslie, *History of English Thought in the Eighteenth Century* (London: Putnam, 1876).

Still, Judith, *Justice and Difference in the Works of Rousseau: 'Bienfaisance' and 'Pudeur'* (Cambridge: Cambridge University Press, 1993).

Stout, Jeffrey, *Democracy and Tradition* (Princeton: Princeton University Press, 2004).

Talon-Hugon, Carole, *Descartes ou les passions rêvées par la raison: essai sur la théorie des passions de Descartes et de quelques-uns de ses contemporains* (Paris: Vrin, 2002).

Tavris, Carol, *Anger: The Misunderstood Emotion* (rev. edn, New York: Simon and Schuster, 1989).

Taylor, Charles, *A Secular Age* (Cambridge, Mass.: Harvard University Press, 2007).

—— *Sources of the Self: The Making of the Modern Identity* (Cambridge, Mass.: Harvard University Press, 1989).

Tuck, Richard, *Natural Rights Theories: Their Origin and Development* (Cambridge: Cambridge University Press, 1979).

Villaverde, M.-J., '*Vitam impendere vero*: de Juvénal à Rousseau', *Études Jean-Jacques Rousseau* 4 (1990), 53–70.

Wade, Ira O., *The Clandestine Organization and Diffusion of Philosophic Ideas in France from 1700 to 1750* (Princeton: Princeton University Press, 1938).

Wallace-Hadrill, Andrew, ed., *Patronage in Ancient Society* (London: Routledge, 1989).

Weil-Bergougnoux, Michèle, ed., *Séminaire Robert Challe: Les Illustres Françaises* (Montpellier: Université Paul-Valéry Montpellier III, 1995).

Weinbrot, Howard D., *Menippean Satire Reconsidered: From Antiquity to the Eighteenth Century* (Baltimore: Johns Hopkins University Press, 2005).

Werner, Stephen, *Socratic Satire: An Essay on Diderot and 'Le Neveu de Rameau'* (Birmingham, Ala.: Summa Publications, 1987).

Wiel, Véronique, *Écriture et philosophie chez Malebranche* (Paris: Champion, 2004).

Williams, Raymond, *Marxism and Literature* (Oxford: Oxford University Press, 1977).

Williams, Rowan, *Dostoevsky: Language, Faith and Fiction* (Waco, Tex.: Baylor University Press, 2008).

Index